2/06

D1304848

Savannah Ga. Dec 22. 1864

To his Excellency,
President Lincoln.

Dear Sir,

I beg to present you as a Christmas Gift, the City of Savannah with 150 heavy guns and plenty of ammunition; and also about 25,000 bales of Cotton.

W. T. Sherman
Maj Genl.

By the same author:

JAMES MOORE WAYNE: SOUTHERN UNIONIST

STORM OVER SAVANNAH

JAMES JOHNSTON, GEORGIA'S FIRST PRINTER

A
PRESENT
FOR
MR. LINCOLN

The Story of Savannah
from Secession to Sherman

BY

Alexander A. Lawrence

THE OGLETHORPE PRESS, INC.

SAVANNAH, 1997

Copyright 1961 by the Ardivan Press, Inc.

Reprinted 1997 by The Oglethorpe Press, Inc.
326 Bull Street
Savannah, Georgia 31401

1-891495-00-3

Lawrence, Alexander A.

A Present for Mr. Lincoln

The Story of Savannah from
Secession to Sherman

1. Civil War - Georgia - Savannah

The Oglethorpe Press honors the memory
of Judge Alexander A. Lawrence of Savannah,
scholar, lawyer, jurist and friend.

We thank the family of Judge Lawrence
for their support and cooperation.

For Alex, Jr., and Margo

FOREWORD

AN HISTORIAN who moves from the era of Colonial or Revolutionary Georgia into the period of the Civil War looks about with feelings somewhat akin to those of the explorer who "Silent, upon a peak in Darien" gazed out at the Pacific for the first time.

Such is one's first impression of the vastness of source materials compared with those of the earlier epochs. I suspect that there is almost as much in the way of manuscripts still lying in attics and trunks as have found their way into the archives of libraries and institutions up to the present. A rewarding technique (certainly, at Savannah) is to stop people on the street and inquire whether they have any letters or diaries of the Civil War period. An unexploited wealth of letters and diaries of soldiers who accompanied General William T. Sherman to Savannah in 1864 exists in the Midwest. Whether research be in the area of manuscript, newspaper or of published materials one can be sure of only one thing—that he has not done much more than get below the surface.

By and large, I have let people speak for themselves throughout this book. They say their say better than anyone else can. For this reason I have retained their misspellings and peculiarities of speech. I have seldom intruded with my own opinions. This is not a study; it is the story of Savannah in the struggle told for the first time and, I hope, without visible prejudice.

For Confederate seaports like Savannah and Charleston the war possessed a continuousness, an immediate presence, lacking in most places. For three years before Sherman came the enemy was at Savannah's doorstep. During that period the city fought a microcosmic war of its own, relying to a considerable extent upon its own manpower, initiative and resources. I have used the military and naval events around Savannah mainly as background for what soldiers and civilians, in high place and low, thought and said and did. Savannah from Secession to Sherman is by no means so parochial a subject as might be supposed. Mirrored in these pages will be found not only the face of Savannah but the visage of the Confederacy itself.

The author is indebted to many persons for help on this book. My obligation to the following is especially large: Mrs. Lilla M. Hawes, Director of the Georgia Historical Society; Miss Elizabeth Hodge and Miss Margaret Godley of the staff of the Savannah Public Library; Mrs. Mary G. Bryan, Director of the Georgia Department of Archives and History; Mrs. Susan B. Tate of the staff of the University of Georgia Libraries; Colonel Allen P. Julian, Director of the Atlanta Historical Society; Mrs. Mary R. Davis, Acting Chief, Special Collections, Emory University Library; Miss Faye Locke of the staff of Duke University Library; John J. de Porry, Falls Church, Virginia; Miss Helen Burr Smith, New York City; James N. Adams, Springfield, Illinois, and Quinn C. Smet, Madison, Wisconsin. Dr. Spencer B. King of Mercer University and Dr. James C. Bonner of Georgia State College for Women made helpful suggestions after reading the manuscript. My deep thanks are also due Mrs. Barbara B. Kehoe and Mrs. Norma Berry Meehan who typed the manuscript.

ALEXANDER A. LAWRENCE

Savannah, Georgia

CONTENTS

A
PRESENT
FOR
MR. LINCOLN

1.

"We will sing the requiem of these United States"

⋙ THE ORATOR'S voice rose higher now. The spell of his art transfixed his listeners. "I am tired of this endless controversy. I am wearied with seeing this threatening cloud forever above our heads. If the storm is to come, and it seems to me as though it must, be its fury ever so great, I court it now in the day of my vigor and strength."

The applause died. The speaker resumed. "If any man is to peril life, fortune and honor in defense of our rights, I claim to be one of those men." That he was in earnest time would verify. "Let it come now, I am ready for it. Put it not off until tomorrow, or next day, we shall not be stronger by waiting." He gloried in the nation's "heroic birth, and youthful struggles, and in the grandeur of its maturity." He was a Union man. But he would "peril *all*," he added— "ALL, before I will abandon our rights in the Union or submit to be governed by an unprincipled majority." [1]

Revolutions require orators and Francis S. Bartow of Savannah was a gifted one. Of the voices in Georgia that clamored for secession none was more persuasive than this forty-four-year-old attorney. Experience before juries had given him an easy facility with words. "He was a lawyer of the first ability," said William Starr Basinger who added, "Above all, he was a noble soul." [2]

The occasion of Bartow's speech was a Breckinridge rally in Savannah on September 17, 1860. Within a few months Lincoln and the "Black Republicans" (as appeared all too clear) were to hold the reins of national government. The speaker's purpose seemed to be to prepare Georgians for disunion quite as much as to persuade them to vote for Breckinridge.

The turmoil that possessed the minds of Savannah's inhabitants at the prospect of a sectional government seemed strangely out of keeping with the outward languor, the timeless serenity, of the place itself. "A tranquil old city," William Makepeace Thackeray called it, "wide-streeted, tree-planted, with a few cows and carriages toiling through the sandy road, a few happy negroes sauntering here and there, a red river with a tranquil little fleet of merchant-men taking in cargo, and tranquil ware-houses barricaded with packs of cotton,—no row, no tearing Northern bustle, no ceaseless hotel racket, no crowds, drinking at bars." Another English visitor, William Howard Russell, saw it in 1861 as "a delightful, quaint city, spread out like a large Indian cantonment." The numerous squares and the oaks, the magnolias and the Pride of India made it difficult "to believe you are in the midst of a city." [8]

The serenity of the outward scene masked, however, the bustling spirit of commercial enterprise in Savannah. Three railroads now connected the city with other points—the Georgia Central, the Savannah and Charleston Railroad and the Atlantic and Gulf line. They were pouring the treasures of King Cotton into the city's lap. There were two iron foundries, two shipyards, railroad shops, four cotton compresses, a rice mill and several sawmills. But the key to prosperity was, as always, the tawny Savannah that coursed round the great bend where the city stood, on through the wide marshes, and down to the sea eighteen miles away.

"I glory in the prosperity of Savannah," wrote a visitor in the Savannah *Daily Morning News* in March, 1861. It was his first trip there in seven years and the growth of the city surprised him. Handsome residences had been erected as far south as Gaston Street. What had been a wooded area below the town was now a fountained park—"the scene," he added, "of more life and animation on a pleasant afternoon than marks the busy Bay and its commercial surroundings." By 1860 the population had grown to 13,875 whites and 8,417 slaves and free Negroes.

The populace, or at least the Caucasian portion of it, was a fallow field for the prophets of disunion. Secession had no organized opposition in Savannah. The inhabitants of that city were determined not to submit to a purely sectional Administration. They were almost of one mind on that subject, looking to their leaders solely as to "the *method* of resistance," said Charles H. Olmstead.⁴ The idea that the people were unwillingly dragged into secession by their leaders was not the case with Savannah, he added. In fact, such a contention was "almost ridiculously untrue" of the South in general, asserted William Basinger.

"The telegrams announce the fact of Lincoln's election by a popular vote!!! . . . We are on the verge of Heaven knows what," wrote Mayor Charles C. Jones, Jr., on November 7, 1860. The "astounding news" that Lincoln and Hamlin had been elected by large majorities in the North produced "intense excitement" in the city, reported George A. Mercer. The place was in a "perfect turmoil" was the way another resident described it.⁵

The day after the election a notice was posted at the office of the Savannah *Morning News* announcing a public meeting on November 8 to inform the representatives in the legislature of the views of the people. Several hundred citizens signed the call. It was the first such meeting held in Georgia. More than three thousand Savannahians turned out. They filled Masonic Hall and milled in the contiguous streets. "Brass bands were playing, rockets soaring, bonfires blazing; in fact the old town seemed to have gone crazy," recalled Olmstead.

One after another speakers set off roars from the crowd as they addressed themselves in favor of the resolutions Francis Bartow presented, the first of which declared that "the election of Abraham Lincoln and Hannibal Hamlin . . . ought not to be submitted to." Finally, Judge William Law was called to the platform. Conservative in his views and up to this time opposed to secession, he was a man who could not be swayed by clamor or prejudice. Amid an expectant silence he calmly reviewed the pros and the cons of the situation, the dangers attendant on breaking up the Union, on the one hand, and the wrongs to the South, on the other. When Judge Law announced, "I give to these resolutions my hearty endorsement," a wild shout went up in the hall and echoed back from the throng in the streets. Men yelled until their breath was gone and "hugged each other with passionate embraces," said Olmstead. "I am not exaggerating," he added, "but telling of what I saw and heard in what was probably the most thrilling gathering in my life's experience." [6]

A few days after the Savannah meeting, the General Assembly of Georgia took a far-reaching step: it appropriated a million dollars for the defense of the State. In December it created the office of Adjutant and Inspector General. The post was tendered to a Savannah-born officer, Henry C. Wayne. "The State needs your services, will you come to her?" Governor Joseph E. Brown telegraphed him at Washington. "Under this invitation," said Major Wayne, "how could I hesitate? To have hesitated would have been recreant to my family, to the land of my birth, to my name and to my pledge to some of my friends. . . ." [7] He was the first Georgian, according to Brown, to respond to the "call of his State, when the dissolution of the Union was seen to be inevitable."

Before he resigned from the Army he talked over the decision with his father, Mr. Justice Wayne of the United States Supreme Court. The Savannah jurist approved his son's course though he himself had decided to remain on the Federal bench. "To break up the Court," he explained, "would be to the injury of many private rights, involving much money before it." On November 13, 1860, Judge Wayne held court in the Customs House at Savannah for the last time. On his return to Washington he was reported as saying that four-fifths of the people in his native city were opposed to immediate secession. [8]

The modifying adjective saved the venerable justice from a miscalculation of the sentiment at Savannah. A correspondent of the New York *Times,* writing on November 21, reported that "with the exception of eight or ten citizens here, all are in favor of secession." Persons differed only as to time and manner. "It was," wrote Mercer in his diary that November, "the sad but settled conviction that the General Government had failed in its objects of equal protection, that the northern states had broken their solemn covenant." There was nothing left but for Georgia to reassume her position as an independent State, added the young attorney.

As to this, Democrats and ex-Whigs were of a single mind, at least in Savannah. The temper of the community was expressed by Bartow in a letter published in the *Republican* on November 27. "We have been 'wounded in the house of our friends,'" said this former leader of the American Party, "and I think we had better have a house of our own where treacherous friends cannot assail us." A potent Democratic spokesman in Savannah was Henry R. Jackson. Replying to pro-Union arguments, Jackson wrote that month, "They, not we, have violated law. They, not we, have dissolved the Union." [9]

In early December Dr. Richard Arnold, noting that "the feeling here is not noisy but it is deep," assured a Northern friend that "with the fanatics who rule you and would rule us, we are ready for war to the knife and the knife to the handle." Three weeks later this Savannah physician declared, "It is a practical question with us, not only as to existence and prosperity, but whether we are to [be] disfranchised of our liberties and subjugated to domination of the Black Race." The Southern mind could not disassociate the Republican Party and that policy. "We can't stand Black Republican rule," wrote Henry C. Wayne in the winter of 1861. The thought of living under such a regime was too much even for inveterate Unionists. The mother of Mayor Jones revealed to her son that when he was a small boy she had pledged him in front of Washington's statue in Independence Hall at Philadelphia to support and defend the Union. "That Union has passed away," she now told him, and he was free from his "Mother's vow." [10]

All creeds at Savannah seemed to be of one mind. The Rector of St. John's Church told a congregation that while his heart trembled in contemplating a dissolution of the Union, if no other remedy for the problems of the country could be found, "we will sing the requiem of these United States." Bishop Verot of the Catholic Church rejoiced in secession while blaming the Northern Protestant clergy for bringing on "this deplorable state of things." A priest who visited Savannah that winter complained on his return to Atlanta that some of the Catholic clergy there had tried to make a secessionist out of him. One of them, a certain Father Whelan, had even hinted darkly of "tar and feathers." [11]

The good Peter Whelan was, of course, joking. Others in Savannah were not. Secret vigilant committees, using such names as "Rattlesnakes" and "Hyenas" and composed of the town toughs, created "a reign of terror" for men of Union sympathies.[12]

Events moved rapidly in December. On the 21st the General Assembly of Georgia approved an act reciting that "the present crisis in our national affairs . . . demands resistance." The legislation provided for an election in January of delegates to a State convention to consider proper measures. The day before this action was taken South Carolina seceded from the Union. "Carolina has done all we could desire; and we are now left without excuse," Alexander R. Lawton commented to the Governor. "I pray that Georgia may not disappoint the hopes of the South!" [13]

An enthusiastic demonstration took place at Savannah in honor of the neighboring State on the night of December 26. Most of the houses were illuminated and the whole population seemed to be out in the streets. Many citizens wore secession rosettes and badges. A feature of the celebration that Mercer disliked was the appearance of women in a decorated car. It smacked too much of French and Northern customs, he thought. Two large banners were displayed in Johnson Square. One contained a coiled rattlesnake, a motto concerning Southern Rights and the words "Don't tread on me." Another banner depicted the American eagle about to strike at a female figure (South Carolina) while another female figure, which represented her sister Southern states, interposed herself in protection. "Touch her if you dare" was the inscription.

At Charleston two days later came the evacuation of Fort Moultrie by the Federal troops and their occupation of Fort Sumter. "The whole city has been wild with excitement ever since Sumter was taken," reported a Savannahian.[14] The action came like an "electric shock," declared the Savannah *Republican*. That paper which had been urging conservative action in the South was ready to endorse secession. "We might have been quieted by a milder course," said the editor, "but there are none of us so degraded as to submit to being whipped into submission."

Bartow was speaking at a secession meeting in Atlanta when a dispatch arrived reporting the destruction of Fort Moultrie by the Federal garrison. In the middle of his speech (which an Atlanta newspaper called "truly eloquent and sublime") the telegram was handed to him. To cries of "no! never!" he asked, "Is this gallant, noble state of South Carolina, that had the boldness to take the lead in this matter, to be left to the cold calculating of the co-operationists of Georgia?" When the excitement subsided, Bartow (with what the paper called "biting sarcasm in his lip") resumed. "Yes," he said, "while you *talk* of *cooperation,* you hear the thunders of the cannon, and the clash of sabres reach you from South Carolina." [15]

At least one Savannahian would have left that "gallant, noble state" to her own devices. Edward C. Anderson disapproved entirely of the rash course of the politicians of the country, North and South. He thought that "Georgia especially had been led by the nose by South Carolina." If his state seceded, she would have trouble with her neighbor within two years, he predicted. If South Carolina did not have her own way in any Southern confederacy, she would "secede again from the new government." [16]

In mid-November the Savannah *Republican* had come out strongly in favor of a national convention made up of three delegates from each State in the Union—the "wise and prudent men of the country." The paper recommended that the meeting convene in Independence Hall on Washington's Birthday, hoping that the delegates might catch the "patriotic fire" that had animated the "noble founders." The editor felt confident a plan could be adopted, protecting all interests and bringing peace to the land. During the previous month the newly elected Mayor of Savannah, foreseeing Republican victory and an "intestine war," expressed the hope that God would influence the minds of fanatical men so as to avert what he called a "direful calamity." [17]

But voices of conservatism went unheard in the clamor of the times. According to Basinger, "the number of those opposed to secession was infinitesimal." In the election of delegates from Chatham County to the approaching State Convention Union sympathizers had no other way of expressing their view than to stay away from the polls. On January 2, 1861, three staunch secessionists were unanimously elected—Francis S. Bartow, John W. Anderson and Augustus Seaborn Jones.

Significantly perhaps, all three were active in the military establishments of the city.

2.

"The Rubicon is passed—a new nation is born!"

⮜ THE SAME day the election of delegates to the State Convention took place an important decision was reached in a law office on the bay in Savannah. A note from Colonel Alexander R. Lawton, commanding the 1st Regiment of Georgia Volunteers, brought his adjutant hurriedly from a counting house desk. Entering the room, Charles Olmstead found the assembled group "conversing in low tones, with grave and serious faces." Among them was an angular, sallow-complexioned man, Joseph Emerson Brown, Governor of Georgia. He had been called to Savannah after a telegram from Senator Toombs in Washington warned that Fort Pulaski was in danger of being occupied by Federal troops.

The question of its seizure was a ticklish one. It was the property of the United States and Georgia was still in the Union. State security was paramount, however. "Colonel, you will take possession of the Fort tomorrow," confirmed the Governor as the meeting broke up.[1] Viewed in any light, State seizure was an act of hostility against the Federal government—the most overt step that had been taken by any Southern State up to that time.

The following day one hundred and thirty-four men from three military companies, the Chatham Artillery, Savannah Volunteer Guards and Oglethorpe Light Infantry, embarked by steamer for Fort Pulaski. The crowd that turned out to see the expedition off was so large the volunteers had difficulty making their way to the riverfront. Every window and balcony, every vessel at the wharves, was crowded, according to Basinger. "This," commented Captain Bartow as he surveyed the scene, "is the beginning of a glorious history."

Charles Olmstead would never forget their entry into the Fort. "I can shut my eyes," he wrote many years later, "and see it all now, the proud step of officers and men, the colors snapping in the strong breeze from the ocean; the bright sunlight of the parade as we emerged from the shadow of the archway; the first glimpse of a gun through an open casemate door: one and all they were photographed on my mind. . . ." As the troops marched up to the Fort the sun broke through heavy clouds—an "auspicious omen," one of them said in a letter to the *Morning News.* The night before, Henry R. Jackson of Governor Brown's staff had preceded the volunteers to Cockspur. Later he could contemplate with satisfaction that he was the "first rebel, 'so called,' actively engaged upon land or water, at the South." But as Jackson proceeded down the river in a row boat through heavy rainfall, it seemed to him an evil portent of things to come.[2]

Whatever vaticinations the elements might evoke in men's minds, the seizure of Fort Pulaski was heartily approved at Savannah. "No language can express our delight in the sense of security and of certain triumph inspired by the prompt and energetic, though wise and well-considered course adopted by the Governor," said the *Morning News* on January 3. But for Brown's timely arrival in the city the occupation of Pulaski, declared the editor, "would have been effected by a spontaneous uprising of our people."

The sole occupants were an ordnance sergeant and a caretaker. Captain William H. C. Whiting, USA, whose responsibilities included Pulaski, was away from Savannah at the time of the seizure. On his return to the city he went down to Cockspur to investigate. He could report to his superiors that he was received there by Colonel Lawton with "great civility." In February the State authorities seized the Oglethorpe Barracks in which Whiting's quarters were located. With a civility equal to the previous occasion, Lawton assured that officer, "Please consider yourself at liberty to occupy, with your employes, such apartments as are necessary for your convenience while you are closing up your business here." [3] The Mississippi-born Whiting was soon to close his business with the United States Army. In February he accepted a commission as major in the Provisional Army of the Confederacy. He became the beloved "Little Billy" of his troops and died a vain, heroic death near the close of the struggle.

"The Convention meets today," wrote Olmstead from Fort Pulaski on January 16. "God grant that its deliberations may be fraught with nothing but honor to old Georgia." [4] There was no real doubt of the outcome at Milledgeville. Reporting the secession of Alabama, the Savannah *Morning News* announced on January 12, 1861, "The Rubicon is passed—a new nation is born!" The only question now was "what line on the map will be the Northern boundary of our glorious Southern Confederacy."

At Milledgeville the secessionists won out over those who favored a convention of the Southern states rather than immediate withdrawal from the Union. The Chatham delegation voted on each roll call to leave the Union. While the cheers of a jubilant populace rang through Savannah that night, Mercer recorded in his diary, "This Saturday the 19th of January 1861 is become the most memorable day in our annals. . . . Georgia is free, and determined to remain equal, free and independent." A Negro brass band serenaded the Mayor, Colonel Lawton and other officials. The people, according to a resident, "kicked up a big noise generally." The excitement in the city in the early part of January far exceeded what Judge D'Lyon had seen there in 1815 "when the British were at our door." [5]

On January 31 John Boston, Collector of Customs at Savannah, resigned that office in a letter to President Buchanan in which he expressed regret that "the fanatical delusion" of a portion of the citizens of the United States made his action a duty. He gave permission for the flag of Georgia to be hoisted over the building. The version of the State flag was raised to "hearty cheers by the Custom House officers and the citizens in the streets." The *Morning News* reported on February 2, "While the coat of arms of our own State is the prominent feature of the banner, the seceding states, as they come into the constellation of our Southern Confederacy, will find their appropriate places in the arch of strength or the bow of promise that spans our glorious banner of free and independent Georgia."

In March the State Convention reconvened at Savannah. While in the city, the delegates took a day off for a steamboat excursion to Fort Pulaski. On the way back they were entertained by a Negro who told stories and sang songs of his own composition. He was particularly amusing, a correspondent reported, in the way he ridiculed Lincoln, Greeley, Harriet Beecher Stowe and Frederick Douglass. When the delegates pretended to present him with his freedom, he tactfully declined the proffer.[6]

If Alexander H. Stephens' ideas about Confederate fundamentals were to prevail, it was the slave's last chance to be free. In March, 1861, the Vice President of the Confederate States of America revealed the word at Savannah in his famous "Cornerstone Speech." The largest crowd ever assembled at the Athenaeum came to hear him—"such a tribute to distinguished talent, patriotism and private worth, as few men have ever received," reported the *Morning News*. The "corner-stone" of the Confederacy, Stephens told the audience, "rests upon the great truth, that the negro is not equal to the white man; that slavery—subordination to the superior race—is his natural and normal condition."

Meanwhile during these weeks the jostling between North and South had become more and more ominous. In January the New York City police seized several cases of guns purchased for the State of Georgia through Gazaway B. Lamar, a Savannahian living in the North. Governor Brown retaliated by ordering the seizure of all vessels at Savannah owned by citizens of New York. His action was described by the New York *Herald* as "the most grave and momentous event that has yet occurred, in the progress toward civil war," while the *World* declared that the Governor's order was "worthy of some half civilized Asiatic satrap, or some petty potentate of the Barbary states." "I tell you," wrote Gazaway Lamar from New York, "there is a latent feeling of opposition generally prevailing against the South . . . and if they do not make war it is not for want of inclination but of power. I would bet 100 to 5 that a telegram that an attack had been made on Ft. Sumter and repelled by loss of 5000 men of the South would cause an illumination even in this city, and much more in the West and New England." [7]

Early on the morning of April 12, 1861, a mortar shell burst over Fort Sumter in Charleston harbor. "Our community was intoxicated with joy," wrote George Mercer, who was never happier in his life. The contest between North and South, as he saw it, was one "between faith and infidelity, between constitutional liberty and mobocracy." While he foresaw a "dreadful civil war," the Confederacy was not to be "so easily subjugated as they imagine and we will teach them the truth if they require a century to learn the lesson." The South was in the right and "God will defend us." [8]

Never were a people surer of who was in the right or where God stood. Declaring that the firing on Fort Sumter was forced upon the South, a Savannah lady wrote in April, 1861, "We are conscious that we are in the right, and may trust our cause with the Judge of all the earth." [9]

As to God's favor she had the word of Bishop Stephen Elliott of Savannah. Singularly handsome, impressive in physique and possessed of magnificent presence as a speaker, this Episcopal prelate rendered yeoman service to the Confederacy in the pulpit. No one was more deft in associating God and the cause of the South. "The conflict in which you are about to mingle is one waged upon the holiest grounds of self-preservation and self-defence," Elliott declared in June, 1861. "We are fighting to prevent ourselves from being transferred from American republicanism to French democracy. . . . We are fighting to protect and preserve a race who form a part of our household, and stand with us next to our children. We are fighting to drive away from our sanctuaries the infidel and rationalistic principles which are sweeping over the land and substituting a gospel of the stars and stripes for the gospel of Jesus Christ." [10]

3.

"We are a miniature Sparta"

≈IN FEBRUARY, 1861, Francis S. Bartow, now Chairman of the Military Affairs Committee of the Provisional Congress of the Confederate States, wrote a note to Colonel Lawton from Montgomery. "Will the armament of the forts be increased, and from what source? How much powder has the State of Georgia on hand, & what materials for making powder? Is there any one in Georgia disposed to establish a powder mill & where?" Lawton passed the inquiries on to Adjutant General Wayne with the comment, "I can give only a vague reply." [1]

The letter bespoke the topsy-turvy state of military affairs and lack of preparedness for war in the South. While Savannah shared in the general unreadiness for the struggle it was far better prepared than most communities. A strong military tradition existed, and the city boasted nine volunteer companies. They made up the 1st Volunteer Regiment of Georgia. Commanded by Colonel Lawton, a graduate of West Point who took up the career of law, it was less a regiment than a legion. "In the thought of every volunteer," according to William Basinger, "the Regiment was only a convenience." The company was the real object of "his affection and pride." [2]

The oldest of these independent companies was the Chatham Artillery. The members prized two handsome brass field pieces that President Washington, impressed by what he called the "present dexterous Corps of Artillery," had presented to them following his visit to Savannah in 1791. The Savannah Volunteer Guards was the oldest infantry company in the State. *"Ah! quels beaux soldats!"* Lafayette had exclaimed when they paraded for him on his visit to Savannah. With the approach of war in 1861 their handsome dress outfits were discarded for uniforms of coarse, gray cloth. Bartow admired this service dress so much that he insisted in Congress on the adoption of gray as the prescribed color for the uniform of the Confederate States Army.[3]

The Republican Blues of Savannah had made an excellent impression in New York when the company marched down Broadway during a visit in the summer of 1860. "We have never seen a finer, more gentlemanly set of men," *Leslie's Illustrated Newspaper* reported. The Blues could not return that compliment in respect to certain elements in New York. Only by physical resistance were the visitors able to prevent the Negro servants they brought along from being taken away.

The Georgia Hussars claimed a more ancient lineage than either the Guards or the Republicans, though they were not organized under that name until 1816. Several months before hostilities began they discarded the handsome dress uniforms and adopted a service uniform made of "Georgia cassimere." It consisted of dark blue pants and a duck-tail sack coat with large silver buttons.[4] The members tendered their services to Governor Brown on January 3, 1861, with the request that the company be listed as the first accepted military unit in the State.

Other established military units in the city were the Irish Jasper Greens, the Phoenix Riflemen, the German Volunteers, the DeKalb Riflemen, and the Oglethorpe Light Infantry. As conflict with the North approached, the ranks of all of these organizations were filled. The Savannah Volunteer Guards and the Republican Blues would each become a battalion. The Oglethorpes, the Georgia Hussars and the Jasper Greens were to add a second company.

Volunteers poured into newly formed outfits—the City Light Guards, Washington Volunteers, Tattnall Guards, Irish Volunteers, Coast Riflemen, Emmett Rifles, Savannah Artillery, Blue

Cap Cavalry and the Montgomery Guards. The Savannah Cadets, made up of boys of twelve and fourteen years of age, "are armed with muskets, drill beautifully, and now act on fire alarm duty," reported Mercer in August, 1861. Numerous ephemeral companies came into existence, bearing such names as the Chatham Rifles, Rattle Snakes, Bay Rangers, Hyenas, Buen Hombres (Spanish), Garde Internationale, Dr. Jim Stewart's Sharp Shooters and Warsaw Rifles.

"Our soldiers are diligently preparing for the conflict," wrote Mercer in April, 1861. "Our drill rooms are open nightly; companies drill every afternoon; three corps were on the parade ground last night exercising by moonlight." In the midst of all this warlike work "it was pleasant to walk in the shady park," reported William H. Russell of the London *Times*.[5] But even there, he complained, children in the charge of nurses were playing at soldiers. "We are a miniature Sparta and every man is a soldier," wrote Mercer that August.

A parade of the fourteen Savannah companies comprising the 1st Volunteer Regiment of Georgia was described by the *Morning News* on March 22, 1861, as "the largest body of uniformed volunteer troops ever assembled under one command in Georgia." Led by Colonel Lawton, over one thousand soldiers marched in the column, making "the most imposing and gratifying military display we have seen in Savannah."

The display of military might was entirely a State show. There was little Confederate strength and less organization in the city. On April 11 Bartow telegraphed the Confederate Secretary of War concerning the great uneasiness felt at Savannah because no general officer had been assigned to command the defenses. It was important, he said, that the Confederate authorities should have control of Fort Pulaski. Secretary Walker replied that he had received no notice that the Fort had been transferred by the State to the Confederate government. Furthermore, he had heard nothing from his requisition on Governor Brown for one thousand men for the defense of that post. "We have troops here ready to enter the service of the Confederate government," replied Bartow.

"Don't wait on the Governor. We want the orders and authority of our government." [6]

On April 13, 1861, a general officer was assigned to the command of Savannah, Fort Pulaski and the vicinity. Alexander R. Lawton was commissioned a Brigadier General in the Provisional Confederate Army and given command of the district. His principal concern at the moment was the brick fortress at the mouth of the Savannah. Strenuous efforts had been under way since January to put it in defensible condition. Slaves contributed by planters on the coast had been engaged in clearing mud out of the moats and in other tasks. William H. Russell who visited Cockspur that spring found the entire garrison of 650 soldiers at work. Some were building sandbag traverses, others were rolling stores and casks, and still others were mounting ten-inch columbiads. The guards he saw at the landing were described by him as "tall, stout young fellows, in various uniforms, or in rude mufti in which the Garibaldian red shirt and felt slouched hats predominated." They were armed with smoothbore 1851 muskets, the bayonets, barrels and locks of which were bright and clean. During a tour of the Fort the correspondent noted that the officers were "sharp in tone and manner to their men as volunteers well could be." [7]

The garrison was anxious for the enemy to appear. "The largest cannon we have carries a ball weighing one hundred and twenty-eight pounds. Don't you think such a ball would be a welcome message to any vessel of the honorable Mr. Lincoln?" wrote a Columbus volunteer that April. "The boys are in good spirits 'Spilin' for a fight," he added. From Fort Pulaski Lieutenant James Barrow wrote the same month, "When we get them all down here [the cannon] and mounted we will then be able to defy a whole fleet of vessels. The sooner after this event the vessels come the better pleased we will be for we shall have an opportunity of sinking some of the abolition scoundrels." James Branch, another officer stationed there, informed his mother that the guns he commanded at the Fort would prove to the "Northern Branches that if I am as they think a Traiter that I am at least a *man*." [8]

Less than a mile from Pulaski, across the south channel of the Savannah River, lay sandy Tybee Island. Recognizing its importance to the defense of the Fort, troops were stationed there and a battery built. The island was in some ways a pleasant post. There was a "constant breeze from the sea . . . broad beach for drill" while the "surf bathing was delightful," wrote Mercer in the summer of 1861. There Charles Olmstead got his first command. A conscientious officer, he would inspect the pickets stationed along Tybee beach hourly each night. There were few lonelier sentinel posts in the Confederacy during this summer of '61. "As I rode from one to the other in the black night, with the bare sand dunes on one hand and the rolling waves of the ocean upon the other I seemed to be the only person in the Universe," said Olmstead.[9]

About three miles below the city stood another brick fortification on the Savannah. "The position of Fort Jackson, between this work and the City of Savannah, has caused some uneasiness among our people," Lawton had written from Cockspur Island in January, '61, pointing out that the occupation of that post by Federal troops would cut off communications with the city." [10] Before the end of that month a company was sent to garrison it.

The Savannah River was but one of three approaches to the city by water. South of Little Tybee Island lay Wassaw Sound into which Wilmington River and Tybee Creek emptied. Those streams connected with the Savannah River four miles below the city. To protect the entrance to the sound a battery was erected on the north end of Wassaw Island. It was described as a "well constructed" octagonal work with platforms for eight guns.[11] For further protection against attack by way of the Wilmington River works were thrown up at Thunderbolt, four and a half miles southeast of the city, at the head of the mainland on the Wilmington River. While it was an earthwork, it was a heavy one.

Another access to the mainland southeast of the city was through Ossabaw Sound and up the Vernon River—the same route the French had taken when they landed during the American

Revolution. To seal that particular approach a fortification was erected on Green Island in the summer of 1861 by three hundred Negro laborers furnished by Captain Screven of the Savannah Volunteer Guards. The Great Ogeechee River also flowed into Ossabaw, and twelve miles south of Savannah it afforded a landing place on the northern bank. A vital railroad stood there. To protect the railroad line a fortification was begun in June, 1861, at Genesis Point on the south bank some miles downstream.

Lieutenant Charles C. Jones, Jr., of the Chatham Artillery (who doubled as Mayor of Savannah during 1861) thought that General Lawton was disposing his forces around Savannah to poor advantage. An isolated company posted here and there, with no reserve corps to support it, could do little more than watch the movements of the enemy, he pointed out. What was needed was a regular system of fortification at the most accessible points, with heavy, well-manned batteries and with reserve forces to support them in the event of "hostile Demonstrations." [12] With the means he possessed, which were not considerable, Lawton was striving during this first summer of the war toward just such an end.

In August, 1861, a Savannahian reported that "the engineers are getting the coast in splendid order now. It will soon be bristling with guns from Tybee to Fernandina." [13] A correspondent in the *Morning News* on September 5 of that year predicted that "when the works of defence which have begun are completed Georgia may be considered secure from an invasion by sea." The *Republican* was more sanguine. A few days earlier, it assured the public that "within one week from today no Federal fleet will be able to enter a harbor or inlet, or effect a landing of troops on the coast of Georgia."

But what of naval forces? With a seacoast 3,500 miles long the Confederacy went to war without any semblance of a Navy. To be sure, officers from the old Navy were plentiful. Their choice of allegiance was a hard one, even for men like Edward C. Anderson who had resigned his commission several years before the war and had come back to Savannah to live. "I had been reared under

the U. S. flag in the Navy," he said, "and was to the innermost
recesses of my nature attached to its folds." But the die was cast,
he added, "and my lot as a Southern man with it."

For officers who did not go with their native states Southerners
had only contempt. During the course of the war Anderson ran
into Lieutenant Commander Edward E. Stone of the U. S. Navy
aboard a truce ship. A former Savannahian, Stone had chosen
the Northern side in the struggle. When he bowed in recognition
to Colonel Anderson the Confederate officer assumed an expression
of such utter contempt that Stone looked "abashed & sheepish."
Of another officer who forsook the South William Basinger wrote
later, "I do not wish ever to see him again." He was alluding to
Stephen Vincent Benet of Florida who had attended the University
of Georgia with him. Later Benet graduated from West Point. "I
consider that he was a traitor to his country," explained Basinger.[14]

The most prominent of the seafaring Georgians who came back
was Josiah Tattnall. Born sixty-five years before on the plantation
of Governor Tattnall near Savannah, he had served under the
Stars and Stripes for forty-eight years. In China during 1859
Tattnall had gained fame with his phrase, "Blood is thicker than
water." He was handy at phrases. "Yes, I have reached the Styx,
and I think I have the penny," the old sea-dog told a clergyman
who informed him that his illness was fatal.

At a banquet in Boston a few years before the war he had
exclaimed, "Palsied be the hand of him who attempts the dissolution of this glorious Union." His choice was a difficult one. But
Tattnall could not fight against the land that had given him birth.
As he put it, he could suffer no "consideration or feeling or interest" to interfere with his duty to his own State, on what he
called "this momentous occasion."[15]

He was bitterly assailed in the North for this choice. "The
traitor Tattnall" one of his naval associates called him. A particularly vicious article appeared in the New York *Times*. Paulding
Tattnall defended his father in the public prints. The "Republic of
America" was a thing of the past, "its Government a corpse," he
argued, contending that unless officers renewed their oath of

allegiance under a different form continued service was voluntary —not a matter of duty.[16]

In February Tattnall was commissioned Senior Flag Officer of the Georgia Navy. Of all hyperboles, "Navy of Georgia" must be accounted one of the most hyperbolical. It was non-existent. Adjutant General Wayne had shopped around the North trying to purchase vessels. W. B. Hill had been sent to Philadelphia to purchase ships and war materiel under instructions to communicate with "our confidential agent Mr. Henry Simons, 105 Arch Street." In telegrams he was to refer to schooners as "lumber" and to steamers as "iron." [17] Neither "lumber" nor "iron" was to be had in the North—nor much of either in the South.

"So there is one Steamer for our Navy to begin with," Wayne could inform Commander C. Manigault Morris of the Georgia Navy on February 19, 1861. She was the *Everglade,* purchased at Savannah for $40,000. A paddle-wheeler, 122 feet in length and of 383 tons burden, she had been a passenger vessel in the inland waters. According to an advertisement, the main salon of the *Everglade* was fitted up in "a most elegant style" while adjacent to it was "a most convenient dressing room for the ladies." One could boast less of her boiler—at least in 1861. With care, said Morris, it would "last three years." [18] By mounting two smooth-bore cannon on her deck the *Everglade* was converted into a fighting ship. Renamed the *Savannah,* this former river-boat became the flagship of the Georgia Navy.

"I took command of the Steamer *Savannah* this afternoon, with officers and men numbering forty-five," John McIntosh Kell wrote on February 28, 1861. Two weeks later he was able to say that his complement of officers and crew, now totalling sixty-one, would be "a formidable body of men" when he got them well drilled to their arms. Their uniform, at least the one prescribed by Adjutant General Wayne, was the same as the "U S service with exception of the buttons and except the eagle on the chapeau." [19] The crew was armed with fifty Maynard rifles, cutlasses, pikes and Colt revolvers.

The prescribed "cruizing ground" of the *Savannah* was from

the Savannah to the St. Mary's River. The Adjutant General ordered visits to "such islands and harbors as may be thought best with a view of giving confidence to the planters along the coast." The maiden voyage of the *GS Savannah* down the coast created more consternation than confidence. When she anchored at Sunbury one day, the terror-stricken inhabitants were certain the Yankees had arrived. "One of them actually took to the woods," said Kell.[20]

John Newland Maffitt assumed command of the *Savannah* when she was transferred to the Confederate States service in May. "A more absurd abortion for a man of war was rarely witnessed," he said. Others had the same opinion. "A single shell from one of the gun-boats outside would have blown her up," claimed James D. Bulloch.[21] The other vessels in Tattnall's squadron were even more ludicrous. The *Sampson* and the *Resolute* were both old tugs that were converted to warships by the addition of a cannon. Like them, the *Huntress* was a side-wheeler with her engine and boiler on deck.

Called on for an opinion, Lieutenant Maffitt "unhesitatingly condemned the whole squadron save as provisional gun-boats." Tattnall's ideas on that subject were not basically different. The Commodore "often makes holy vows that he will yet sink each and all those d—d old tubs off the bar," it was reported by a former resident of Darien. If he did not say it, the Flag Officer probably thought as much. "I suppose," wrote a friend, "no officer of his rank and quality was ever doomed to the indignity of such an inefficient command." [22]

Maffitt recommended that vessels of proper capacity be built and purchased immediately, and that propellers be bought in England and in France with "powerful engines to be taken for gunboats . . . & adapted to our waters." Easier said than done. When William Howard Russell visited Fort Pulaski on May 11, 1861, he pointed out certain weaknesses in the position to General Lawton. "The Commodore," Lawton replied, "will take care of the Yankees at sea, and we shall manage them on land." Josiah Tattnall was present. "Where are the ships?" he interjected with a rueful smile. "I have no fleet! Long before the South has a fleet to cope with the North, my bones will be whitening in the grave!" [23]

On his way down the Savannah River that year to board the racing yacht *America* for an important mission to England, Major Edward Anderson could only sympathize with the envious midshipmen he saw on Tattnall's flagship. They were "doomed" he recorded in his diary on May 31, 1861, "to pass their inactive lives in the tranquil waters of the Savannah without the chance or prospect of honorable service from the very nature of the worthless craft they were attached to."

4.

"I go to illustrate . . . my native State"

⤺ THE DEFENSE of Georgia, for Joseph E. Brown, transcended the military exigencies of the Confederacy elsewhere. In that respect a sour note injected itself into his plans. Virginia was to be the first theatre of war and the traditional military organizations of Savannah wanted to be there when the shooting started. "Many of our men are burning to fly to the assistance of old Virginia," reported Lieutenant Mercer in April, 1861. Their wishes made little difference to the Governor. He was determined "to keep all our troops in and near Savannah for the protection of the City and coast," Mercer complained. Savannah could have twenty full companies in Virginia "if only permitted to leave." [1]

Camping around the city was not the way some Georgians wanted to fight the war. The commander of the Wrightsville Infantry wrote to a delegate in the Confederate Congress asking his help in getting the outfit moved from Savannah to some place *"where there is a prospect of a fight."* A member of the Volunteer Guards proposed to go back home to Thomas County "till I can see some necessity for my services or go to Virginia where there is a pressing demand for men." From the same post another soldier wrote that "like the troops every where else the men are anxious to go to Virginia." Meanwhile, he hoped that the "Yankees will change their programme and come this way." Personally, he was ready for them. "I put several bullets through a piece of paper about a foot square at a hundred yards," and he was sure he "could do as well for the 'brethren' of the North." [2]

General Lawton informed Governor Brown in June, 1861, that "the 'rage' for Virginia is now so great that it is difficult to impress upon our troops the duty of defending our own State." Confessing a desire to be "where grander military movements are in *progress*," Lawton nevertheless pointed out that a soldier "has no right to *select* his post of duty." A few weeks earlier Adjutant General Wayne had written privately to President Davis about the situation in the 1st Regiment of Georgia Volunteers, "a fine Regiment consisting of the flower of the City, of all classes." It was disintegrating by what he called "desertions to Richmond and Norfolk." If the President would call upon Georgia for a regular regiment detailed to service at Fort Pulaski, things could be arranged locally by Wayne and it might help to keep the outfit intact.[3] A member of that regiment wrote in the *Morning News* on April 27, "Service is what they want, and what they will have. . . . If Governor Brown will not use us, other Governors will."

Two Savannah companies were hell-bent on getting to the front. When President Davis was inaugurated, the Hussars had proffered their services to the Confederacy, proposing to put themselves in Virginia fully equipped without cost to the government. "Got no use for cavalry," replied Secretary of War Walker.[4] After First Manassas when it became clear that cavalry were badly needed the offer was accepted. However, the equipment of the Hussars belonged to the State and Governor Brown refused to give his consent to their leaving Georgia. The men furnished their own horses, pistols and sabres. The privilege of fighting outside Georgia cost them an estimated $25,000.

That the Oglethorpe Light Infantry got to Virginia was entirely the result of the efforts of Captain Francis S. Bartow who had no intention of enduring the "inglorious ease" to which he claimed Governor Brown had relegated the Savannah companies. The Governor had refused to tender their services to the Confederacy for the period of the war. However, in the spring of 1861 the Confederate Congress passed an act authorizing the President to accept the service of independent commands smaller than regiments. As soon as the bill became law Congressman Bartow telegraphed the news from Montgomery. That night the Oglethorpes met at Savannah. "Amid a storm of enthusiasm and excitement" they unanimously offered their services to the Confederate States.[5] Bartow personally took the telegram announcing the decision of his company to President Davis. The offer was accepted.

Governor Brown now went into action. The arms of the Oglethorpe Light Infantry belonged to Georgia. (The United States government had furnished them to the State originally.) On May 14 the Governor issued an order prohibiting any company from taking equipment furnished by the State beyond its borders without his consent. The *Republican* thought Brown had selected an "unfortunate time" to stand on punctilio. "From the beginning a misunderstanding seems to have existed between him and the Confederate authorities, to be found, with no other State." It was high time this business were brought to a close, added the editor. "He is a picayune of a man," wrote Judge Levi D'Lyon. "He has grown entirely too large for his Breeches." [6]

To the anger of Governor Brown his edict was ignored. "I take my departure to-day with my Company, the Oglethorpe Light Infantry, for Virginia, under the orders of the President of the Confederate States," Captain Bartow informed him on May 21. He hoped the blessings and commendation of every one in Georgia would follow him. "I go to illustrate, if I can, my native State; at all events, to be true to her interests and her character." [7]

Great enthusiasm marked the entrainment of his company. According to the *Republican,* an "immense multitude" turned out. The other military companies marched with the members to the Central Railroad depot while the band played "Bold Soldier Boy." A flag made by some ladies was presented to the outfit. Captain Bartow accepted it with a few remarks. "Tears coursed down many a rugged cheek," reported the *Morning News.* "I have not led them to this fight. They have led me," said Bartow, pledging in their behalf that "should they fail to bring back to you this flag, it will be because there is not one arm left among them to bear it aloft." [8]

One woman was so moved she scribbled a bit of verse which appeared a week later in the *Morning News* with the explanation that it was "Impromptu." The opening lines read:

> Go forth! ye warriors, to the battle field,
>   Not e'en one inch to Lincoln yield.
> Fight for your country, fight for your lives,
>   Fight for your mothers, fight for your wives,
> Fight for your sisters, fight for your babes,
>   Tread down the dastard horde of Old Abe's.

The day after the company departed a "Weeping, Hoping Mother" wrote, "We send them from us with willing though weeping hearts, *knowing,* being assured, that they will front the foe unflinchingly, and never surrender." The Oglethorpes were sure of that. "We are drilling hard; and should we go to Manassas Gap, I think the O.L.I. will give a good account of themselves," wrote one of its members from Richmond. From the trip northward that spring many of these young men were to come home, if at all, in wooden boxes. "They left their dead and wounded on every battlefield from Manassas to Appomatox," wrote an historian of the company.[9]

The malice of the Governor followed Bartow to Virginia. "You have carried away from Savannah . . . some of her bravest and best young men," charged Brown in a letter written on May 29. "Should the city be attacked or destroyed in your absence, I fear you would not receive the commendation of these mothers and sisters, whose sons and brothers you took from that city to fill places in Virginia, which thousands of others would gladly have occupied." With "little time and less inclination" to reply to what he termed "the insolent missive," Bartow nevertheless penned a long reply from Harpers Ferry. "I assure you, in passing," he told Brown, "that I shall never think it necessary to obtain *your* consent to enter the service of my country. God forbid that I should ever fall so low."[10]

In June, a few weeks after the Oglethorpes left town, the Pulaski Guards departed for Virginia. They went with the blessings of

Bishop Elliott. "Ye may go to battle without any fear, and strike boldly for your homes and your altars without any guilt," he assured the members. "The church will sound the trumpets that shall summon you to the battle."

It was to the sound of company drums and not to the trumpets of the church that the Oglethorpes went into battle two months to the day after they left home. Meanwhile they had become part of the 8th Georgia Regiment made up of a number of independent companies from the State. Captain Bartow became Colonel Bartow. Shortly afterward the Savannahian was given command of a brigade of five regiments, including the 7th, 8th and 9th Georgia. By courtesy he was now General Bartow though he did not yet have a Brigadier's commission.

"I trust, if God spares my life, I shall set foot again upon the soil of Georgia and be well assured," he had informed Governor Brown, "that I no more fear to meet my enemies at home than I now do to meet the enemies of my country abroad." Having made a pledge to the people to meet all the consequences of secession, he was bound, he said, both by honor and duty to be "among the foremost in accepting the bloody consequences." While the opposing armies were concentrating for the first big battle of the war Bartow had a talk with a Virginian. The latter remarked that the odds were against the Confederates. "We shall not count the odds," rejoined the Georgian. "I shall go into that fight with a determination never to leave the field alive, but in victory, and I know that the same spirit animates my whole command." More than once, according to Thomas R. R. Cobb, Bartow informed his wife that he wanted to die on the field of battle defending the liberty of his country.[11]

Such were the feelings of the man who on July 20, 1861, reached Manassas Junction. The train had taken all night to make the last twenty-five miles. "I have disliked the looks of a freight car ever since," said Berrien Zettler. The night before the battle Bartow talked to his old company—"B.B.B.'s," people called them, for "Bartow's Beardless Boys." "Our Captain (God bless him!) treats us more like his children than like soldiers," one of them had written half complainingly from Richmond. It was not unnatural. There was scarcely a married man in the whole lot and most were under twenty years of age.[12]

According to Zettler, Bartow gave them "a fatherly talk." He had secured for his old company the honor of being in the opening of the battle which would begin early the next morning and he was sure they would acquit themselves well. "But remember, boys," he warned, "battle and fighting mean death, and probably before sunrise some of us will be dead." En route to Virginia that night was a letter from Savannah that John L. Branch would never receive. "My heart akes dreadfully I am so sad to think of the fate of the First Georgia Reg.," Mrs. Branch wrote. "May God protect you, My dear, dear boy is the earnest prayer of your fond Mother."[13]

As Private Berrien Macpherson Zettler lay on his blanket that night he looked up at the stars and thought of the morrow. He was "homesick," he had to confess. Nearby was Julius Ferrill. "Such a manly, whole-souled, little fellow" one of his officers had never seen in all his life. As Ferrill lay down to sleep that night he, too, probably looked up at the stars and was homesick. Perhaps frightened, too. What was it that Captain Bartow had said the day they left Savannah? "They were going to lay themselves down to sleep on the bosom of Virginia."[14]

Sunrise came and nobody was dead. In fact they hadn't even been in a fight. Colonel Bartow moved about nervously and then rode off. Returning about eight, he announced, according to Zettler, "Get ready, men! the battle has been raging for two hours on our extreme left, and we must go there at once." McDowell's effort to flank the Confederate line had become apparent. The 8th Georgia marched at double quick for five miles through the heat and dust with Bartow frequently galloping up to troops already in position to inquire, "Is this our extreme left?" He finally found it in a corn field on the brow of a hill. At this point a Union battery opened on the regiment—its baptism of fire. "If my hair at that moment had turned as white as cotton it would not have surprised me," wrote Zettler.

The 8th Georgia participated in some of the hardest fighting of the day. Along with the men of Bee and Evans the regiment bore for some time the brunt of the Union attack. It suffered heavily

(207 casualties out of five hundred men) and became badly dis-
organized. But when the battle was over Beauregard would say,
"I salute the Eighth Georgia with my hat off." Of seventy-eight
members of the Oglethorpes who went into action that day six
were killed, twenty wounded, and twenty-nine hit but not badly
hurt. Julius A. Ferrill, John L. Branch, George M. Butler, William H. Crane, Bryan Morel and Thomas Purse had attended
Sunday School together at the Independent Presbyterian Church
at Savannah. They were to be there once more—in February,
1862, the day their mass funeral took place. "All young, all un-
married, all gentlemen, there was not one of the killed," said a
Savannah newspaper, "who was not an ornament to his community and freighted with brilliant promise."

There was another casualty among the Oglethorpe Light Infantry. At a critical moment in the battle its former captain rode
up to Beauregard. "What shall I do, tell me, and if in the power of
man, I will do it," Colonel Bartow asked. "Take that position,"
the General replied, pointing left and forward.[15] The 7th Georgia
had now come up and its colonel, Lucius Gartrell, inquired where
he should go. "Give me your flag, and I will tell you," answered
Bartow. Leading that regiment to its stand, he exhorted, "Gen.
Beauregard says you must hold this position and Georgians, I appeal to you to hold it." Not long afterward he was wounded in
the leg. Remounting another horse, Bartow waved his cap about
his head and called upon the men to advance upon a Union
battery. Then he was hit again. His talent for phrase-making did
not fail him at the end. To those who gathered around Colonel
Bartow said, "They have killed me, boys, but never give up the
field!" He emphasized "never," wrote a correspondent in the *Morning News* on August 1, with "his peculiar and stirring manner,
that all who knew him will so feelingly recall."

President Davis' wife volunteered to break the news to his
widow. Before she could say a word the latter covered her face
with her shawl. "Is it bad news for me? . . . Is he killed?"
Later Mrs. Bartow confided, "As soon as I saw Mrs. Davis's face
. . . I knew it all. . . . I knew it before I wrapped the shawl
about my head." A week after his death Colonel Bartow was

buried at Savannah. Four gray horses drew the hearse which bore the coffin. All the military turned out and an "immense concourse of citizens thronged the Bay," according to the *Morning News* which called it the "most solemn and imposing spectacle we have ever witnessed in Savannah." [16]

While Bartow was perhaps "not wholly free from minor defects," said the Milledgeville *Southern Recorder* on July 30, "his name is immortal, and will be ranked in future years among the purest patriots and most chivalrous men who ever served in council, or commanded in the field." According to Mayor Jones, "None ever for a moment doubted his bravery—and he has left to our army and to his country, a signal illustration of true Southern valor." [17]

While grieving for the dead ("I am truly living in a graveyard," wrote Jones), Savannahians gloried in the famous victory. The good Lord was responsible. "Our hearts are filled with gratitude to God," said the Mayor's mother. "God be praised," exclaimed Olmstead.[18] In a sermon entitled, "God's Presence with our Army at Manassas," Stephen Elliott affirmed that "God was evidently there, strengthening the hearts of our struggling soldiers and bringing the haughty down to the dust."

One of the happiest of Southerners was Edward C. Anderson who was in Liverpool when tidings of the victory came. Jumping into a cab, he drove rapidly "to Prioleaus to give him the news and to run up the Confederate flag on his housetop." Inspired by a half crown tip, the cabman mounted to the top of the carriage and "made the welkin ring with his cheers." [19] In roseate prospective, another Savannahian envisioned a bright aftermath of the Confederate victory in Virginia. "Arlington possessed & Washington threatened if not taken," predicted William Duncan. How much farther north Confederate arms would go depended on the circumstances. In any event, Philadelphia should be asked to contribute "by way of a levy of ten millions to help pay the expenses of the war." [20]

The war did not end on July 21, 1861. Within four months it was to come much closer to Savannah than Manassas.

5.

Coming of the Vandals

⇐ AT THE end of October, 1861, a large Union fleet sailed southward from Hampton Roads. "In so righteous a cause as ours, and
against so wicked a rebellion, we must overcome all difficulties,"
wrote its commander upon his departure.[1] Since the moral armament of the enemy was quite equal to Flag Officer Du Pont's, something more was needed to assure victory to the cause of righteous-
ness.

Du Pont possessed it—seventy-four vessels of all kinds, including gunboats, frigates, sloops of war, transports and colliers.
Aboard the troop ships were twelve thousand men under command
of Brigadier General Thomas West Sherman.* "Probably it was
the most carefully prepared and most complete expedition ever
put afloat," wrote Mercer, "not so large as Philip's Armada but
far more thorough."[2]

Every precaution had been taken to conceal the destination of
the fleet. The captains sailed under sealed orders. Men could only
guess at the objectives. An exception must be made in the case of
Bradley Sillick Osbon who went to Washington to obtain permission to accompany the expedition. While waiting to see the Secretary of the Navy this New York *Herald* reporter espied on a desk in
an outer office a chart of Port Royal, South Carolina. "Mr.

---

* Not to be confused with General William Tecumseh Sherman, the
better-known Union General.

[34]

Welles," said Osbon, while the old gentleman stared at him in surprise, "will you kindly give me a letter to the commanding officer of the expedition that is going to Port Royal." [3] The South was as well informed as this brash Northern reporter. "I have just received information, which I consider entirely reliable, that the enemy's expedition is intended for Port Royal," Secretary of War Judah P. Benjamin telegraphed to South Carolina the day after it sailed.

For a base on the south Atlantic coast the naval authorities selected a harbor that three centuries before Jean Ribaut had pronounced "one of the greatest and fayrest havens of the worlde." Port Royal was scarcely twenty-five miles from Savannah on paper and but a few more by water.

When news of the destination of the fleet reached Commodore Tattnall, his cockle-shell steamers paddled over to Port Royal Sound—the *Savannah, Sampson, Resolute* and *Lady Davis.* "Miserable affairs," Edward Anderson called them—"so conspicuous with their deck cabins . . . as to render it impossible for the enemy to miss them." [4] From Savannah also went four hundred fifty troops under Colonel William H. Stiles.

To protect Port Royal Sound earthwork batteries had been erected at each side of its entrance—Fort Walker on the northern tip of Hilton Head, and three miles across the water at Bay Point, a battery named Fort Beauregard. The works were poorly planned, complained Lieutenant John Maffitt who had recommended that the cannon be spread out along the beach rather than concentrated. He had also urged that a prize brought into Beaufort, the *A. B. Thompson,* be converted into an ironclad floating battery and anchored in the middle of the channel. [5] As befell most of the recommendations Maffitt made, they were not followed.

Commanding the troops on Hilton Head Island was Thomas F. Drayton of South Carolina. Commanding the *USS Pocahontas* which took part in the attack on the Confederate defenses was Charleston-born Percival Drayton, his brother. Evil tongues at Savannah would connect that relationship in rationalizing the results of the battle. ("The people say that General Drayton did not fight hard, because he had a brother who commanded one of the enemy vessels in the attack.") [6] The causes of Southern disaster were deeper rooted than the Drayton consanguinity.

November 7, 1861, was an exquisite Indian summer day. "No breath of wind marred the smooth surface of the ocean, and it shone like a thousand mirrors," wrote a Confederate soldier. With the forty-eight-gun *Wabash* in the van the Union ships made a majestic spectacle as they steamed on an elliptic course past the land batteries, slowing down to fire a broadside each time they came opposite. For four hours the Union fleet pounded away at the forts. The *Wabash* alone fired 880 shells. "I will repeat to the day of my death, that the second assault of this ship . . . for rapidity, continuity, and precision of fire, has never been surpassed in naval warfare," wrote Commodore Du Pont. "Such utter destruction probably never overtook a fortification," a Northern officer said of Fort Walker.[7]

For the South it was a day of humiliation. The Confederacy received an elementary lesson in seapower. "The battle of Port Royal," reported the commander of Fort Walker, "has been lost, but the enemy, I sincerely believe, have paid very dear for their success." [8] The dear price of victory consisted of damaged rigging on several of the ships, a few holes in hulls and eight seamen killed and six seriously wounded. The marksmanship of the Confederates was "wretched," asserted Maffitt. They had never practiced at a target and knew so little "about the exercise of the carriages that they failed to throw them out of gear—& thus all the 8 10 and 11 inch guns recoiled off the slides."

The Confederates departed somewhat hastily. "Yes, sir," yelled Bradley Osbon from his perch high up on the *Wabash,* "they are taking to the woods as fast as their legs can carry them." It was no exaggeration. Hearing from aloft a cry that the defenders were leaving, Commander Steedman of the *Bienville* hurried to the top of the wheel-house. "Sure enough," he confirmed, "they were scampering as fast as their legs could carry them." [9]

Across the water at Fort Beauregard the withdrawal was somewhat more leisured. Captain Stephen Elliott, Jr., of the Beaufort Artillery had time to write a note requesting (with an appropriate Latin quotation) that the enemy kindly treat the soldiers who could not be removed. He explained to the victors that the defenders chose to leave the untenable position so that they could "assist in establishing the Southern Confederacy" to better purposes than was possible at Bay Point.

Aboard the Union transports the soldiers sang hymns and shouted "Glory!" reported Osbon. "When our men went on shore and planted the Stars and Stripes," wrote a New York soldier, "then you ought to hear the Chears ring from the fleat lode and long." [10] Carnival scenes took place there. On getting ashore a New England private was greeted "by a peculiar and strong smell" which he afterwards learned came from quantities of whiskey that "the rebels had purposely spilled." Apparently not all of it had been spilled. The scene on the beach was "a perfect pandemonium" said another Northerner, with guns going off, "some fired by drunken marines and others by disorderly soldiers, men screaming, yelling and rushing about in perfect disorder." [11]

The pandemonium of the Federal landing hardly exceeded that of the Confederate departure. "The rebels ran in the extremest fright, abandoning almost every thing but the clothing on them," reported Colonel Joseph R. Hawley of the 7th Connecticut. [12] Confederate confirmation of the disorder was not lacking. "The confusion in retreat was awful," declared Maffitt. No provision had been made for a probable defeat, he claimed. The troops were evacuated so hurriedly they could not return to camp for their blankets and knapsacks.

The penchant of Savannahians for faultfinding is reflected in letters of the time. "Genl. Draytons conduct is severely commented on & our Col Stiles faces worse," wrote William Duncan. "Many ill natured remarks are made of him which I cant trust on paper but some of which would make you laugh." All the talk about Stiles having two horses shot from under him was "simple nonsense," said Charles C. Jones, Jr., who added that "Randolph

Spalding is represented to have been so drunk that he could not take command of his Regiment when ordered to the relief of the Port Royal Batteries." [13]

Maffitt's only compliments were reserved for Tattnall's naval squadron. The mosquito fleet "boldly engaged the overwhelming force of the enemy with a gallantry that was unprecedented." The lieutenant was incensed that Du Pont in his report "had not the generosity to do justice to the daring and chivalric exertion of his old Commander—nay . . . he speaks slightingly, and gives no credit for a brave enemies bold assault with miserable vessels mounting but two light guns each." A Savannah lady was just as much put out over another enemy slight to Tattnall. When a shell struck the flagship, the venerable Commodore dipped his flag three times in salutation. This civility, complained Mrs. George W. Anderson, had not been returned by Du Pont.[14]

On the part of one Confederate naval officer there was too much boldness, thought Tattnall. The guilty party was none other than John Newland Maffitt. While Commodore Tattnall was ashore at Bay Point on November 5 the lieutenant took the *Savannah* too near the enemy gunboats. On the *Seneca* Commander Daniel Ammen personally sighted one of the guns. The ball ricochetted across the water and struck the Commodore's flagship in the hog braces. According to Ammen, Lieutenant Maffitt was "half seas over." Tattnall was exceedingly wrothful. As soon as he could get back aboard he had Maffitt placed under arrest. The latter claimed that his orders were that no "sounding" by the enemy was to be permitted. "I saw the Yankees sounding & went at them," he explained.[15]

Back at Savannah the inhabitants listened excitedly to the cannonade at Port Royal. With their customary capacity for foolish optimism they believed the forts capable of withstanding any naval force. Panic is the word for the reaction there to the debacle. It was impossible to describe, said a Savannahian. "The fleet was hourly expected & the decision with most was to burn their dwellings & let the Yankees have smoking ruins to welcome them." [16]

Large crowds gathered in the streets and around the newspaper and telegraph offices. Outgoing trains were packed. "The Cars twice a day are loaded down with women & children bound to the Interior," wrote Mrs. George Anderson. "You would be surprised," said another resident, "to see how deserted our town is. The church today looked like it does in yellow fever time." [17]

"We are all in confusion, every body running 'hither & yon,' " wrote William Duncan the day after the disaster. "If the enemy comes between us & the fort which they can do in 12 hours as I have said, we are at their mercy (?) & would have to capitulate on their own terms." George Mercer complained that "there were men (?) here who counseled the evacuation of the Green Island battery *and even of Fort Pulaski,* and who believed that Savannah could be captured by a single gun boat." The enemy was not in disagreement. "That Savannah could have been taken by a regiment within forty eight hours after the Port Royal affair I have not the least doubt," affirmed a Union naval officer. [18]

The gunsmoke had not yet settled over Port Royal when Robert E. Lee reached Coosawatchie and assumed command of the Military Department of South Carolina, Georgia and Florida. He is said to have commented that if he had been there in time, "there would never have been a single gun fired, nor a man or gun on the island." [19] To have surrendered Port Royal without a fight would merely have shifted the accent of Southern reaction from one of anguish to anger.

Disaster, despair and disorganization greeted General Lee in assuming command of the Department. After a tour of the coastal defenses south of Savannah to Amelia Island, he described them as "poor indeed." In the next four months he would accomplish much in establishing a workable policy for the defense of more than two hundred miles of the south Atlantic littoral.

In the course of duty Lee was to visit Savannah several times. To most people in Georgia who met or saw him he was but another Confederate general. Letter writers and diarists frequently mention his name, little else. His innate simplicity was recognized by a soldier who observed him during an inspection tour of St.

Simons Island. "We were visited the other day," he wrote, "by Gens Lee, Lawton, and Mercer and a good many other little puffs, Gen Lee was dressed very plainly while his inferiors were dressed within 'an inch of their lives.'" Olmstead alone seemed to sense unusual qualities in the man who was to command the Army of Northern Virginia. His description of Lee as he saw him that fall at Fort Pulaski was written long after the war. "Tall in stature, straight as an arrow, well knit and vigorous in frame yet graceful and easy in movement, a well shaped head just beginning to be touched with gray." In Lee's face kindliness and sweetness of temper were blended with firmness of purpose and dignified reserve.

If these physiognomic qualities made any such impression on Olmstead in 1861, he did not reveal it in a letter he wrote about Lee from Fort Pulaski on November 21. His character, however, left a contemporaneous imprint on Olmstead's mind. A man who could so "thoroughly & delicately appreciate the feelings of one in a much humbler sphere than himself" was "just the one to lead others." An accompanying remark by him hints that not everyone agreed on the subject of the military officer some people were calling "Granny Lee" as a result of failures in western Virginia. "I would like to have you tell Mrs. Philbrick about this," requested Olmstead, who thought it would give her greater confidence in the General.[20] Mrs. Philbrick probably required more assurance than that. The weeks that followed Lee's assumption of command seemed merely to compound disaster.

Garrisons were withdrawn from exposed positions on islands and large areas of the coast abandoned. The troops on Tybee Island had been evacuated in the retrenchment following the Port Royal fiasco. Before many days Union gunboats were at the mouth of the Savannah River. On November 24 the *Seneca, Augusta* and *Pocahontas* crossed the bar and anchored off Tybee where a picket was still stationed. "About ten o'clock," a Confederate private wrote in his diary, "the Yankees commenced to shell us and kept at it for about two hours, when we retreated from the Island under fire of their shells. . . ."[21] At forty-five minutes after three p.m.," he continued, "thirteen surf-boats loaded with men landed on the Island, and raised the Stars and Stripes." *

A few days after this incursion Du Pont's gunboats reconnoitered the two sounds immediately to the south of Tybee. Early in December a landing force went ashore on the north end of Wassaw Island where the Federals ascertained that the Confederate battery located there had recently been evacuated and destroyed. Captain Rodgers' flotilla then proceeded to the mouth of the Wilmington River. From that point they could see, glistening in the sun, the bayonets of Confederate soldiers on the ramparts of a fortification on Skidaway Island. Six days later the same gunboats reconnoitered Ossabaw Sound. On Green Island an eight-gun battery and an encampment of about seventy-five tents was observed. The sight of the enemy calmly making their observations from a safe distance was "very aggravating," wrote Basinger who asserted that had they attacked the battery they would have been "signally defeated." Among the Guards at Fort Screven that day was Private Joseph C. Thompson. For this young Savannahian the appearance of the gunboats was an exciting event. "I went in the Battery and took charge of my gun and gave the orders as cooly as if I was at drill," he proudly informed his father. "Tell Mother," he added, "I went . . . ready to die like a man and a Soldier, with the only present she gave me, next my heart, my Bible." [22]

The evacuation of Tybee and Wassaw greatly perturbed Savannahians. "Where are our men?" complained a correspondent in the *Morning News* on November 26, 1861. "Do we intend waiting until the Hessians march up Bull Street before we repel them?" The Milledgeville *Union* asked, "Will the gallant Savannah boys,

* Sixty years later a seaman on the *USS Augusta* who had hoisted the flag at Tybee wrote to Savannah to inquire whether it was the first occasion the Union colors had flown over Georgia soil after the commencement of the war. Colonel Charles H. Olmstead, still in life, replied that quite possibly it was a fact, recalling how, from the ramparts of Fort Pulaski which he had commanded in 1861, he watched "with natural anxiety" the raising of the American flag at Tybee.

and those from the interior who are stationed near Savannah, permit the Yankee invasion of Tybee to pass without making an effort to dislodge the vandals?" If words counted, at least one soldier was willing to try to dislodge "the vandals." A member of Harrison's brigade craved the opportunity. "I would like to get a fair chance at one of the nigerish looking Yankeys. I would make him do worse than bite the dust." [23]

Many Savannahians would have agreed with the view of Union Captain Charles Henry Davis who thought it "incredible" that the Confederates should yield up such an important position as Tybee "without a blow. . . . With this post in our possession the fall of Fort Pulaski is only a question of time." There was talk of trying to retake Tybee with the State troops. The plan was abandoned, however. On November 29 a Savannahian wrote, "A thousand men marched down from their camps today to the river to embark for Pulaski intending to make an attack on them tonight, but in two hours they were marched back, why or wherefore we have not yet learned." [24]

Apparently the Confederate authorities had persuaded the Commanding General of the State forces not to make the attempt. The decision to abandon island positions held by manpower sorely needed elsewhere was sound. Too large a force was required at Tybee (three thousand to five thousand men, Charles C. Jones, Jr., estimated). It was in reality no different from other islands which George Mercer described as "nothing but a trap." Jones wrote later, "The art of war, on the coast of Georgia as well as elsewhere, was learned only after a vast and useless expenditure of labor, treasure and valuable time." He was more outspoken in 1862. "It does seem to me," he wrote to his parents, "that all our operations on this Coast have been mere military experiments, conceived in ignorance, and brought forth none the more wisely— mere jackleg performances." [25]

Throughout these weeks Federal gunboats remained in Tybee Roads. Occasionally Tattnall would venture out toward them with his "mosquito fleet," fire a few shots and scurry back under the protection of Fort Pulaski's guns. But for his natural grace and dignity it might have seemed mere bravado, said James D. Bulloch. The enemy did not make that concession. "My cousin Tatnall," wrote Captain Drayton, USN, "takes a look at me with his squadron every now and then, showing an immense admiral's flag to our admiring and wistful gaze, but as he does not leave the protection of Pulasky there the matter ends." [26] The game ended when Tattnall's communication with Savannah was endangered by Federal encroachments up the River.

Five miles above Fort Pulaski a stream known as Mud Creek entered the Savannah River. To the northward the creek joined Wright River, a loop of which passed close to New River. A manmade channel known as Wall's Cut had been dug to connect the two streams. By means of this channel the Savannah River became part of a continuous system of inland waterways leading to Port Royal Sound. Through these creeks and through this cut Lieutenant Colonel John Maitland and his Highlanders had reached Savannah in September, 1779, in time to save the town from its French and American besiegers.

Aware of the potentialities of this waterway, which permitted the bypassing of Fort Pulaski, the Confederates had sunk a large brig across Wall's Cut between rows of piling. The importance of the route was not lost to the enemy, at least not to General Thomas Sherman's topographical officer, James Harrison Wilson, West Point, '60. Equipping himself with a cutter from one of the nearby plantations which he manned with "ten stout sea-island negroes," he could make, despite his indiarubber bed, "eight or nine miles an hour and on a spurt could pass an ordinary steamer." His oarsmen knew the waters for fifty miles up and down the coast as one of them expressed it, "like de palm of my hand." Not many of the waterways held secrets from Lieutenant Wilson, least of all Wall's Cut and Mud Creek. Its importance he had duly reported.[27]

Wilson got the job of removing the obstructions, a project in which he was assisted by a detachment of the 48th New York under Colonel Oliver T. Beard. After hard labor by the men and equally hard profanity by Beard the brig was raised and the piling removed. The work was carried on so quietly that it was not until late in January that the Confederates waked up to the fact that a path was open for gunboats into the Savannah River above Pulaski.

The provisioning of the Fort against a siege became an immediate necessity. On the bright and beautiful day of January 28 Tattnall's flotilla steamed down the Savannah on the mission of convoying two supply ships to Pulaski. A unique engagement in naval annals ensued—a battle simultaneously fought by three separate squadrons in three separate rivers. At the time Tattnall came down the river six Union gunboats were trying to work their way into the Savannah from Wright River by way of Wall's Cut. Three miles to the south a force of seven gunboats commanded by Union Captain Davis was in Wilmington Narrows where it had been halted by the piling placed by the Confederates.

Both squadrons opened on the Confederate vessels. Fearful that the Union gunboats in the Wilmington Narrows might get past the obstructions and cut him off, Commodore Tattnall headed back to the city with the *Savannah* and the *Resolute.* Meanwhile the *Sampson,* convoying two slow-moving supply ships ran the gauntlet of fire to Fort Pulaski. The provisions were delivered. That accomplished, Lieutenant Joel S. Kennard brought the vessels back to Savannah under heavy fire.

According to the *Republican,* the *Sampson* was struck by rifle shells four times. Two passed through her, a third lodged on her deck and a fourth exploded in the store-room "breaking up things generally but damaging no one." It was a wonder the side-wheeler was not blown up as her cylinder was vulnerable for a distance of twelve feet above the water. Lieutenant Kennard "displayed qualities that day that would have made him a man of rank anywhere," said Olmstead.[28] Enemy praise for the Confederate naval officer was not lacking. "A plucky fellow," attested Captain Davis.

The presence of Union gunboats at Wall's Cut and in Wilmington Narrows was part of an effort to cause the Confederates to think Savannah was to be attacked so as to bring about the evacuation of Fernandina and Amelia Island. With Davis's squadron came transports carrying 4,200 troops. What all this elaborate deception accomplished is difficult to see as Fernandina was already in the process of being abandoned. However, some Union officers seemed satisfied. Captain Davis reported that Savannah was thrown into a state of alarm. His excursion up Tybee Creek to the Narrows had also revealed that there were no residents remaining on Wilmington Island. Commander Daniel Ammen had personally performed the feat of snipping the telegraph line connecting the city and Fort Pulaski, an accomplishment which "greatly alarmed the people in Savannah." [29]

While these feats were being accomplished the lice-ridden Union troops crowded aboard transports in Wassaw Sound were having a hard time of it. "For sixteen days," wrote Sergeant Charles K. Cadwell of the 6th Connecticut, "we were fed on salt pork and beef, and no vegetables, with hard tack that was full of vermin. . . ." According to an officer, "their drinking-water was from camphene casks, where it had been put months before" and was "so foul, that the strongest tea could not conceal the nauseating flavor and smell." Spotted fever broke out in the 6th Connecticut. There were several deaths every day.[30]

If this naval demonstration alarmed Savannahians, what happened two weeks later added mortification to fear. When the *Ida* went down to Fort Pulaski on February 13 her crew got a surprise. She was fired on by a Union battery lately erected at Venus Point on Jones Island. The little steamer was in the south channel of the Savannah and made it safely to the Fort. A few days later another Federal battery was built on Bird (or Oakley) Island athwart the south channel. There was to be no more communication by ship between Savannah and Pulaski. The two batteries and the Union gunboats in Mud Creek formed a triangle, reported the *Republican* on February 25, that could not be "passed by any vessel in our service."

The batteries were thrown up atop a marshy ooze which Confederate authorities had pronounced impractical as a site for heavy guns. William R. Boggs, the State military engineer, complained that when he suggested fortifying the islands he was informed by General Lawton that it was not possible "to stand on them, much less occupy them, and that a gun would sink out of sight." [31] The construction of batteries in alluvial slime had not been easy. "Incredible difficulty" was involved in dragging cannon across the marsh to Venus Point, declared Lieutenant Wilson. "A task any rational man would pronounce impossible," another Union soldier called it. "Many fell in the mud and refused to rise, in most cases could not," he added.[32] Equal difficulties attended the erection of the battery on Bird Island. But after a few nights of hard work in bitter weather Battery Vulcan on Venus Point and Battery Hamilton on Bird Island were in existence.

In Savannah there was talk of joint land and naval operations against Bird Island. The proposal was the subject of a lengthy discussion on the night of February 26 at a conference attended by Lee, Lawton, Tattnall and others. Major Anderson strongly opposed the idea. "The hopelessness of the thing struck me at a glance," said the former naval officer who envisioned boats capsizing, crews drowning and other catastrophies, all for the sake of driving the enemy from an island which "we would not possibly keep possession of."

Writing to his son concerning the enemy movements, Robert E. Lee commented that it was "grating to see his progress unopposed by any resistance we can make." He was anxious to "wake the Navy up in some way," wrote Anderson. Something Lee had said in that vein had apparently gotten back to Tattnall and had miffed him. At the council of war a vote was taken unfavorable to the project. The proposition was left open, however, out of deference to the Commodore who did not want to withdraw "even from a hopeless expedition." [33]

On the morning after the conference Lee called upon Tattnall at the latter's headquarters at the corner of Bull and Bryan Streets. The two men remained closeted for some time. As General Lee came out Anderson heard him say that "all was right." Apparently the Commodore's ruffled feelings had been smoothed. The feasibility of a joint expedition was referred to a board of officers which unanimously recommended against the project.

The continuing encroachments by the Federals in the winter of '62 convinced many that an attack on Savannah was at hand. To some people those in command seemed to be making it easy for the enemy. The batteries on Green and on Skidaway Islands were abandoned in March. On the 25th of that month a Union flotilla ascended the Wilmington River and a landing party went ashore on Skidaway Island. Commander John P. Gillis reported that he found there a "strong bastioned work for ten guns, with bomb-proofs, trenches, etc.," recently abandoned. After hoisting the Union flag the party returned to the gunboats.³⁴

Leaving Savannah as rubble was an idea that had staunch pro-ponents. Apparently the talk was more than bravado. When Howell Cobb visited the city in February, '62, he and General Henry R. Jackson agreed that, if captured, it must be "a dearly bought victory and one of ashes." Governor Brown informed Gen-eral Lee on February 8 that were he a Savannahian, he would de-fend the place to the end and leave it in "smoking ruins when driven from it." But the idea of destroying Savannah was op-posed by the more thoughtful. The Augusta *Constitutionalist* interposed a vigorous protest. Such a step would produce no seri-ous disadvantage to the enemy, it argued, and would inflict "a stu-pendous, permanent injury upon the people of the city and the state." ³⁵

Those who feared for Savannah did not reckon, however, with the problem of divided command between the Union land and naval forces at Port Royal or with General Thomas West Sherman, USA. A classic in fatuity was the remark he made in February, 1862. "My opinion," he informed General McClellan, "is that you have about crushed this rebellion already." Not many Union offi-cers had a good word for this Rhode Island soldier. "If the general commanding were a man of vigor and genius, we would be in the city of Savannah in a fortnight," claimed a naval officer in De-cember, '61, complaining that Thomas Sherman constantly found

fault with the volunteers and disparaged his means.[36] Colonel
Joseph Hawley informed Gideon Welles that he "damned and
goddamned his officers before the men themselves." The Hartford
soldier-editor expanded on that subject in a letter to his wife. He
was, Hawley said, a "dyspeptic domineering uneasy fault finding
man with a certain apparent energy . . . but not much fixed
purpose." [37]

The enemy were also among the critics of the Union commander. "Gen. Sherman," the *Morning News* declared on
January 10, 1862, "seems to be pre-eminently endowed with one
attribute at least of generalship—caution." When Thomas Sherman took counsel, it was usually with his fears. "No one is more
anxious than myself to push on and crush out this rebellion," he assured headquarters in December, '61, but "some judgment and
proper prudence [has] to be exercised in this matter." He was not
his own master. "My master," he explained, has been "the exigencies created by want of means and facilities."

He had been at Hilton Head only a few days when he informed
the War Department that ten thousand additional troops were
needed to make his foothold secure. Ten more regiments of infantry along with one cavalry and one artillery regiment would
do the trick. With the forces he had his strategy was necessarily
confined to protecting the position already won.

It was not that Thomas Sherman lacked larger designs. He envisioned what he called a "great dash" on the north side of the
Savannah River and the occupation of that country. That accomplished, the siege of Savannah from the southern side of the
city would be easy. "Every day's delay now is a sad loss," he
warned in January. As he had pointed out a few weeks before,
"Those fellows are getting stronger and stronger every day." Indeed, by the end of February the General was crediting a report by
deserters that there were no less than 65,000 Confederate troops
around Savannah.[38]

In January Sherman thought he had discovered the solution to
the problem of an assault on the city. He conceived the plan of a
joint operation up the Savannah River by a combined land and

naval force. The city would be taken by a *"coup de main"*—a phrase that sounds somewhat incongruous on the lips of this stolid though courageous Rhode Islander. He urged Du Pont to cooperate in his plan. "Will it not be possible to go in there now with a sufficient force to make it a profitable job?" he wrote to the Flag Officer on January 16. Pressing his point, he sent a second letter that day. The Confederates were hard at work (Sherman had learned) building fortifications across from Fort Jackson. "Now is the time before these batteries can be completed," he urged. Before the day was out he wrote a third letter to Du Pont. "Savannah, commodore, is a great point for us and the cause." He was aware of the fact that the Navy was occupied with the project of sinking old whaling vessels brought down from New England ("the stone fleet") in order to block up the harbors of Charleston and Savannah. But he was sure Du Pont would "not let any secondary matter" interfere with his plan.[39]

The Commodore was willing. He had sailed under strict orders from the President concerning "cordial and effectual cooperation between the officers of the two services." But it was necessary, of course, to know whether the proposed route was practicable for his gunboats. Du Pont sent one of his trusted officers to find out. On the night of January 17 John Rodgers, accompanied by Sherman's topographical officer, James H. Wilson, made a reconnaissance of Wall's Cut and of Mud Creek. Wilson reported the passage practicable for gunboats and light transports. Still unconvinced, Commander Rodgers reported that a more thorough survey was necessary.[40]

Ten days later the Navy killed the project. In a second report Rodgers stated that while the route was practicable at high water, once the Union gunboats got into the Savannah River they would be cut off from "retreat or help" except when the tide was flooding. In that event they would have to withstand "all that the South can bring against them." (The might the Confederacy could hurl consisted of a former river passenger boat and two tugs converted into war vessels, the whole squadron being no match for the smallest of Du Pont's gunboats.)

Much disappointed, General Sherman expressed the opinion that had the attack been made Savannah would have resisted but a few hours. Commander Daniel Ammen concurred in respect to the Wilmington Narrows route. "There would have been nothing in the way but Fort Jackson, a little old brick fort that would have been knocked down by half a dozen heavy shells."

It was to be Thomas Sherman's last chance. In February General McClellan told him to forget about an attack on Savannah and to concentrate upon an alternative objective he had proposed.[41] Sherman now turned his attention to a project for which his talents well suited him.

6.

The Brick Fort and the Rifled Cannon

≈ LIKE A fang of the serpentine Savannah, Cockspur Island extrudes at the mouth of the river. The marshy strip has not been without historic associations. There in 1736 John Wesley preached his first sermon in the New World. As the threshold of Georgia, the importance of Peeper Island, as it was first known, was early recognized. In colonial days Fort King George stood there. It was succeeded after the American Revolution by Fort Greene. The latter vanished in the great hurricane of 1804. A quarter-century after its destruction a new fortification designed to be impervious to elements as well as to enemy was commenced. Eighteen years later, after the laying of twenty-five million brick and the expenditure of around $1,000,000, Fort Pulaski was completed. With its masonry walls seven and a half feet thick it was impregnable by all known standards.

Among the Army engineers assigned to this project in the initial stage was a second lieutenant just out of West Point. Thirty years after his last service there Robert E. Lee, now a full General in the Confederate Army, returned to Cockspur Island. On November 11, 1861, he came to inspect the Fort, returning on two occasions that month and again on January 6.

An incident connected with one of his visits revealed his character in "most beautiful light," a soldier informed his wife. As Lee walked up to the Fort with Governor Brown, General Lawton and Commodore Tattnall, followed by several other high ranking

Army and Navy officers, he espied a familiar face. Standing near
the outer bridge at the demi-lune, hand drawn in salute, stood the
former coxswain of the barge that had carried him between Cockspur Island and Savannah many years before. "I ought to know
that man. Why Francis! is that you?" said the General, smiling
broadly as he advanced with hand extended. "Just like I was one
of his best friends," boasted Francis Circoply, now captain of the
little steamer *Ida.* Lee took the time to introduce his old acquaint-
ance to each of the distinguished visitors. "It will doubtless be a
tradition in his family for many a year to come 'how Gen. Lee
met grand father,'" wrote Olmstead.[1]

Lee made several suggestions in the way of strengthening the
Fort against attack. As he left after one of his visits the Virginian
looked over at Goat Point on Tybee seventeen hundred yards
away. "They will make it pretty hot for you with shells," he observed, "but they cannot breach your walls at that distance."[2]

The day after General Lee's third trip to Pulaski in the fall of
1861 other eyes gazed across the same stretch of water. They included those of a New England private who was in a detachment
sent to Goat Point as a guard. From there Elias A. Bryant of
Francestown, New Hampshire, could clearly discern the sentinels
pacing the ramparts and the "secesh" flag waving from the flagstaff. Fort Pulaski looked as though it was about as far away from
him as "Mr. E. P. Bryant's is from the Mountain View House."
More calculating and experienced eyes than those of young Bryant
probed the Confederate stronghold that day. To Captain Q. A.
Gillmore, USA, had fallen the task of deciding whether it was
practicable to reduce the Fort from Tybee Island. A solidly built,
six-foot Ohioan who had been graduated at the top of his class
from West Point, he had a head that reminded John Chipman
Gray much of "the busts of Socrates without having the pug nose."
On his return to Hilton Head Captain Gillmore reported the results of his survey of the problem: "I deem the reduction of that
work practicable by batteries of mortars and rifled guns, established on Tybee Island."[3]

In 1863 Gillmore was to write to Horace Greeley of the

Tribune listing his military achievements up to that time, among them "the Reduction of Fort Pulaski in violation of what was *supposed* to be correct military principles, & in opposition to the opinion of my seniors as recorded & now in my possession." If one thinks less of him for this mode of seeking promotion, there is no question of his superiors being skeptical about breaching a masonry wall at a distance of over eight hundred yards. General Joseph Totten, Chief Engineer of the Army, expressed the belief that "the work could not be reduced in a month's firing with any number of guns of manageable calibers." In endorsing Gillmore's plan for the reduction of the Fort General Thomas Sherman agreed with everything "except possibly the use of rifled guns, until their effect has been fully tested. . . . All that can be done with guns is to shake the walls in a random manner." From Tybee Island on December 29 Joseph Hawley informed his wife, "Gen. Wright wouldn't have me say it aloud . . . but he says the only way to take Fort Pulaski is *to bury it in iron*." [4]

Quincy Adams Gillmore was not the only man who thought the Fort could be reduced. Captain John Hamilton, USA, predicted that Pulaski "would be reduced in three days from the time fire was opened." As General Sherman's chief of artillery, Hamilton badly wanted to have charge of the project. However, Gillmore was brevetted a Brigadier General and Hamilton who had seniority in the regular Army was directed to report to him. If Sherman's action was much to Gillmore's "disgust & embarrassment," as Hawley wrote, it was even more so to Hamilton. The latter strenuously objected. When General Sherman asked him what might be done to rectify things, he replied, "I see no way out of the difficulty except for you to appoint me a major general and direct Gillmore to report to me." [5]

Gillmore became famous; Hamilton remained obscure. The truth is nobody forsaw the real effectiveness of rifled cannon on brick walls at that distance. Gillmore frankly admitted it later. "Had we possessed our present knowledge of their power, the eight weeks of laborious preparation for its reduction, could have been curtailed to one week," he reported.

It was, indeed, to use Colonel Hawley's phrase, "no light job." The mortars, weighing up to seventeen thousand pounds each, were unloaded from ships onto barges which were towed ashore by rowboats through the surf. They were dumped at high tide. Ropes were made fast and when the tide was out the cannon were dragged to high land. According to Hawley, it took two hundred men two hours to move one of them above high water mark, a distance no further than from his barn to his house back in Connecticut.[6] They were then transported at night to the battery sites, as far as two miles away. Two hundred and fifty soldiers were barely sufficient to move one of the huge mortars or columbiads on sling carts along causeways built across swamp and marsh.

A letter from a soldier in the 7th Connecticut thus described the tenor of life on Tybee during this period: "Pulaski shoots at us occasionally and the boys rather like it; for nobody gets hurt, and relics accumulate; earthworks slowly rise; a gun gets mounted frequently; fleas bite continually; once in a while a mail comes in; somebody shoots an otter or an eagle; teams and mulecarts work eighteen hours a day, drawing great loads of shot and shell two miles; and the beach is strewn with all the implements of war." "Oh this is a grand life," wrote Colonel Hawley that March. "Every day we hear the sublime bass of some heavy gun."[7]

Eleven batteries were constructed over a stretch of a mile and a half running from the northwest point of Tybee eastward almost to the lighthouse. Thirty-six guns were mounted in the Union works, their distance from the Fort varying from 1,650 to 3,400 yards. As already mentioned, the batteries erected west of the Fort on Jones Island and on Bird Island had isolated Pulaski. Since early in February, 1862, it had been on its own. On the 17th of that month General Lee assured the commanding officer that the safety of the garrison would be an anxious consideration. For the present communication with the mainland would have to be by light boats across the marshes or "by any other mode by which you can further accomplish it."[8]

Within the Fort was a garrison of three hundred and eighty-five Confederates, "fine looking men and the officers perfect gentlemen," according to a Connecticut soldier.[9] Of the five companies stationed at Pulaski four were from Savannah: Company "B" of the Oglethorpes, the Washington Volunteers, the Montgomery Guards and the German Volunteers. The other company stationed there, the Wise Guards, had arrived at the Fort early in February, having volunteered for duty at the beleaguered post.

Commanding the garrison was a twenty-four-year-old Savannahian, Charles H. Olmstead. After a visit to Fort Pulaski in 1861, Edward C. Anderson had gone away shaking his head over the bald-browed young commandant. Amiable enough and correct in his social relations, he lacked "what Navy men call 'vim,' " said Anderson who thought he needed "a stiffer head than the one on his own shoulders to advise him." But Olmstead was levelheaded and intelligent. Popular with the rank and file, he was elected colonel of the 1st Georgia Volunteer Regiment in December, 1861. He had worked hard to carry out the recommendations Lee had made. "It was a busy time for all of us—every man was at work from early morning until night fall at the hardest kind of labor," said Olmstead. Blindages of heavy timber were placed around the entire circuit of the interior to protect the casemates from shell fragments. Ditches were dug across the parade ground and traverses erected to catch rolling shells. Unnecessary embrasures were bricked up. The weeks dragged by in toil and drill. "The boys have been at work all day and have worked hard. Officers and all at work," commented W. L. Landershine on April 7. "Boys still at work, they do it very cheerful," he noted in his diary the next day.[10]

Gun crews acquired a paternal feeling for their cannon. Lieutenant Theodorick W. Montfort was much amused by the "endearing epithets" the men gave them. He was not immune to the same affection. "I really feel attached to my guns," he wrote, confessing that they "feel to me as part of my family." He painted on them in large white letters the names "Elizabeth," "Louisa" and "Sarah." Montfort reported that the cannon are "petted & rubbed with as much care as a mother ever did her child." A little Irish private kept his brass field piece polished until it shone like a mirror. "Wallace, you keep your gun in fine order," Colonel Olmstead complimented him one day. "An' well I might yer honor," he replied, "for me fâther was a bombardier." [11]

The sense of isolation was strong at Fort Pulaski, the only link with the mainland being an occasional mail brought in with extreme difficulty through the marshes. "I am now virtually a prisoner," reported Montfort on February 18. The gaunt lawyer from Macon County was a man of "genial kindness" and "full of funny stories." But in the loneliness of isolation he thought bitter thoughts. Cogitating upon the "mercenary Race that are seeking to subjugate us," he admonished his wife: "Teach my children to hate them with that bitter hatred, that will never permit them to meet under any circumstances without seeking to destroy each other." [12] Poor Montfort! He would not live to teach his offspring that or anything else. In March he informed his family that his lungs were "getting weaker every year." That year, at the end of his long road home from Northern prisons, Death was waiting.

Gathering for a smoke in the evenings, the Confederate officers were wont to discuss their situation. The conversation frequently turned to the prospects of outside aid. For at least one man hope lay over the horizon. "There is a prospect," Edward W. Drummond wrote in late March, "of our soon being set free again as our friends in Savannah are using every effort to drive the Yankees from our midst." He was hopeful of "relief by the river." Our "boats and barges must be near completed. God speed them." [13]

Much store was laid by a floating battery then under construction at Savannah. In April, '62, General Lawton detailed an officer to serve on the "floating battery to open communication with Fort Pulaski" and to afford "relief to our brother soldiers now confined in the Fort." But the feeling of most of the officers was that there was little likelihood the Fort would be relieved. "If Gin'ral Lawton or some other gintleman would only build a plank road," Private Wallace offered. [14]

In the minds of some people hope in another shape than floating batteries existed. If the enemy should "stay on the river till April & May the musquitoes & sandflies will trouble them &

later the fever & malaria will do the work," predicted a Savannahian.[15] The *Morning News* expressed hope on April 5 that the State troops would not be disbanded or withdrawn until "the Yankees are driven from our coast by the heat and, to them, deadly malaria of summer." Lieutenant Montfort was of the opinion that before their provisions gave out at the Fort "the yellow fever will come to our assistance & run them off." In March he looked "more to Providence sand flies, musquitoes & sickness relieveing us than to any one else."

The day General Lawton assigned an officer to serve on the new floating battery (April 9) the Federals were busy completing preparations for the bombardment. The only help from the mainland the garrison would have now was prayer. Plenty of that was available. "Would to Heaven it were in our power to go to the support of our brave brothers in the Fort. . . . May God protect them," Charles R. Hanleiter wrote in his diary.[16]

Throughout March and the early part of April little had been seen of the enemy on Tybee. What they were up to was no secret at Cockspur. It surprised the Federals that nothing was done to impede them. "They must have known what we were at & the ground that one can stand on is so limited that they *must* know *where* we are at work," wrote Colonel Hawley in March. "Yet they have not fired a gun for weeks."

The profile of the dunes on Tybee remained unchanged but the hum of activity at night at Goat Point was audible to the Confederate pickets. Early on the morning of March 22 Lieutenant Hussey scouted the area and discovered a battery under erection near King's landing. The site was shelled from the Fort.

Tybee was not the only site of Union batteries. On April 9 a party sent out from Pulaski discovered a mortar battery under construction on Long Island westward of Cockspur. "They must intend attacking us soon or they would not have had the powder and all there," wrote a member of the garrison. On April 6 Lieutenant Montfort had reported a formidable enemy battery a half mile in length about 1,900 yards from the Fort. "We have more to fear from this Battery than all others," he thought. Edward

Drummond wrote, "They now have a string of Batteries along Tybee Beach . . . and are no doubt contemplating the destruction of this fort." He was of the opinion, however, that they could do no damage. "All they can do is fire away and we will let them fire." [17] Such was not the feeling over at Tybee. "We begin to feel very confident of the result," wrote Joseph Hawley on March 20. "And then," he added, "we shall begin to think of Savannah."

There was a last minute rush by the Federals on April 9 to complete preparations. Without the aid of lanterns and under "a moon struggling to look down through misty clouds" men were busy at all the Tybee batteries until a late hour that night. At the Fort there was similar activity during this period. "There is something sad and melancholy in the preparation for Battle," Lieutenant Montfort wrote—the surgeon "whetting his saw," the making of lint, and the scattering of sand around guns to "drink up human blood as it flows from the veins & hearts of noble men."

At 5:30 a.m. on April 10, 1862, Lieutenant James H. Wilson, USA, seated himself in the stern of a boat on Tybee. He bore a communication addressed to the commanding officer at Fort Pulaski. At this point General Henry Benham called out in a loud voice, "Take your seat in the bow of the boat, Captain Wilson." The Lieutenant did not turn around. With greater emphasis Benham shouted, "Take your seat in the bow of the boat, Major Wilson." The Lieutenant did not stir. The order was then addressed to "Lieutenant Colonel Wilson." The cocky young West Pointer who revelled in chronicling the foibles of superiors and who did not see why it mattered where he sat in the boat turned around and explained that he was a lieutenant.[18]

As the craft slowly made its way across the choppy waters of the south channel there was little doubt at Pulaski about the purpose of the mission. That morning when a soldier went outside the Fort he saw "the boys standing in groups making remarks on the appearance of things." The dunes in front of the Federal batteries had been levelled overnight and the guns were unmasked.

"We knew that the Ball would soon be opened," wrote W. L. Landershine in his diary that day.[19]

The communication Lieutenant Wilson bore was signed by Major General David Hunter, a fifty-nine-year-old professional soldier who had recently succeeded Thomas Sherman in command. Pointing out that the number, calibre and completeness of his batteries left no doubt of the outcome, the immediate surrender and restoration of the Fort to the authority and possession of the United States was demanded. "It is hoped," said Hunter, "that you may see fit to avert the useless waste of life." A half-hour to respond was allowed.

Even the enemy had to concede that Olmstead's answer was well phrased. "In reply," he wrote, "I can only say that I am here to defend the Fort not to surrender it." Upon reading the response General Hunter, according to a New York *Times* reporter, went to the door and blandly said to Gillmore, "you may open fire as soon as you please." Captain Adam Badeau, who until lately had been a war correspondent for the New York *Express,* was given the assignment of delivering the order. The bespectacled aide mounted a horse (a type of transportation to which he was unaccustomed) and galloped off. On reaching Porter's battery General Grant's future biographer half fell from his mount. He threw the reins over a pile of shells and rushed forward, shouting "Commence firing!" It was 7:40 a.m. The discharge of the first guns shook the island. Badeau's frightened steed galloped madly off and was last seen "disappearing in the neighboring marsh," tradition having it that he "never returned." [20]

Further down the line a German officer mounted the parapet with drawn sword. With a dramatic flourish he signalled the discharge. In the excitement, the matter of opening the embrasures in the sand ridge had been overlooked. Some of the shot ended up almost as far from Fort Pulaski as it was when fired.[21]

The first of 5,275 shells fired from Tybee arched high over the water from Battery Halleck which was manned by a detachment of the 7th Connecticut. "A nutmeg from Connecticut; can you furnish a grater?" someone had written on it. The shot passed over the Fort and exploded above the old hospital building, according to Corporal Landershine. The same young soldier set down his thoughts when the bombardment commenced. They were of anxiety and worry over his mother and those at home who were without means of learning who had been killed or wounded. That night as the Savannahian laid down his pen the thought was still uppermost in his mind: "My Mother, how does she stand the anxiety?"

The mortar fire was ineffective. The story was about the same with the columbiads. It was different with the rifled cannon. Dust soon began to fly from the face of the southeast angle, known as the *pancoupé*. Their shells "bored into the walls like augers," reported a naval officer.[22] As the bombardment continued, the area on which the rifles concentrated began to assume what the correspondent of the New York *Herald* called a "mottled aspect." The wall seemed "to have the small pox," he wrote—"blotches appearing all over it."

Around 8:30 a.m. a shell carried away the halyards on the flagstaff of the Fort. The Confederate colors fluttered down amid cheers from across the water. Twenty minutes later the flag reappeared on the ramparts at the northeast angle. Two members of the garrison had sprung upon the parapet under what Corporal Landershine called "a perfect shower of shot and shell" and raised the flag on a temporary staff rigged to a gun-carriage.[23] But for the fact that ordnance experts had learned to increase the velocity and range of shells by rifling cannon barrels Lieutenant Christopher Hussey and Private John Latham might have achieved a fame history denied.

All day on the 10th the firing continued—seven to a minute and four hundred to an hour, Hawley estimated. The Union gun crews would jump to the parapets after each shot to watch the effect. There was not much danger to them. The fire from Fort Pulaski, while fairly steady, was "wild and did but little harm," reported James H. Wilson. He and Lieutenant Horace Porter would sit on the parapet and watch the flight of the shot until they were a short distance away, "when we would jump down and take cover, or sit fast and allow them to pass over our heads."

By noon forty-seven scars could be counted on the southeastern face of the Fort. The damage there was such that Gillmore was convinced his rifle guns would breach the wall. Near sunset the New York *Herald* correspondent thought he could detect a small gleam of sunlight through the masonry at one point. At sundown the fire ceased except for a few pieces fired periodically during the night to prevent repairs to the Fort.

Olmstead now had an opportunity to inspect the exterior. In the first hour of the bombardment, after a shot struck the outer wall, he had noticed an ominous bulging of bricks inside the Fort. But he was not prepared for what he now saw. The damage was "worse than disheartening." Near the southeast angle the wall was almost entirely shot away at one point revealing the interior of the casemate. Two other casemates were in nearly the same shape. Meanwhile, his ability to reply to the enemy had diminished. Of the twenty guns that bore on Tybee only one-half were now serviceable. The dismounted cannon "lay like logs among the bricks." [24]

Shortly after daybreak the batteries were back at it. "At 7 o'clock two shots came through the wall," a member of the garrison recorded in his diary. "Now and then a cartload of masonry rolled down; then everybody yelled in triumph," wrote Colonel Hawley. "And what a scream ran down the line when the first hole appeared." The moat was so filled with masses of brick that a person could have walked over it "dry-shod," reported the Savannah *Republican.* In two hours a breach had been opened near the southeast angle large enough to admit two people abreast. By eleven o'clock it was eight or ten feet square—big enough to drive a coach and four through, according to that paper. Another hole of almost equal size was opened by noon. Three casemates had been breached by 1:30 p.m. Shot were "pouring through," said an officer in the Fort, "and peppering our Magazine which cannot stand it long." [25]

All except four of the parapet guns of the Fort had now been dismounted. A like situation existed in the casemates. Corporal

Samuel Law informed the *Republican* that a "braver and more determined garrison" was not to be found. There was "a continued contest," he said, "as to who should man" the remaining guns.[26] But the gallantry with which the cannon were served was equalled by the ineffectiveness. None of the Union pieces was damaged and only one man was killed.

In Savannah windows rattled with the cannonade. People gathered on rooftops to watch. The din of battle almost but not quite brought respite to the private war that was waged between the two Savannah newspapers during the South's struggle with the North. "The Republican has not a word against Governor Brown yesterday. Perhaps the editor has magnanimously determined to reserve his fire while the Yankee batteries are playing upon us," observed the *Morning News* on the 12th.

Belief in the impregnability of the Fort had been practically an article of religion at Savannah. It was not confined to the laity. Before returning to his headquarters in Carolina the afternoon of the first day of the bombardment, General John C. Pemberton, CSA, remarked that Olmstead was wasting his ammunition in replying. "Yet he is an experienced Artillerist," was George Mercer's dry comment on the Commanding General's observation. Henry C. Wayne had expressed the view (at least Mercer so recorded) that Fort Pulaski could not be damaged from Tybee. Apparently the Adjutant General of Georgia changed his mind during the attack. Able to distinguish by ear between the direction of artillery fire and noting the diminishing volume from Pulaski, he openly predicted that the garrison could not hold out very long. This was practically treason. Thought was believed to be the offspring of wish. Feeling in Savannah reached a point where personal violence upon Wayne was a possibility.[27]

The story one may question; the fact of popular faith in the brick fortress one cannot doubt. "The enemy have been bombarding the fort since early this morning, seemingly with no effect," reported Captain William D. Harden from near Savannah on the first day of the attack. Writing at 1 p.m. the second day of the bombardment, a Savannahian informed a friend that the firing had been renewed that morning "with vigor, said to be from Pulaski chiefly & a report from a person from a mile below fort Jackson just recd is that we have silenced all the batteries on Tybee except one." A member of the Chatham Artillery, which was stationed at the Isle of Hope, predicted that day, "At present rate, it will be a long time, I think before any material impression will be made upon the Fort. No breach can be effected. . . ." Noting the cessation of fire in the early afternoon, he conjectured that the Federals had abandoned their efforts.[28]

At Pulaski, Colonel Olmstead had heard a commotion shortly before 2 p.m. It was in a casemate some distance away. He sent Captain Guilmartin to investigate. The officer returned with the report that a shell had exploded in the passageway leading to the magazine and that the ordnance squad had scattered in panic. On two other occasions shells struck there.

The position of the defenders was desperate. There was no hope of relief and the means of resistance were small. Considerations such as the difficulty of an assault by enemy infantry were outweighed by the possibility of disaster in the shape of the explosion of the magazine. All of the officers agreed that it was useless to resist any longer. "With an anguish of soul" that was to return in dreams during the remainder of his days Olmstead decided to give up. The first the men knew of the decision was when they saw their commandant and another officer pass by with a rammer and a white sheet. At approximately 2 p.m. the flag came down.

The Union troops went "crazy," reported Hawley. "Stop that firing. The white flag! The white flag!" they shouted. "Glory to God." Concerned for his reputation at Savannah, Olmstead explained to his wife, "We fought until the outer wall of two casemates was entirely down . . . while those terrible rifle projectiles had free access to the brick traverse protecting our magazine door." It was only a question of a short time, he added, "whether we should be blown in the air or not." [29]

He was correct in surmising that Savannahians might not understand. "Never," commented Charles C. Jones, Jr., at the time, "did man or officer have a better opportunity of giving a name to

History and honor to his country than did Olmstead." If he himself had been in command (Jones speculated), he would have nailed the colors hard and fast and fought to the bitter end. Then he would have withdrawn what was left of the garrison and "blown the whole concern to atoms." [30] Had Olmstead perished in the ruins of Pulaski, "he would have lived a Hero for all time," added Jones.

"I yield my sword but I trust I have not disgraced it," Colonel Olmstead remarked to Major Charles C. Halpine (the celebrated "Private Miles O'Reilly" of Civil War literature) at the surrender ceremony. The Savannahian's "soldierly and subdued" bearing won the sympathy of his captors, said a reporter of the New York *Times.* "Some of the others," he added, "were not equally felicitous." According to Olmstead, Captain McMahon unbuckled his waist belt and threw it and his sword on the table with the remark, "Take it! I wore it in Mexico." [31] The captured officers, though greatly chagrined, "talked as boldly and defiantly as ever," reported the New York *Herald.*

The correspondent of the *Herald* was not present at the surrender ceremony which took place in the dim, candle-lit headquarters in the Fort. His ability to report what happened to a rival reporter offset his disappointment. George Washburn Smalley of the New York *Tribune* had seated himself in the boat that was to take General Gillmore over to the Fort. "Put that man with a white hat out!" came a cry from land. "Put him out, he has no business there." Gillmore ordered the correspondent ashore and Smalley had to wade back. "The scene," gloated the *Herald,* "gave immense satisfaction to the crowd, who laughed heartily at the well deserved treatment the *Tribune's* representative received."

It was, indeed, a painful experience for this former stroke of the Yale crew, graduate of Harvard Law School and close associate of Wendell Phillips. Eventually Smalley got over to Pulaski. There he obtained an interview he did not seek. A captured Confederate officer asked him who he was and was informed that he represented Horace Greeley's *Tribune.* "What! that old abolition sheet." There was an affirmative response. "And we're going to be written up by his gang?" They were. "Well," said the Confederate, "I could have stood the surrender, but this humiliation is too much!" [32]

"Alas!" exclaimed Lieutenant William Murray Davidson, "our Fort is gone! I was sure, long ago if the Enemy were allowed to remain on Tybee unmolested, they would erect Mortar Batteries there that would eventually batter the Fort down!" But others found it hard to believe Fort Pulaski had been battered down. General Lawton was unwilling to give full credence to reports that came back about the extent of the damage. Early on the second day of the bombardment Corporal Samuel Law, a brave and resourceful soldier, reached the Fort in a small boat accompanied by a member of the Signal Corps. After the surrender Law and the signalman headed back through the marshes toward Savannah. They arrived there with news of the defeat and of the great damage to the walls. "I must express my belief," said Lawton, "that they gave an exaggerated account of the injury done to the fort, owing, perhaps, to the very exciting circumstances under which they must have entered and left it." [33]

George Mercer believed every word and more. What he called a "mortifying and stunning blow" was in his eyes an epochal event. "The whole system of warfare is revolutionized," he declared. "Brick is no longer of any avail." The science of war "has leaped a century forward and all are behind the age." [34] In a more measured appraisal General Hunter reported, "The result of this bombardment must cause a change in the construction of fortifications as radical as that foreshadowed in naval architecture by the conflict between the *Monitor* and *Merrimac.*"

7.

"A stronger place even than Charleston"

☙ "THE PEOPLE of Savannah, at least, are now satisfied of their ability to hold the city against any odds," Felix G. De Fontaine, a Charleston war correspondent, had written on March 1, 1862. Two weeks earlier a Savannahian had reported that General Lee "says that the gun boats cannot pass all these [batteries]." [1] The loss of Fort Pulaski shook this confidence. The defeat threw people into a state comparable to what the Port Royal disaster had occasioned five months before. "I can give you but a faint idea of the consternation the capture produced," a correspondent wrote on April 12—"women are leaving and property of all kinds is being sent off." [2]

Talk of destroying the city rather than allowing it to fall into enemy hands was renewed. "All old men, women & children should be sent from Savannah and those only left who are willing to see the city one mass of ruin & desolation," wrote an officer. On the alternative of burning or surrendering William Duncan found himself changing his mind frequently. "Sometimes," he said, he was "all for burning—then again 'cui bono' & all for surrender." [3]

General Pemberton urged that martial law be proclaimed at Savannah. Richmond passed his recommendation on to Governor Brown. The latter had no objection, provided the local authorities wanted it. City Council did not. The General reiterated his request in a telegram to Lee in Virginia and was informed that in view of local objections President Davis "does not feel justified in making the declaration until it becomes a positive necessity." [4]

Dissatisfaction with the military leadership at Savannah intensified. "The enemy is slowly but surely extending his coil around the devoted city," Captain Hanleiter wrote in his diary on April 19. "Unless more energy is displayed by our Commanders within the next few days, than has yet marked their administration, it will be useless to attempt a further defense of the city." Doubt as to whether the military authorities meant to defend Savannah took possession of many minds.

General Lawton attempted to remove the "erroneous impressions" which he said seemed to exist among a portion of the community concerning its defense. If the gunboats should pass the batteries, any demand to surrender would be steadily refused and the enemy resisted "so long as I am left with any force," he assured City Council. The announcement seemed to satisfy everyone except a Sandersville editor. Pointing out that Lawton had been at Savannah for a year and apparently had just discovered he was there to defend it, the writer was at a loss to know the cause of rejoicing unless it was because "this long delayed and remote spark of intelligence has at last, after a tediously tortuous journey, arrived at headquarters." [5]

"The key to the state," Savannah must be "defended at all hazards," declared Governor Brown in urging the Secretary of War to send at least eight thousand additional Confederate troops there. One thing was beyond question: his State forces were in no position to defend the city. The end of the period of enlistment of many of Brown's regulars coincided with the crisis on the coast. "Georgia's boasted bulwarks, the State troops, are melting away like morning mists," wrote a Confederate officer that April. "At a time when every one should be doing all in their power for their Country, they are looking to nothing but self." [6]

Forcing men to fight was repugnant to many Georgians. "I volunteered for six months and I am perfectly willing to serve my time out and come home and stay awhile and go again, but I don't want to be forced to go," reported a soldier from his camp near Savannah. Writing shortly after the fall of Fort Pulaski, Major Edward R. Harden said, "The army here is in great excitement at the passage of the conscript law of Congress declaring that every white male citizen between the age of 18 & 35 throughout the Confederate States are in the service." According to Harden, everybody was opposed to the "tyrannical conscription law." [7]

No one was more opposed to the draft than Governor Brown who fought President Davis as hard as he did the North and apparently with more malice. It did not add to his popularity at Savannah where the opposition was already sufficiently strong to have given the county to E. A. Nisbet by a narrow margin in the gubernatorial election in 1861. According to Mercer, the calling up by Brown that fall of three additional regiments of six-months volunteers had killed volunteering for the war. Its purpose, he claimed, was merely to promote Brown's own popularity. "A demagogue & a humbug," William Duncan labelled the Governor in June, 1862, accusing him of "aiming at the presidency." While President Davis "pants for the deliverance of his country," Governor Brown's "heart is fixed upon himself," charged the *Republican* on June 21 of that year.

By March, 1862, the volunteer system had produced in Chatham County at least thirty-one companies. "All the trades and professions are stripped and every able bodied man is in service," wrote Mercer in April. This was not entirely accurate. Felix G. De Fontaine attended a "draft" held at this period on the parade ground south of Forsyth Park. It is better to let "Personne," as this Charleston war correspondent signed his articles, describe the scene in his own style.

> The Colonel now takes his place in the centre, and from the back of a magnificent horse, in a few well timed remarks calls for volunteers. He said it was a shame that a Georgian should submit to be drafted, and dishonorable to a citizen of Savannah to be forced into the service of his country. He appealed to their patriotism, their pluck, and their-self. He told them of good clothes, good living and fifty dollars bounty, and on the strength of these eloquent considerations

invited every body to walk three paces in front. Nobody did it. An ugly pause ensued, worse than the dead silence between the ticking of a conversation. The Colonel thought he might not have been heard or understood, and repeated his catalogue of persuasions. At this point, one of the sides of the square opened and in marched a company of about forty stalwart Irishmen, whom their Captain, in a loud and excited tone, announced as 'The Mitchell Guards—we volunteer, Colonel in a body.' The Colonel was delighted. He proposed 'three cheers for the Mitchell Guards,' and the crowd indulged not inordinately in the pulmonary exercise. The requisite number did not seem to be forthcoming however, and the Colonel made another little speech, winding up with an invitation to the black drummer and fifer to perambulate the quadrangle and play Dixie. Which they did, but they came as they went—solitary and alone, not the ghost of a volunteer being any where visible in the Ethiopian wake. . . .

As a *dernier ressort* the Colonel directed all who had excuses to advance to the centre and submit them for examination. And then, for the first and only time during the occasion, there appeared to be the most wonderful unanimity of sentiment. . . . Every hand held its magical bit of paper, from a stable or a foundry to the daintily gloved extremity of the dry goods clerk, just from his counter. Young and old, rich and poor, neat and nasty, Americans, Englishmen, Irishmen, Germans, Frenchmen, Italians, Israelites and Gentiles, all went to make up the motley mass. What a pretty lot of sick and disabled individuals there were to be sure! Swelled arms, limping legs, spine diseases, bad eyes, corns, toothaches, constitutional debility in the bread basket, eruptive diseases, deafness, rheumatism, not well generally—these and a thousand other complaints were represented as variously and heterogeneously as by any procession of pilgrims that ever visited the Holy Land.[8]

A contrast to this spectacle was a review of the State troops stationed around Savannah by Governor Brown on April 4 of that year—one of the "most gratifying and impressive spectacles ever beheld in Georgia," reported the *Morning News,* "a glorious

demonstration of the military power of our glorious old State."
One hundred and twenty companies of infantry participated in the
parade which ended, said a private, with "a warm and affetind
speach" by the Governor. "I believe," added the soldier, "the troops
will all reinlist after they have gone home & saw their folks." [9]

Soldiers' letters during this period reflect a determination to
beat back any attack. Writing the day after Pulaski fell, an officer
doubted the rumor as to its capture, but "there is one thing," he
added, "they are afraid to come out on land and fight us a fare
fight." Another soldier informed a "cosin" in March, '62, that he
had "never seen narry Yankee yet." He did not "think that we will
while we stay hear, tho thear no telling which way the wind may
blow." He promised that if they should come, "we will give them
the best that we have in our shop." When his regiment was called
out one night as the result of a false report, still another volunteer
reported, "I never saw men more anxious for a fight, in all my
life . . . we would have given the vandals a hot reception." [10]

Letters to newspapers reflect the same resolution. "If the homes
of our people are to be desolated with fire and sword, fight at the
first onset—fight amid smoke and flames, and then fight among
the rubbish of our city," exhorted a soldier in the two local papers
on April 22. A correspondent in the *Morning News,* after ana-
lyzing the Fort Pulaski disaster, declared, "Courage, then—never
surrender the city—and stand to your arms, and stand by one
another, and stand by your country and stand by your State."

In an article captioned, "Savannah Never to be Surrendered,"
the *Republican* suggested that commanders of the river batteries
assemble their garrisons and swear the men "never to abandon a
gun so long as it sits on its carriage, and a soldier is left to man it."
This proposition drew a rejoinder from a soldier who advised the
editor to "lay down his air gun and pick up a musket. . . . We
are *volunteers* from Georgia, absent from respectable and comfortable homes, and came without consulting *Mr. Republican,*
to defend our homes and our country at large and expect to do it
to the last." They needed no oath, he said, to make them fight for
all that was near and dear.

Those who believed Savannah would be attacked reckoned without General David Hunter. The commander of the Union's Department of the South suffered from the occupational disease that frequently beset Civil War generals—over-estimation of the enemy and under-estimation of their own strength. A few days after the surrender of Pulaski, he informed the Secretary of War that there were thirty thousand Confederates at Savannah and that large forces stationed at Charleston and Augusta could be concentrated there. Naturally, he asked for reinforcements. With them he hoped to be able to report in a few weeks the fall of both Charleston and Savannah. Meanwhile, why they did not attack him, knowing as they did his situation, was a mystery to Hunter.[11]

The General was getting his intelligence as to Confederate strength from the newspapers or perhaps even from the observation balloons he was sending up around Savannah.[12] From whatever source his information was derived, it was erroneous. In early June, '62, approximately thirteen thousand troops were stationed around the city. This force was drastically reduced by the departure of six regiments for Virginia on the 7th of that month. Following the battle of Seven Pines orders had been received by General Lawton to get ready to move five thousand troops to Richmond on the shortest notice. "My men to the number designated are ready to march at once, and I earnestly request that I may be ordered to Virginia with them," he telegraphed back.

Having endured for more than a year the frustrations and the back-biting associated with the Confederate command at Savannah, Lawton must have welcomed the opportunity to combat his enemies in the open field. His troops arrived in Virginia in time to take part in the Peninsular Campaign and he led the Brigade (Lee's largest) in the severe fighting that summer until he was badly wounded at Sharpsburg.* "A better brigade never, in the history of this war, appeared on the field of battle," said Charles C. Jones, Jr.

* Upon General Lawton's recovery in 1863 he accepted the post of Quartermaster General of the Confederacy, a position in which he rendered services of a high order.

The departure of the brigade left only five thousand effectives with which to defend Savannah, reported General Pemberton. The transfer of so many troops alarmed the City Fathers. The Mayor *pro tem* "solemnly" protested to Richmond that the place was in a "helpless condition" and at the "mercy of the enemy." [13]

The apprehensions for Savannah's safety proved groundless. The enemy had no intention of attacking. General David Hunter's pen was mightier than his sword. "A fine, gallant, and manly old fellow," said a Union officer, he was "more interested in abolishing slavery than in putting down the rebellion." Two days after Pulaski fell Hunter issued an order declaring that all persons of color on Cockspur Island were free and were entitled to the fruits of their own labor. On May 9 he expanded the territorial application of his edict when he proclaimed "forever free" all persons heretofore held as slaves in Georgia, Florida and South Carolina. [14]

Hunter gained great applause in Abolitionist circles. His soldiers were less enthusiastic. A volunteer wrote in May, 1862, that his order had caused "wild excitement in the various camps." The officers were almost unanimously opposed. "Had I known 9 months ago what I know now, I know I wouldn't be here now," wrote this German-born soldier who considered it "a shame for the entire American people and especially a disgrace for the military . . . that the Government, after it had promised the people that they would have nothing to do with slaves, and then broke their word." Hundreds of thousands would have remained at home had they known what would develop, he added. Percival Drayton, who disliked slavery, criticized an edict which could "merely irritate without freeing a nigger." It was very much "as if Jeff Davis was to inform the crew of the *Pawnee* that they were all absolved from their allegiance to our government." [15]

Not yet ready for emancipation, President Lincoln revoked the proclamation. Later General Hunter acting on his own responsibility enrolled a regiment of blacks in the Union service. Congress upheld his action. The enlistment of Negroes to fight against their masters drew a quick response from Richmond. Hunter was pronounced an outlaw to be held for execution as a felon should he be taken prisoner.[16]

There was to be no opportunity to capture him around Savannah. Aggressiveness was no part of his strategy. The nearest thing to a battle in that theatre was a skirmish on Whitemarsh Island.

Within a week after the fall of Fort Pulaski General Gillmore sent James H. Wilson to the island to learn more of its topography and about affairs there. The lieutenant had an escort of several companies of the 8th Michigan Volunteers, totalling about 415 men. They were needed. Landing at Whitemarsh on April 16, the force was attacked by around eight hundred Confederate troops armed with Enfields. When the bugles sounded charge, the Federals mistook it for retreat. In the resulting confusion the enemy advanced rapidly and delivered "a steady and destructive fire." However, order was soon re-established and the Confederates were held in check for an hour or more.

It was the first combat experience for the future conqueror of Selma, Montgomery, Columbus and Macon. Wilson never forgot how the blood of Lieutenant N. Miner Pratt spattered in his face when the Michigan officer was shot in the head while cheering on his men. Ten Union soldiers were killed and thirty-five wounded while the Confederates had four killed and fifteen wounded. Wilson was pleased to report, however, that in the end the enemy was driven from the field.[17]

Colonel Marcellus Douglass of the 13th Georgia Regiment also made a report of the skirmish. In it he described how 800 to 860 troops of the 8th Michigan were held at bay and finally forced to withdraw by a small force of Confederates who fought them for hours before reinforcements arrived from Causton's Bluff. Night came on and "having only about 60 men with cartridges and physically able to fight," Douglass deemed it imprudent to pursue the enemy to their boats, "knowing their overwhelming force of 800 men."

Only when Hunter is heard from is one inclined not to call it a drawn battle. Informed about the expedition, he sent a message which, stripped of official jargon, failed to show complete satisfaction. Although he was disposed to praise, the General "is compelled to feel that . . . the results . . . either from information gained or the known injury to the enemy, are not a compensation for the great loss to ourselves which has been suffered in this affair." [18]

Meanwhile, progress in strengthening the harbor's defenses was being made. "The city is getting better fortified every day," said a soldier on February 28, 1862. "The longer the Yankees delay their attack the harder it will be for them to come up to the city." De Fontaine was agreeably surprised when he visited Savannah to see the steps taken to fortify the place. He had heard so much about its defenseless condition he was prepared to find it almost ready to fall into the hands of the enemy. Instead, he found Savannah "a stronger place even than Charleston." [19]

Fort Jackson, which was described by General Beauregard as "a very weak old work," was bolstered by a battery erected on the Savannah River a short distance eastward. After visiting this new battery (Fort Lee) in February, 1862, Anderson dubbed it "the mud valley." Later a railroad was built to the site. It became a powerful work, according to Colonel Anderson, "able to withstand all the force the Yankees might venture to bring to bear on it."

On a small island in the Savannah River across from Fort Jackson a battery called Fort Cheves was constructed, while on nearby Barnwell Island Fort Lawton was erected. A mile further up the Savannah River toward the city a work was built on Fig Island. At Savannah itself a battery was erected at the eastern end of the bluff.

The problem of defending the city against attack other than by way of the Savannah River was a difficult one. The lacework of rivers and creeks afforded many landing places to the enemy. As General Lee informed his son in February, 1862, the waters around the city made it "one of the hardest places to defend I ever saw, against light draft boats." A board of general officers pointed out in 1863, "The city is approached not only by the Savannah River but by the Augustine Creek, the Wassaw, the Vernon, and the Ogeechee Rivers to within distances ranging from 4 to 12 miles." The defensive works on these water courses were mutually dependent, continued the report. If one fell and the enemy should land, the others could be taken in reverse. This was especially true of Fort Jackson and Fort Lee on the Savannah River, both of which were untenable should the enemy effect a lodgement along Augustine Creek.[20]

To provide against that danger an earthwork was erected at Causton's Bluff about a mile south of Fort Jackson. Covering seventeen acres, Fort Bartow, as it was called, was one of the largest and most complete works of its kind on the coast. While inspecting the site in the winter of '62 Lee's career almost came to an end. A cannon supposed to be able to throw a projectile five miles was being tested. It exploded on the first shot. The upper half sailed over the General's head, burying itself in a swamp three or four hundred yards away. Several men were killed and wounded.[21]

When Lee was transferred to Virginia that March his last instruction to Lawton was to urge the utmost expedition in completing these projects. Work on them had accelerated that winter with the arrival of William R. Boggs, an Army engineer in the service of the State of Georgia. General Lee's plan for an inner line around the city had not been carried out. On reaching Savannah Boggs had procured a good map of the county. With it as a guide, a pocket full of fencing nails and a hatchet in his belt, he had gone out and verified the map. Boggs had then laid out what he called a "first rate" interior line of defense. It ran from the Savannah River on the east around to Laurel Grove Cemetery on the west, a distance of nearly four and a half miles, averaging one and a third miles distance from the city.

"We are building a large Fort cald fort Bogs . . . below Savannah on the River," wrote an officer in March, '62, adding that when completed it would be "the best one in the state." Three days later another soldier expressed the opinion that when the work was finished Savannah would be impenetrable by the enemy as they "will have to pass Forte Jackson, Boggs & 5 or

6 batteries scateried up & down the river, besides, 5 or 6 gunboats." [22] Situated on Brewton Hill along the Savannah about a
mile east of the city, Fort Boggs was on the extreme left of the
interior line. It was, according to Major Basinger, "one of the finest
field works constructed on either side during the war."

Much of the labor on these works was performed by State
troops. Going out at eight in the morning, the soldiers worked
until an hour before sundown. The sight of Savannah militia performing hard labor was highly enjoyable to the men from the interior. As the city boys threw up mud with their spades while
working in their broadcloth coats, silk cravats, fine starched linen
shirts and calfskin boots, they reminded one volunteer of a "piny
woods salamander." [23]

Slave labor, however, was principally relied on in erecting
these defenses. At one time more than two thousand Negroes
were working on the fortifications around Savannah. Frank Vizetelly, the artist-correspondent of the *Illustrated London News,*
sketched a gang working on top of an earthwork. As the Negroes
paced slowly forward and backward with their rammers they kept
perfect time, he reported, to some such ditty as:

> I dont like the lowland gal;
> Tell you de reason why?
> She comb har hair wid a herring-bone,
> And dat dont please my eye.

> But I do like de mountain gal;
> Will you hab de reason why?
> She comb har hair wid de tortoise-shell
> And har movements am so spry! [24]

Planters from the interior loaned slaves for this work. When
the volunteer system of procuring labor proved inadequate, the
draft became an issue. The question of Negro impressment was
creating quite a stir, reported John Wright Carswell in the summer of '62. "The men that dont go to war, it appears are equally
reluctant to send their darkies. . . . They seem to think it too
sickly about Savannah." Carswell had a stock reply to such ob-

jectors. "I think we can very well afford to risk the negroes when we send our sons," he would tell them.[25] The labor draft was extensively resorted to at Savannah in 1863. A report of the District Engineer that summer showed that the impressed force around the city amounted to 2,005 Negroes.

The fall of Pulaski spurred the work of obstructing the Savannah River. At Four Mile Point below Fort Jackson the north and south channels were blocked by sinking huge wooden cribs filled with paving stones removed from the ramps along Bay Street. Sixteen vessels were scuttled nearby. A short distance below Fort Lee a row of heavy piling was placed across the Savannah. More cribs were sunk there. Torpedoes were laid in the area.

The fall of the year 1862 saw the addition of another type of obstruction on the Savannah River. The floating battery *Georgia* (formerly "Ladies Gun Boat") was placed in service in October. Moored in a crib near the upper end of Elba Island and below the obstructions, she was able by warping to bring a broadside to bear upon either channel of the Savannah.

On October 1, 1862, the *Morning News* reported that two gunboats came up within three miles of Fort Lee and Fort Bartow and "shelled the marsh in every direction." According to Charles C. Jones, Jr., one shell burst directly over the battery still under construction at Fort Lee. The Negroes at work there "dropped wheel barrows, spades, shovels, hods . . . and came tumbling down head over heels. . . ." Their lives, he added, were much more endangered by "their lofty and precipitate tumbles" than by the projectiles.

It was the only thing in the way of "excitement that has happened here in some time," said a Confederate. "I shall be very willing to have a brush with them, for we have been doing nothing long enough." [26] There was to be no brush, much less battle. The Union strategy—or lack of it—kept the city in continual fear of attack. "Their menace is a feint," wrote De Fontaine, "and thus far it has been successful in keeping upon the coast thousands of men who would otherwise have swollen the ranks of the Confederate armies in Tennessee and Virginia."

The pattern of things during the weeks that followed the fall of Pulaski was to be that of the ensuing year. In February, 1863, Governor Brown informed the Confederate Secretary of War that an early attack was feared. "As you are aware," he complained, "we have a very inadequate force there for its defense." [27] Other old, familiar refrains were heard. Last ditch defense was still the order of the day. In November, 1862, the Legislature resolved that Savannah should be defended "street by street, and house by house, until if taken, the victors' spoils should be alone a heap of ashes." Alluding to the plans of the "Nigger Ginral" [David Hunter], the *Morning News* declared in February, '63, "The seaport of the Empire State is not for them. It will be defended while a Georgian can raise an arm and only surrendered when a heap of smouldering ruins."

Firm resolution to defend Savannah continued to be evidenced in letters of soldiers stationed there. A Berrien County sergeant wrote in March, '63, "We are well drilled now and will be able to meet the enemey at any point and at any time two to one, and Show them that the Confederate boyes are allways ripe and ready for the application of cold Steal." Describing a review by Beauregard of the troops in Savannah in February, Alfred Hartridge said "it was a beautiful day, & a more beautiful sight, to a soldier, to see column after column of our gallant men passing in review before the old hero, to see thousands upon thousands of glistening bayonets casting the dancing sunbeams from battalion to battalion. . . . A grand sight, and who that saw it could dare to say Savannah can be taken?" [28]

Time had indeed lessened that possibility—from the water, at least. In addition to the completion of the interior line the outer perimeter of defenses had been strengthened. New forts were constructed. At Beauregard's suggestion a battery was thrown up at Greenwich along Augustine Creek and a large earthwork was erected on Rose Dhu Island to prevent any approach to the mainland by way of the Little Ogeechee or the upper Vernon. [29]

Lamenting the failure to move on the city after the victory at Port Royal, Union Flag Officer Du Pont expressed the opinion in the fall of 1862 that if necessary troops had been provided for joint land and naval operations, Savannah and Charleston would have been captured with scarcely any loss of life. "The difficulties to be overcome now," added the Rear Admiral, "have increased a thousandfold." [30]

During that interim, time and the Savannah River had flowed placidly by Fort Pulaski. The garrison of the fortress was drilled to a high state of proficiency. The historian of the 48th New York Regiment never saw "a crack regiment of militia or any other body of soldiers whose evolutions surpassed those of the Forty-eighth when at drill in Fort Pulaski." Drilling was dull but there were respites. After a review of the outfit by General Ormsby Mitchel in September, 1862, the men were treated to the oratorical talents of the new Commanding General of the Department of the South. Hinting of activity to come, this soldier-astronomer ("Old Stars," he was called) assured the assembled troops that he had served in the field and understood it perfectly.[31] "I have fought the enemy through 400 miles of territory and never known what it was to be checked or turned back." *

Besides oratory, there were weekly dramatic productions, photograph-taking, band concerts, duck hunting and fishing. There was also baseball. The team the regiment fielded was a "fine success." [32] Perhaps it was even a history-making one. Its defeat of the nine representing the 47th New York at Fort Pulaski by a score of 20 to 7 on January 3, 1863, was probably the first baseball game between organized teams ever played in Georgia.

The reduction of Pulaski meant more to the North, however, than providing a military playground along the south Atlantic coast. The blockade of Georgia's principal gateway to the sea became much easier with the Fort in Union hands.

---

* He would soon know. In October, 1862, a force of four thousand five hundred troops commanded by General Mitchel was turned back by a little over five hundred Confederates at Pocataligo, S. C., in a movement on the Charleston and Savannah Railroad.

8.

The Blockade and Savannah

≈DANIEL AMMEN of Ohio and Edward C. Anderson of Georgia had been as brothers in the United States Navy. Their friendship continued after the Savannahian resigned and went into business. Before Lincoln's inauguration Anderson met his old friend in Baltimore. The two men had a frank but courteous discussion about the impending struggle. Ammen privately thought the views of the Southerner were "utterly and hopelessly insane." "When a war had begun," he warned Anderson, "nineteen out of twenty in the North who were now actually friendly to the South would practically be converted into John Browns." Entertaining such convictions as he did about the preservation of the Union it was probable, retorted the Savannahian, that he "would be down on the Southern coast in some vessel trying to blockade." "God forbid that we should have a civil war, but, should it occur, that is just where I will be," Ammen assured him.[1]

Before the year was out *USS Seneca,* Ammen in command, crossed the bar and anchored in Tybee Roads, the first Union warship to do so after commencement of hostilities.

But the story does not end there. The scene shifts—two weeks back, to the pre-dawn of November 12, 1861, and to a locale in the Atlantic off the coast of Georgia.

A black-hulled, black-funnelled vessel eased shoreward through the Gulf Stream. Aboard her was an important military cargo—14,000 Enfield rifles, 1,000 short rifles, 500 revolvers, 3,000 sabres, four pieces of ordnance, 233,000 cartridges, two million percussion caps and 17,000 pounds of powder. The outer blockade offered little trouble. Faintly outlined by the moon, a large frigate was seen anchored at sea across the steamer's course. At full speed the runner passed, like a spectre, astern the warship. As she drew nearer the coast a fog set in as thick as and about the same color of "mulligatawny soup," recounted James D. Bulloch, a passenger. "There was not a sound," he wrote, "but the throb of the engines and the slight 'shir-r-r' made by the friction of the ship through the water, and these seemed muffled by the dank vaporous air."

All at once the silence was shattered by an "unearthly" sound— "a shrill prolonged quavering shriek" which to the tense men aboard the runner seemed "as loud and as piercing as a steam-whistle." A cock in a hen coop on the ship was heralding the approach of dawn. Hands grabbed quickly for the noisy chanticleer. A neck was wrung. From another coop a second, then a third cock sounded. "In utter desperation," recounted another passenger, "we pitched the coops overboard." [2]

By daybreak the smell of salt marshes reached the steamer. As the fog drifted seaward the tops of tall pines could be discerned to the west. The landfall was Wassaw. The pilot was more familiar with the channel into the Savannah River than the one through Wassaw Sound. Turning northward, the runner headed for Tybee Roads. Shortly she was over the bar and plowing up the channel, "a big bone in her mouth," as James Bulloch put it. By noon she was safe under the guns of Fort Pulaski amid the cheers of the garrison which lined its ramparts.

"The anxiety about your Uncle Edward worries us all," a member of the Anderson family had written a few days before. Their anxiety was over. From the boat that came ashore upon the arrival of the *Fingal* stepped Edward C. Anderson back from his mission abroad. Rumor had preceded his arrival by several weeks. With the usual roseate outlook of Savannahians concerning military and naval affairs, an inhabitant had written in September, "The steel clad war steamers are expected daily under the command of our fellow citizen Edward Anderson. . . . Should he have occasion to

bring his vessel or fleet into action, you may rest assured that he
will give a good account of himself." [3]

No steel clad war steamer, much less fleet, had arrived. But
the *Fingal* brought in perhaps the most valuable military cargo to
reach the Confederacy during the war. When she tied up at Savannah most of the population of the town turned out in welcome,
said Anderson. As he came ashore the crowd gave him three cheers
and a "tiger," according to a witness. "Joy beamed on every coun-
tenance," wrote his nephew, George Mercer, who regarded the
timely arrival of the vessel as a wonderful instance of "divine
interposition and favor." It removed, he said, the depression caused
by the disaster at Port Royal.[4]

If their Southern contemporaries owed a deep debt of gratitude
to the two Georgians, Bulloch and Anderson, who managed the
venture, posterity, North and South, was to be obligated to them
in a different way. James D. Bulloch later wrote the interesting
work, *Secret Service of the Confederate States in Europe,* in which
the *Fingal* affair plays a prominent part. Edward Anderson kept a
fascinating diary of his activities from the day he slipped out of
Savannah aboard the yacht *America* until his triumphant return
in November, 1861.

A few days before the *Fingal* arrived the seven-hundred-ton
British steamer *Bermuda* escaped from Savannah with a cargo of
eighteen hundred bales of cotton. She had come in from Liverpool
in mid-September. Her arrival caused "great excitement," according to George Mercer. "She saw nothing whatever of Lincoln's
famous blockade," reported Mayor Jones who said that she brought
in eighteen rifle cannon and one thousand Enfield rifles. The
Bermuda's cargo, another Savannahian asserted, included in addition to 6,500 Enfields, "24,000 pairs blankets, 50,000 pairs shoes,
20 Rifled cannon, shot shell & powder, a lot of pants, coats,
drawers & shirts made up." [5]

Another British ship that evaded the blockaders and reached
Savannah that summer bore more important news than cargo from
the Bahamas. On July 2, 1861, the *Republican* quoted the captain
of the schooner *Adeline* about his reception after arriving at Nas-

sau with the Confederate flag flying from the masthead. He was warmly received and encountered no difficulty in clearing with a cargo obviously destined for some Southern port. He was told by the British customs official to pay no attention to the threats of the Yankee consul at Nassau.

It was good news for the blockade-running fraternity—this evidence of a hands-off policy by the British at a point less than three days by steamer from Savannah or Charleston. Runners made the most of this opportunity in the summer of 1861. During that period the blockade was, to borrow a Union naval officer's phrase, "a perfect farce." [6] According to Edward C. Anderson, "the shore fever was in full blast." Captains of blockading vessels feared shoal waters so much, he said, that they seldom ventured inside twenty fathoms. "Hurrah for Abraham's blockade!" the *Morning News* exulted in August, '61. The occasion was the arrival of the Northern brig *Santa Clara* which was brought into port by a prize crew after her capture by the Confederate privateer *Jeff Davis.*

During that summer the acting British consul at Savannah reported that besides being too few in number, "the vessels used by the U. S. Government for blockading seem to be too large for that purpose." Stations were often left vacant. "The absence of the blockading fleet is of frequent occurrence, sometimes as long as one or two weeks in good weather," wrote the Confederate Customs Collector at Savannah in the fall of 1861. [7]

The situation reversed itself when Port Royal fell. After the Union Navy secured that base for operations Savannah was doomed as an important blockade-running center. The city's chief contribution to such activity following that event was the organizational and financial abilities of Gazaway B. Lamar. He was the brains and Savannah the headquarters of an international cotton speculation syndicate with agents in London and Paris. Lamar incorporated the Importing & Exporting Company of Georgia which by the end of 1863 was operating five fast steamers. [8] But none of this blockade-running activity took place at Savannah. Geography took care of that.

"I will cork up Savannah like a bottle by placing a frigate in the roads opposite Tybee and out of range from Pulaski," Flag Officer Du Pont had written in 1861 after the Confederates evacuated Tybee Island. On December 4, 1861, he had reported, "Savannah is completely stopped up." [9] A few days before, the New York *Tribune* had been able to announce that the city "is not only hermetically sealed, but is at our mercy." Late that year two blockade runners, the *Admiral* and *Cheshire,* were captured off Tybee.

However, there were other water approaches to Savannah. One was by way of Wassaw Sound, the other via Ossabaw whose tributary rivers afforded access to landings below the city. But it was not hard to blockade these waters, too. The truth was, as Flag Officer William W. Hunter of the Confederate Navy put it, "there is no part of the Atlantic coast which may be more effectually blockaded than Savannah." [10]

The *Fingal* was never able to get back out. After taking on a cargo of cotton she went around to Thunderbolt in December, '61, in the hope of getting to sea by way of Wassaw Sound. Several Union warships were waiting there for her. Had there been a "little dash" on the part of the Navy she could have "steamed out unmolested over Tybee Bar while the enemy's vessels were watching for her off Wassaw," thought Anderson. At any rate, the *Fingal* returned to Savannah. "Unless there be some changes in the political relations of the United States with the courts of Europe," reported Bulloch at the time, "I consider the port of Savannah as completely closed to commerce for an indefinite time." [11]

Getting in or out at night, however, was by no means impracticable. Blockade-runners succeeded in getting through the north channel of the Savannah within gun shot of Fort Pulaski. The *Kate,* which made forty-one trips between Confederate ports and the West Indies, accomplished it in 1863. During August of that year the *Oconee* (formerly the *CSS Savannah*) ran aground in sight of Pulaski while trying to get to sea. She returned up the Savannah River without being detected. Two weeks later this steamer escaped at night on an attempted voyage to Nassau where it was planned to pick up a cargo of iron for a new ram. The *Oconee* carried a cargo of 323 bales of cotton. The opinion had been expressed by Lieutenant Kell concerning this former flagship of the Savannah squadron that she would "never be a good sea-boat." Her first venture upon the high seas was proof of the fact. The night after she got into the Atlantic the *Oconee* sprung a leak and foundered off St. Catherine's Island.[12]

The greatest obstacle to blockade-running was shallow water. As Michael P. Usina of Savannah pointed out, "When we ran the blockade, there were no lights and no marks by which to ascertain the channel. All we had was a lead line." Most captures around Savannah resulted from vessels running aground. In August, 1862, Aaron Wilbur informed his wife, "The steamer *Emma* of this port started out to run the blockade—got aground last night & the Federal barges put off after her & the men on board set her on fire. She had on board 600 or 700 Bales of Cotton all lost." A fine vessel of about five hundred tons burden, the *Emma* grounded at the southeastern extremity of Jones Island near the mouth of the Savannah River.[13]

Shoal waters bested ships of extremely light draft. In September, 1863, the side-wheeler *Jupiter,* one of the fastest of the small Clyde River steamers, became a prize after running ashore off the northeast end of Tybee Island. It was a memorable day for two marines in the boarding party from *USS Cimarron.* The log of that blockader records that the men were "confined in double irons for drunkenness, they having obtained liquor on board the Prize." [14]

In April, 1864, the *Alliance,* a handsome, Clyde-built steamer with two engines and three stacks, grounded off Daufuskie Island trying to get in at night with a cargo of soap, medicines, liquors, glass and salt. Drawing only five and a half feet of water, she was piloted by John Makin, one of Savannah's most experienced pilots.[15] The most important of such prizes was the *Lodona.* Built in England shortly after the war, this large iron-hulled steamer was one of the first blockade-runners with a reduced silhouette. On August 3, 1862, she attempted to run in past Tybee but turned back to sea after being struck by a shell fired from the battery at the Martello tower.

The next morning the *Lodona* entered Ossabaw Sound. The log of *USS Unadilla* tells the rest of the story. "At 8.15 anchored in Florida passage . . . at 10.30 made a steamer from the Mast Head standing up the Ogeechee River—got under weigh & stood for her. At 11.10 made her colors English with a white flag at the mizzen. As we approached saw that her colors were Union down & that she was aground in Hell Gate." From the Beaulieu battery Captain Hanleiter sadly watched the "infernal little Gun Boat" come alongside this "large steamer." She was taken "bloody handed," as her master put it. Aboard her was a cargo of salt, tea, clothing, drugs, watches, starch, soap, tin plate, paint and quinine. Converted into a blockader, the *Lodona* later rendered useful service to the Union in blockading the same waters.[16]

Another ironical denouement in blockade-running involved the *Rebecca Hertz.* Designed, built and owned by Savannahians, the schooner was considered a "very handsome little craft." During the latter part of the war she ran the blockade out of Savannah loaded with cotton. Late in December, 1864, she returned to port with a cargo of tea, sugar, salt, coffee and pepper. Anchoring opposite the gas works one evening, the crew of the *Rebecca Hertz* discovered the American flag flying over the city.[17]

A somewhat related case was described by the *Republican* on November 23, 1864. It reported that the *Bertha* ran the blockade into the Savannah River the same night several Union steamers had gone to Venus Point for the purpose of exchanging prisoners. Her master concluded the city had fallen to the enemy and the schooner was abandoned.

Most of the blockade-running at Savannah after 1861 was by sailing vessel. Much of it was of a paltry sort. An example was the schooner *Glide* which grounded at the mouth of Tybee Creek one night in February, 1863. "A poor little pilot boat," said Captain Percival Drayton, "we had to take her, according to law although it seemed a shame to trouble such a mite of a thing."[18] She carried seventy-two bales of cotton and, what the captors valued almost as much, "the late papers."

Other instances of petty blockade-running included the sloop *Evening Star* captured in Wassaw Sound in 1863 with a cargo of seven bales of cotton and a crew of three men; the schooner *Swift* taken in the same waters in '64; the *Persis* (twenty-two bales), and the thirty-five-ton *Arletta* which grounded off Tybee trying to get in during March, 1864. The Navy put in a claim to the cargo of the latter which included whiskey. The Army, however, got there first and retained possession.[19]

In a reminiscence of blockade-running Henry Blun described the voyage he made to Nassau. Advised by his physician to seek a change of climate, he purchased a sailing vessel of ten tons burden and obtained a six-months furlough from military duty. After refitting the ship (named *Maggie Blun* for his daughter) Blun sailed from Savannah in April, 1864, with a cargo of thirteen bales of cotton. The little sloop crept out through Ossabaw Sound in a northeast gale. There was no sign of the blockaders usually on that station. During the rough passage to Nassau a sudden jibbing of the boom knocked two of the crew overboard, the master being drowned. With Blun at the helm the rest of the trip, the *Maggie Blun* reached Nassau where her cargo fetched $1,200.[20]

Another Savannahian who became interested in blockade-running was Hermann L. Schreiner. An easygoing, amiable man who conducted a music publishing business in the city, he was the most prolific of the South's composers during the war. Among Schreiner's better-known productions was "General Lee's Grand March." The very last man in the world for deeds of adventurous daring, he decided in 1863 to embark on the career of a blockade-runner. Colonel Olmstead was instructed to allow his vessel, a small craft loaded with cotton, to pass down the Wilmington River to Wassaw. Olmstead had a hard time keeping a straight face when the German-born composer reported to him. His nautical costume was unique. "He wore," wrote Olmstead, "a tarpaulin hat, a pea jacket, a low turn down collar with black silk neck handkerchief, the ends of which fluttered in the breeze, trousers tight in the hip and flowing from the knees down and low quartered shoes. Under his arm was a long spyglass and he looked an ancient mariner from stem to stern; the only incongruity in the 'tout ensemble' being a pair of gold boned spectacles that topped his nose, through which his prominent eyes looked triumphantly into mine." [21] In the end, discretion triumphed over valor. Schreiner returned to Savannah with his cotton.

To such levels blockade-running had descended by 1863. The blockade of the port had been established on May 31, 1861, when the *USS Union* took station off Tybee. By the end of that year it was heavily felt at Savannah. "Our commerce is perfectly prostrated. Many are closing up business," reported a businessman in the fall of 1861. [22]

During the first six months of 1862 the Collector of Customs at Savannah collected no export duties at all while import duties for the first three months of that year totalled only $112.92. The receipts from both export and import duties at the port during 1862 were ninety per cent less than the year before. "Business has played out in Savannah," reported a resident in September, 1862. Two-thirds of the houses were closed and things were "getting worse every day." [23]

Returning to Savannah at this period Olmstead found commerce there "dead," the few stores still open having "depleted stocks and many empty shelves." A visitor in April, 1862, described the ghost town atmosphere that hovered over Savannah. "A strange, mysterious, weird quietude reigns perpetually. Stagnation and paralysis obstruct the channels where business briskly flowed . . . the whole town—every thing—seems to have halted in the precise attitude of one who, with respiration suspended, is listening all agape for some undefined announcement to be made." [24]

European intervention was the subject of much wishful thinking at Savannah. "Certainly if the President insists upon blockading our Ports England and France will interfere," Mrs. H. J. Wayne had predicted. Of that she was sure. "They cannot," she said, "do without our cotton and rice."[25] In February, 1861, Mercer had expressed the opinion that by withholding one crop of cotton the South could damage England more than the United States could by years of warfare. "The close of the year 1861 will terminate the present conflict between North and South," predicted the Savannah *Republican* on October 16. It would be accomplished either by the breakdown of the North or through European intervention.

Throughout the year 1861 the *Republican* frequently advocated an embargo on cotton shipments. It argued that running the blockade would only relieve the shortage in Europe upon which the Confederacy was relying to bring about intervention. There was considerable support for this view in Savannah. "I sincerely hope the blockade will not be raised for a year yet. I want England to realise the fact that 'Cotton is King,' " Duncan had written during the summer of '61. "We must let the North and England understand that not one ounce leaves our ports until the blockade is removed or our independence recognized," declared Mercer in September of that year.

In June, 1862, Duncan ruefully conceded, "England gets along better than I supposed she would on short supply of cotton." Still hopeful, he preferred "to turn the screw on her another season to bring her to her senses." By August, however, this Savannah merchant had abandoned hope of interference by Great Britain. "I give her the back of my hand," was his requiem.[26]

The price lists Admiral Du Pont perused in Savannah newspapers provided an index to the effectiveness of the blockade. And to the depreciation of Confederate currency. Complaints of inflationary prices were universal. "Paper is so high, I have written between the lines," Josephine C. Habersham explained in her diary in the summer of '63. The cost of things both "disgusted" and *"frightened"* her—"58.00 for a summer muslin" and "$195.00 for a dress I could have got two years ago for just $9.00." Coarse gingham was $7 a yard.

"Women have long discarded crinoline as calico is too costly to be wasted in covering a wide expanse of hoops," reported a Hoosier clergyman following a trip to Savannah that year. The clothing supply had been so reduced that the cast-off garments of other generations had been drawn upon. This produced, even among the better classes, he said, a grotesqueness of costume that was ludicrous. A Confederate chaplain, Edmund C. Lee, wrote from Savannah in 1863 that "a nice suit of clothes cost $1000.00." [27] Mercer noted in his diary in February, 1864, "Mrs. Willy Gordon has received from her mother at the north a trunk filled with shoes, clothing etc valued here at $5000.00; it cost north the price of a pair of shoes with us—$150.00."

Soldier as well as civilian found it impossible to make ends meet. General Colston informed his daughter in 1863, "I have to deny myself everything to be able to send you enough to buy bread to put in your mouth." Common undershirts cost $50 apiece at Savannah. Lieutenant Henry Graves complained that his pay of $80 a month barely paid his mess bill and contributed nothing towards his clothing. A pair of boots cost as much as two and a half times his monthly pay. "I am almost persuaded to get married here and go and live with the girl's father." [28]

The shortage of shoes in the Confederacy was such that the *Morning News* commended on October 3, 1862, the "sensible suggestion" of a Georgian that the manufacture of wooden shoes be established in the State. [29] Two days earlier the same paper ran a piece complimenting a girl from a nearby county for doing "her mite" for the cause by fabricating from palmetto a "very beautiful misses' hat" of the latest style. In a popular poem Carrie Bell Sinclair wrote,

> The homespun dress is plain, I know,
>   My hat's palmetto, too;
> But then it shows what Southern girls
>   For Southern rights will do.

A Savannahian reported in 1864 that "the young ladies here wear hats altogether and are having them made out of old white leghorn and straw bonnets." She had neither hat nor bonnet and begged her grandmother to send "anything you can rake or scrape in the way of clothes." Few women could afford to buy them. "Sixty dollars for a straw bonnet—*untrimmed!*" exclaimed Josephine Habersham. "How we would make over old dresses, turn them, add pieces to the skirt, and by trimming make a real nice looking dress," wrote another Savannahian.[30]

Salt was among the scarcest items in the Confederacy and was frequently found listed on manifests of blockade runners. Procurable for 30 cents a bushel in Nassau, salt brought as much as $100 at Charleston in '63. To help remedy the shortage, works were established at many points along the coast, including Thunderbolt, White Bluff and Ship Yard Creek near Savannah. Thirty-four of Captain Hanleiter's company received permission to engage in salt production as long as the work did not interfere with their duties. Using some old boilers found on the Schley place at Beaulieu, the men produced up to five bushels a day.

Inflation rendered the problem of buying food as difficult as that of procuring seasoning. In 1862 flour sold in Savannah for $40 a barrel; two years later a Savannahian paid $125 in Confederate currency for a sack of it. Eggs were fifty cents a dozen in March, 1862, seventy-five cents by October, and $1.50 a year later. In January, 1864, Mayor Arnold informed Beauregard that for a week hardly a house in Savannah had a supply of grits, that article having risen as high as $16 a bushel.

Seafood became a staple in Savannah but it was not immune to this inflation. "Think of it," exclaimed Colonel Anderson after paying $30 in 1864 for four shad which "in the olden time" could have been purchased for fifty cents. "It takes a great deal of Confederate money to buy little or nothing," was the way another Savannahian expressed the obvious.[31] A standing joke, according to Olmstead, was that a housewife going to market needed a basket to carry her money while one hand sufficed to carry her purchases.

While Southerners differed as to the Confederacy's most deadly enemy, it was frequently something besides the North. Worse than "our ruthless Yankee foes," declared the *Morning News* on November 18, 1862, were the "heartless speculators and extortioners

who are sucking the life-blood of our people." In his Annual
Report in 1863 Mayor Holcombe commented on the establishment by the city authorities of a store where provisions were sold
to the public at cost. Explaining the anomaly of a municipality
going into competition with private business in this field, the
Mayor explained, "The spirit of speculation generated by running
the blockade, both by sea and land, accompanied with enormous
gains, soon produced an inflation of prices and an extraordinary
demand for gold, silver and State bank bills to supply the vocifer-
ous calls of the speculator."

Writing to his wife in 1864, a private stationed at Thunderbolt
said that "it looks to me like the Confederate States is compelled
to starve in a short time." He did not care "how soon the starving
commenced, if it would begin on the right ones." [32] The following
month a mob of women with arms marched through the streets of
Savannah demanding food. The riot ended with the ringleaders
in jail.

Invited that summer to the residence of Octavus Cohen, a center
of Savannah hospitality, a Confederate naval officer was impressed
by the grand piano, splendid furniture and costly chinaware and
silver. George W. Gift could not help but contrast these marks of
affluence with "the poverty of their tea table." Persons of wealth
in cities had no more to eat, the lieutenant reported, than was to
be found in ordinary times "in the poorest log cabins in the country." [33]

The decline of the gastronomical art in the city is reflected in
the memoirs of McHenry Howard who came to Savannah in
November, 1864, after an exchange of prisoners.[34] Arriving late
one morning for breakfast at the Pulaski House, a hotel once
noted for its cuisine, the Baltimore officer observed piles of red
shells besides the plates of those who had eaten. Closer inspection
revealed that the guests had been eating boiled shrimp, now a
breakfast food in Savannah.

9.

Fort McAllister Versus Lincoln's Navy

⮜ IN JUNE, 1862, a blockade-runner tried to get into Charleston harbor and was turned away by the squadron outside. A blockader chased her three hundred miles before losing sight of the quarry. She was identified as the *Nashville,* a fast side-wheeler of 1,200 tons which had been seized at Charleston the year before. Converted into a raider, she had been the first vessel to fly the Confederate flag in British waters where she destroyed a Northern merchantman. The seeming ease with which the *Nashville* ran the blockade caused Secretary of the Navy Welles to be lampooned by cartoonists in the North.

A few weeks after the runner eluded her pursuer off Charleston news of interest reached the Union naval authorities at Port Royal. A runaway Negro who lived near the Ogeechee River reported to them that a paddle steamer, bark-rigged, yellow paddle-boxes with a white circle in each, four or five feet in diameter, was at the Gulf Railroad bridge below Savannah. She had come in five or six weeks before. Her crew of one hundred were dressed in uniform as were her officers. She was reputed to have brought in "an assorted cargo, among which were five iron guns and a large quantity of powder." Of passing interest was the information that the Confederate battery on the Ogeechee River had recently been strengthened.[1]

The blockade-runner was the *Nashville;* the battery was Fort

[93]

McAllister. Their history was to be closely interwoven during the next few months.

The first official notice of this Ogeechee earthwork, as far as the Union Navy is concerned, appears to have been on July 1, 1862. The gunboat *Potomska* stopped by Ossabaw Sound that day for a look in. Seven miles up the Great Ogeechee a small schooner which had just brought in a cargo of salt was at anchor. Lieutenant Commander Pendleton Gaines Watmough, USN, headed his ship upstream, keeping a close lookout for "a battery of five guns" he had heard was located "hereabouts." When the *Potomska* reached a point about a mile and a quarter across the marsh from the blockade-runner, the Fort came into view out of a neck of woods There was a harmless exchange of fire after which the gunboat drifted out of range with the ebbing tide. Believing the schooner to be below the row of piling the Confederates had placed across the Ogeechee, Watmough intended to come back after dark and cut her out. However, the runner was upstream from the obstructions and during the evening she moved out of harm's way.[2]

Located at Genesis Point on the nearest bluff of the mainland from the mouth of the Great Ogeechee, Fort McAllister was a key fortification in the defenses of Savannah. It protected the Gulf Railroad bridge and locked the side door to the city. "A truly formidable work; so crammed with bomb proofs and traverses as to look as if the spaces were carved out of solid earth," a Union naval officer described it.[3]

Writing from McAllister in June, 1862, Captain Alfred L. Hartridge of the De Kalb Rifles complained of the "disagreeable" fate of being "stuck in a marsh with no chance of seeing the enemy (but with a glass) among men who are dissatisfied—without an opportunity to get promoted."[4] Things changed after the *Nashville* was trapped in the Ogeechee. The steamer and the Fort were to be among the chief occupations of Du Pont's Union command during the next few months.

Late in July, 1862, the Admiral ordered a reconnaissance in force up the Ogeechee. If the Confederate battery could be silenced, the gunboats were to "continue to the bridge and destroy or capture the steamer." In command of the squadron he placed Charles Steedman, a "perfect lion in voice and bravery in storm or battle," according to Navy associates. Though a native of Charleston, Steedman refused to go with his State when war came. The South Carolina legislature had offered a reward for him, dead or alive.

On July 27 Steedman's flagship, *Paul Jones,* and three other gunboats reached the mouth of the Great Ogeechee. "We shall probably know in a day or two what the pirates are after," commented a contributor to the Savannah *Republican.* Two days later the flotilla steamed upstream and took position below the obstructions in the river. For an hour and a half there was a spirited fire on both sides. The removal of the piling involved "sacrifices not warranted," Commander Steedman reported. More than three hundred shells were fired at the earthwork, according to Hartridge, who said they made cavities "large enough to bury a horse" but did no damage of any consequence, "only ventilating our buildings." The injury to the vessels was even less. "Often & often have I begged the Generals who command this district to let me have a Columbiad," complained Hartridge. "Oh, how earnestly did I wish for it. I would have made them skulk off sooner than they did." [5]

The Fort was not molested again until November 19 when it was attacked by a flotilla under Lieutenant Commander John Lee Davis. Twelve days before, this red-haired naval officer had taken the gunboat *Dawn* up the Little Ogeechee and had shelled and set fire to a blockade-runner at Coffee Bluff. Davis was to add little to his laurels at McAllister. For five hours his vessels bombarded the Fort, the garrison exhibiting "perfect coolness and self-possession under a terrible fire they could not return." [6] The truth was the Confederate battery fired twelve times. The first shot struck the *Wissahickon* midships, six strakes below the water line, forcing her to drop downstream out of the fight. Badly leaking, she was run aground at low tide and patched up. Du Pont, who was sensitive to newspaper criticism, was especially grateful to Lieutenant Davis for "concealing so effectually from the enemy your injuries."

In January, 1863, a confidential dispatch reached Admiral Du

Pont. Five new ironclads were on the way to Port Royal "to enable you to enter the harbor of Charleston and demand the surrender of all its defenses." Successful there, he was immediately to attack Savannah. The execution of this somewhat grandiose strategy was "confidently" submitted to Admiral Du Pont's "eminent ability and energy." [7] At times naval war seemed strangely uncomplicated to Gideon Welles. At any rate, before attacking Charleston it was necessary for Du Pont to test the efficiency of the new craft. Fort McAllister was the place to do it. One ironclad would be used as a starter. The *Montauk* was a two-hundred-foot, monitor-type vessel built at a cost of $400,000 by John Ericsson. A revolving turret housed a fifteen-inch and an eleven-inch Dahlgren.

The operation was entrusted to one of the Navy's best known officers, none other than John L. Worden, the man who had commanded the *Monitor* in her first encounter with *CSS Virginia*. His mission was the capture of Fort McAllister, the destruction of the *Nashville,* and, if possible, the burning of the railroad bridge over the Ogeechee. The gunboats *Seneca, Wissahickon* and *Dawn* and a mortar schooner were also to take part.

Early on the morning of January 27 the squadron took position below the obstructions with *Montauk* in the van and the other vessels strung out behind her. "The mooted question" was to be settled, wrote Bradley Sillick Osbon in the New York *Herald,* "Are ironclads equal to forts?" [8] Osbon had come along under special appointment as "clerk" to Commander Worden, the latter's eyesight still being impaired as a result of the *Monitor-Merrimac* engagement. He was to be his "eyes," said the order permitting him to accompany Worden.

More than three hundred shot were hurled at the Fort, including the first fifteen-inch shells ever fired in war from a naval vessel. "Huge holes were torn in their barbettes, and sand and sod flew every time we fired," reported Osbon. "Nothing disparaging" could be said of the foe who "stand up to their guns in a manner worthy of a better cause." The Confederate artillerists worked mainly on the *Montauk*. The ironclad was struck fifteen times.

However, the shells made little impression, leaving no more than small indentations. It was like "throwing beans against a brick wall," wrote the Northern correspondent.

The supply of ammunition running low, the squadron weighed anchor around noon. "Attack repulsed; nobody hurt in fort," General Beauregard telegraphed Richmond. Worden had been confident of success. There was just one flaw, explained Osbon, "We failed to estimate the power and durability of that fort." But the Navy had demonstrated that a monitor was able to resist shore batteries. Returning down the river to the anchorage, everyone was in such good spirits at getting out on deck in the fresh air once more that they "hardly realised," Osbon said, "how we had revolutionised the navies of the world." [9]

Du Pont saw no advantage in trying again until his ships could get nearer after removing the obstructions and the torpedoes. Worden, however, was still hopeful of success. On Sunday, February 1, he came back for another try. The story this time was much the same as before. Again the Confederates concentrated on the *Montauk* which anchored closer to the Fort than previously. She was struck forty-eight times but with little more damage than before. There was one casualty. At 8:30 a.m. Bradley Osbon was in the pilot house making a note about something or other when it was struck "a tremendous blow." A bolt flew loose and struck the war correspondent on the shoulder. Later, while he was in the wardroom a ball hit directly over his head, driving him with much force into a chair. His "whole muscular system" was "perfectly paralyzed" for about two minutes.

For five hours the vessels kept it up. The shells raised a cloud of dust equal to an explosion of a mine, said a Confederate. "There has been nothing like it since the commencement of the war; indeed, history furnishes no parallel," declared the *Republican*. A fifteen-inch shell passed through a parapet twenty feet thick, burying a man in the sand on the opposite side. According to a contemporary anecdote, a hand first appeared, then a face. Wiping off his mouth, the buried soldier shouted at the top of his voice, "All quiet on the Ogeechee." [10]

There were less humorous aspects of the attack. Major John Gallie who commanded at McAllister was slightly wounded in the face early in the engagement but refused to leave the post. A few minutes later one of the *Montauk's* shells struck a thirty-two pounder where the Savannahian was standing. Either a piece of the trunion or a fragment of the shot took off the "whole top of the head, inflicting as ghastly and terrible wound as can be conceived," wrote Mercer. Gallie's death alloyed the pride with which Beauregard announced the repulse of the most formidable vessel of her class which for hours had hurled "missiles of the heaviest caliber ever used in modern warfare at the weak parapet of the battery." The *Republican* drew an invidious comparison between the brave garrison exposed to shot and shell and the "Abolition troops" skulking "behind and within their iron-casemated turret." In like vein, Mercer had commented after a previous assault, "This cowardly mode of conducting an attack . . . this beating of a man whose hands are tied—is characteristic of the Yankee." [11]

McAllister was a strong work, one which in Worden's opinion would withstand long hammering. "Though but an earthwork, [it] is now really colossal of its kind," another naval officer reported.[12] Resiliency was its chief characteristic. According to Isaac Hermann, the Fort was so "badly dilapidated" after the last-mentioned bombardment that a cyclone appeared to have struck in "full majestic force." But by morning, with the help of slave labor, it was in presentable condition.

Meanwhile, the *Nashville* was still trapped in the Ogeechee. She had come down at this period looking for an opportunity to get to sea. In returning upstream on February 27 she ran on a mud bank around the hair pin bend the Ogeechee makes above McAllister. Strenuous efforts were made to get her free, but, according to Bradley Osbon, "the sturdy labours of the little tug which has been going on through the night" failed to get her off. The Federals immediately noted her predicament.

At daybreak the next day the *Montauk* and two gunboats came up the Ogeechee. Taking position about 1,200 yards from the stranded steamer and 1,000 yards from the Fort, the monitor opened fire on the *Nashville*. The gunboats levelled on the shore battery, the latter on the *Montauk*. The ninth shot struck the *Nashville*. "At 8.03 ceased firing," read the log of the *Montauk*, "the Nashville being well on fire." [13]

At 9:35 a.m. an explosion shook every house in Savannah. The *Rattlesnake* (such was her new name) was no more. "Thus terminated," epitaphized the *Morning News*, "the career of the 'Rattlesnake' whom we fondly hoped soon was to be converted into a sea-serpeant to plague the Yankees on the ocean."

Admiral Du Pont was "extremely gratified at being rid of her." Had this "proverbially fast" vessel gotten to sea she would "doubtless have rivalled the *Alabama* and the *Oreto* in their depredation on our commerce." A mishap to the *Montauk* marred Worden's achievement. Captain George W. Anderson, Jr., who had commanded at Fort McAllister since Gallie's death, reported that the ironclad apparently "passed and repassed with impunity over the spot where the torpedoes were sunk." Appearances had deceived. At 9:10 a.m., as she proceeded down the Ogeechee, there was a "violent, sudden and seemingly double explosion," one of the *Montauk* engineers reported. A torpedo had gone off beneath her port boiler. For a time matters looked serious. In a half-hour there were six inches of water in the fire room. The *Montauk* was run on a bar so that the mud formed a valve under the fracture. Temporary repairs were then made. The damage was "very great," reported Du Pont after a personal inspection of her bottom which he made on "all fours" upon her return to Port Royal.[14]

The once beautiful *Nashville* was now a twisted wreck in the Great Ogeechee. That much the Navy had accomplished. But the earth ramparts of Fort McAllister still mocked the ironclads. . . . Du Pont had already determined to try again. This time the operation would be on a grander scale. One of his ablest officers was given command.

A native of Charleston, Captain Percival Drayton, USN, could intonate "secesh" in the best manner of Yankee scorn. He believed the "horrors" of slavery should cease by law at some named time. He also believed the South was fighting against human progress.

"If we are not successful," he wrote, "I dont want to live, and if we are there will always be something to look to in the great future of our country." [15] As in the case of Commander Steedman, South Carolina had offered a reward for him, dead or alive. The State was not to have the satisfaction of paying it.

Drayton was given plenty of help at McAllister. Three monitors, three gunboats and three mortar schooners were to take part. The ironclads were the *Passaic,* the *Nahant* and the *Patapsco;* the operation was ostensibly designed to try out their mechanical contrivances. "A day's target practice with Fort McAllister," Bradley Osbon called it. More significant perhaps than this newspaper reporter's characterization of the expedition was Du Pont's. "I hope to hear to-morrow that Drayton has taken the fort," he wrote.[16]

On the morning of March 3 the squadron steamed upstream. The mortar schooners which were stationed four thousand yards from the Fort were about as much use as if they had been in New York, said Captain Drayton. The fire from the land battery was concentrated mainly upon the flagship. The artillerists waited until the ports of the *Passaic* were in line—the only chance to hurt her. Four seconds elapsed between the flash of a Confederate cannon and the thud of the shell against his ship, with an interval of about one second between the sound and the impact, reported the meticulous Drayton for whatever the information was worth.

The *Passaic* was hit thirty-four times, the damage being more extensive than the *Montauk* had previously sustained from the Fort's guns. A shell that landed on her deck might have gone all the way through had it not struck over a beam. Another missed a port by only a few inches. The naval practice was less accurate than on prior occasions. Captain John McCrady of the Confederate Engineers reported that of two hundred and twenty-four shells not more than fifty struck home. They cut immense holes but no damage was done which "a good night's work would not repair," conceded Drayton. Three soldiers received slight wounds; one gun carriage was shattered and the garrison's pet tomcat was killed.[17]

"God's hand seemed stretched over the brave men of this little battery," wrote Mercer in his diary. The *Republican* attributed the miraculous escapes to "the Omnipotent Arm" that shields from "harm the cause of the just and oppressed." Captain Drayton might have said the same thing for himself. "The only blood shed on our side," he informed a friend, "was from my face, which was struck by some pieces thrown up from the deck by one of the enemys shot, which came when I was outside directing the firing and which I had not observed in time to get behind the turret."

After seven hours of bombardment the ships pulled anchor and left for good. "I feel very much, of course, the failure, to a certain extent of the attack, which you had entrusted to my direction," Drayton informed Du Pont. Writing to a friend, he explained, "All non combatants think it the easiest thing in the world to pull up piles. . . . No one has yet been found any where at home or abroad that can succeed in doing it, while shot are smashing your boats and killing your people." [18]

In his report to the Secretary of the Navy Admiral Du Pont minimized the failure. "Except that the fort might possibly protect another blockade runner, its capture was of no special practical importance." After all, the operations had produced "important data," useful for the future. Gideon Welles was not impressed. "The information which the rebels derived from that experience was infinitely more valuable to them than any that you obtained was to you," was the Secretary's tart commentary. [19]

The Confederates had, indeed, learned one lesson at McAllister. It would be useful at Charleston. "Iron-clad gunboats have lost their terrors for us!" Mercer informed his sister. [20] "When they do attempt Charleston or Savannah they will hardly place as much reliance as heretofore in their iron-clad monsters," said the *Morning News* on March 9.

The successful defense of McAllister gave a brief lift to spirits in Savannah. There were not many such occasions. War had long ceased to be the fanfare of departing infantry and victorious Bull Runs. It was ever lengthening casualty lists, profitless victories and calamitous defeats, a struggle to the death against an aroused North. "Mamma is very depressed," wrote a Savannahian in 1862, "when she hears of the great preparations at the north & the many praying Christians among their soldiers & people at home praying for them." [21]

In the columns of the *Republican* on August 26, 1863, Peter W. Alexander drew a sombre picture of a country "struggling for independence, without manufactures or diversified pursuits, without a navy, its nationality not recognized by other powers, its ports blockaded, and its whole industrial system embarrassed by a widespread invasion."

Expressing the hope that nobody would have or desire a merry Christmas, the *Republican* declared that "the sun of 1863 goes down in blood" over a country "desolated by the tread of hostile armies and resounding with the lamentations of the bereaved." In similar mood the *Morning News,* describing the sad state of "our once happy land," announced that "the accustomed greeting 'A Merry Christmas' is therefore out of place to-day."

10.

In Camp, Fort and Headquarters

⋙ THERE PROBABLY were never more than fourteen thousand troops stationed at any one time in and around Savannah. The turnover, however, was large. Many thousands of Georgians received in the camps and forts near the city the training that turned them into soldiers.

In 1862 the war correspondent Felix Gregory De Fontaine penned a description of the military scene at Savannah. "Probably there is no city in the Confederacy where you would be so struck by the military air that pervades everything as here," he wrote. "In the Park, if a lady has an escort, it wears a uniform, while in the surroundings of the City where are encamped the various brigades you will see the fine essence of soldierly *esprit de corps.* These regiments, are just such as one might expect to find in Georgia— strong in numbers, and made up of all degrees of humanity from the wealthiest to the poorest and from the white haired veteran to the boy of thirteen.

"Their garments represent every hue that the scriptural Joseph ever dreamed of in contemplating his own historic coat; some wear patched bed quilts that look like dilapidated rag carpets; some have hats without vizors; some red shirts, some white; (a few almost none at all); some wear coats, some don't. . . ." [1]

Of the volunteer units that came to Savannah in 1861 the "Bull Invincibles" of La Grange was unique. One of the members de-

scribed its expedition when the enemy arrived on the coast of
Georgia. Spurred by the headline, "Yankees on Georgia Soil," they
were "red-hot to fight," said W. A. Callaway. "Captain Cato
volunteered to head a company to go to Savannah to drive them
back," he related. After a ten-day encampment near Forsyth Place
at the foot of Bull Street the rations ran out. The military authorities refused to supply them unless they regularly entered the service. "We held a council of war," said Callaway, "and decided by a
unanimous vote that as we had stopped the Yankees, our mission
was accomplished and we had glory enough for one campaign."
With colors flying and "without the loss of a single man," the Bull
Invincibles returned home.[2]

Letters of soldiers fail to reveal much enthusiasm for the city.
It was too hot. The water was not as good as at home. And there
were other complaints. "Savannah is not as fine a City as I expected," wrote a soldier named Wood who described the suburbs
as "filthy." In the eyes of seventeen-year-old Thomas Barrow of
Athens it was an old-looking place with ill-shapen houses and
narrow streets on which the sand was about a foot deep. Scarcely
less critical, his brother, Pope, was of the opinion that if "the test
that was applied to Sodom and Gomorrah was forced upon her
[Savannah] would barely escape the fate of those cities."[3] Tom
thought the inhabitants "a set of stuck up know nothing fools." A
member of the 4th Louisiana Battalion (the misconduct of the
outfit had turned the residents against it) complained in the *Republican* on April 1, 1863, "We came here as strangers and
strangers we have remained . . . the greater portion of us do not
know the name of a man, woman or child in Savannah."

The fair sex of the city fared badly in some eyes. "The ladies
down here are the poorest apologies for beauty I ever saw," declared Thomas Barrow. Since he had been in the city he had yet to
see one to "compare with Miss Livie or Helen." A lieutenant of
Marines found that the romantic light which clothed "all the
female tribe as 'angels on earth,' in his boyish imagination" was
being entirely dissipated in Savannah.[4]

But the chief complaint was not the girls who, according to an

Athens soldier, proved "very attractive to the soldiers eyes." [5] It was insects. An Army scribe writing in the Athens *Southern Banner* in June, 1861, reported that the mosquitoes descended "upon us last night like the hosts of Sennacharib," leaving a man the choice of half-smothering under a heavy blanket or being "literally stung into a fever." Another described the mosquitoes near Fort Jackson as "thick as rice and as large as humming birds."

On the roll of insect enemies fleas and sandflies were close behind. "You can hear them all over the regiment cussing the fleas," a soldier wrote in 1862. "I had pretty near as live [leave] fight the Yankees as the fleas." Both Northern and Southern accounts of camp life in the vicinity describe men getting up in the night and angrily threshing tent poles and trees with their shirts. Sandflies were pestiferous enough to make a man yell. They did as much for William W. Gordon one day on Skidaway Island. "I took a bath this morning & attempted to rub some stuff on the red bugs to kill them but the sand flies on my naked body almost drove me crazy. I fairly hollered." An Athens soldier told his family that there was not a place on his "face and neck an inch square, but is 'brused up' where they have made 'diggs' at me." [6]

The morale of the troops stationed around Savannah was fairly high in the early part of the war. "I came hear to serve my country's call & if I die in the attempt I now I will die in a glorious cause," a private wrote in 1862—"if a country is not worth dying for it is not worth living for." From Skidaway Island a Savannahian informed his wife in 1862, "I must *fight* for our Country; it will *not* do to let these people run rough shod over us. . . . What son of Auld Scotland! can sit tamely in his chair or lay down in his downy couch at night, with such thoughts hanging over his morning slumbers! He that can do this is no Countryman of mine. Away with him!!" [7]

No one was more in love with his cause than seventeen-year-old Joseph C. Thompson. From the battery on Green Island in September, 1861, he wrote his sister, "If they try us I think they will be barking up the wrong tree for I do not believe there is one man in the Guards who would not die before surrender." Private

Thompson amused himself by putting his sentiments into verse, the following being a fair sample of his poetic talents:

> We'll by our Cannon stand,
>   If we dont, why then I lie.
> We'll fight them, to a man
>   And make the Yankees fly.[8]

Bitterness against the North is often reflected in the letters and diaries of soldiers. Returning to his quarters at Skidaway Island after duty on a bitterly cold night in December, 1861, Captain Hanleiter asked himself, "Is it not a shame that men reared to the Arts of Peace, are obliged to stand vigil at such an hour, at such a place, and in such weather in order to protect their homes from invasion by a ruthless horde of marauders professing to be Christians?" A few weeks later this Atlanta officer wrote, "Let Southrons everywhere raise the *black flag,* and neither give or accept quarter on their own soil. Our Independence must be achieved, or every male inhabitant perish." [9]

Few men were in better position to observe the volunteers at Savannah than George Mercer who served on the staff of his father, General Hugh W. Mercer. "Our low country men," Mercer wrote, "are tall, boney, swarthy fellows; they are more useful than showy—strong, hardy, and seasoned, daring and resolute, and soldiers by instinct and habit. Every man of them is familiar with horse, gun, exposure, and hardship." Of the 61st Regiment whose members came from south Georgia, the historian of the outfit would write, "The most of them were taught early how to handle and use a gun, and could kill the fleet-footed deer, panther, wolf, bear, wild-cat and fox running at break-neck speed or could take off a squirrel's head with the old plantation rifle." [10]

The up country soldiers, said Mercer, were "usually rough, un-uniformed, undisciplined men, but hardy and strong and dead shots." He was vastly amused by their comments when they saw a Shetland pony at Savannah for the first time. Another day while a group was drilling on the parade ground south of Forsyth Place the fountain in the park began to play. "They broke and ran to it like quarter nags," he related.

After watching a parade of Harrison's Brigade of State troops Mercer attested that he had "never beheld finer looking men, or men better drilled after two months service." He was particularly impressed by the Bartow Avengers from north Georgia whom he described as "large, robust, finely formed men with those honest, often noble countenances that are so often seen among our rural population."

While the Georgia yeomanry was "exceedingly temperate and tractable" the men were "no respecters of persons, and have little reverence for uniform or rank," Mercer complained. Colonel Charles Lamar's regiment was made up of "quiet, temperate, psalm-singing, simple-hearted men." They were also completely democratic. While encamped on Jekyl Island one of their officers was accustomed not only to mess together with his privates but to cook for them. Another officer did the washing for his mess.

The privates would not hesitate to drop in to see General Mercer at any time on any matter. In speaking of him they would refer to "that ar man." One day when Robert E. Lee was making an inspection tour of the defenses near Brunswick his train stopped at an encampment of the State troops. The soldiers gathered outside, calling loudly for a speech. When this proved unavailing, they crowded into his car and "duly inspected" General Lee, expressing their views in stage whispers. One of them, having satisfied his curiosity, turned toward the door and in a loud tone said, "Gim me room boys. I'se seed the monkey." [11]

The problem of discipline was not confined to rank and file. When Major O. C. Myers approached Colonel E. W. Chastain on official business, the latter exclaimed in the presence of officers and privates (so read the charges), "Go to Hell, God damn you, Dont speak to me. I hate you." In July, 1861, Major Edward R. Harden of Dalton, an officer in the Georgia Army, was tried for leaving his post without permission. He wrote three letters on successive days to Howell Cobb in Richmond. "For God sake, go immediately and see the President," he implored his friend. It was true he had left the Oglethorpe Barracks and had gone to his hotel but he was burning with "bilious fever" and "did not think for three days" to let the other officer know he was ill. Never had a man been so persecuted and hunted down, all the result of an infamous conspiracy on the part of "abominable little Savannah cliques." The officers in his regiment were all on his side but there was "prejudice among the old U.S. resigned officers against the civilians in this Regiment." They were after Harden because he was "an up country civilian." The whole thing was all the more outrageous because, as Cobb well knew, he had done more than anyone "in Cherokee Georgia to promote this secession feeling." [12]

In February, 1862, Adjutant General Wayne, criticizing the "ignorance of military law and discipline" in the Tattnall Guards of Savannah, directed them to be kept in service only "as long as the safety of the City requires it." If necessary, they were to be disarmed and their arms turned over to men "willing to fight as directed by the proper military authorities, and not according to their own individual notions." [13]

Indiscipline was attributed by Alfred Hartridge to the poor calibre of officers who were "generally grossly ignorant of their duty, or not disposed to enforce proper discipline & reform irregularities." [14] In February, 1862, Cornelius Hanleiter wrote in his diary, "There is entirely too much Demagogueism in this Department of the Army. . . . Almost every officer is trimming his sails for future political use." Mercer declared that "ignorant and inefficient officers" were the "curse of our service." Some of those at Savannah were "filthy in person and manners" and would "disgrace any service."

A persistent theme in letters of soldiers was the matter of health, or rather lack of it. During the summer of '62, according to Mercer, only five or six men were present for duty in some companies. In the spring of that year a soldier wrote from Savannah, "Battery Harrison does not seem to agree so well with our boys, not only our company but about half of the Regt. is down with the mumps or something else." [15] Fifty-six members of the Chatham

Artillery were on the sick list at one time. Isaac Hermann related in his recollections that one morning when he blew assembly at his camp near Fort McAllister only one man turned out, the rest of the company being down with chills and fevers.

Soldiers from the rural sections seldom washed or changed their clothes. They gorged on green peaches and watermelons and they spent their pay on raw pies sold by Negro hucksters. Mosquitoes, however, not over-eating or uncleanliness, caused most of the illness. The account book of a local cabinet-maker showed sales in October, 1862, of twelve "stained & trimmed" coffins ($12 each) for deceased members of the 32nd Georgia Regiment.[16] Malaria ravaged Savannah soldiers as much as men from the interior counties. When the Volunteer Guards were stationed at Brewton Hill on the Savannah River Major Basinger was the only man in the battalion who escaped its onslaught. The illness occurred despite the fact that, at his order, every sentry was served at night with a stiff drink of whiskey plentifully mixed with chopped garlic.

Measles were epidemic. Serious complications sometimes followed. A case history, not without poignant aspects, is that of Private James H. Espey of the Georgia State Army. He was "one of the best young men" in his company and possessed "the love and esteame of every one," attested his captain. On January 9, 1862, Espey wrote home from a camp near Savannah that he had been "fiting the measles" but that he had "got them conquerd." On January 15 he said that he was "giting so I can eat very harty." There was no reason for his mother to be "uneasy"; he was going to use every means of "taking cair" of himself. A few days later he reported that he was well although he had not "fuly gained" his "former strenth yet." In early February Espey told his family that he was "out of all dainger of a relaps." Moreover, he had a good chance to be "color barier" of "ower Ridgment." He assured his parents that "if we ever meat the enemy I think we will distinguish ower selve as true Southerners." Ten days later a friend reported to the family that James had "bilious fever." The illness was not considered dangerous. Soon afterward a relative wrote

that he was "verry low" with "pneumonia fever." On February
18 his captain informed his father, "I do not think that you can get
here in time to see your son alive." Espey died, a cousin wrote, "as
easy as a man could with a smile on his face." Just before his death
the young soldier told a friend that "he saw Jesus standing with his
arms open and inviting him to come declaring that all was piece
with him on earth." [17]

"The camp is a peculiar place," wrote a volunteer in January,
'62, "all sorts of men and dispositions of men. . . . Now while I
write there is a variety of amusements in hearing, one party playing at leap frog and singing spiritual songs, some dancing, some
cursing, some reading the bible, some drinking whiskey and all sort
of more evil than good." On Christmas Day, 1861, a soldier reported that he was "tired of seeing so much drinking, quarreling,
cursing and other mischief, going on." A few weeks later the same
volunteer wrote, "Every now & then I can hear them holow out
I have made high low jack & the game" while other soldiers were
"down at the Captains tent having a fratilion some dancing fid-
dling & cracking bones. . . ." [18]

Captain Hanleiter prohibited all card playing in the Joe Thompson Artillery, claiming it had not only become an "intolerable
nuisance" but was calculated "to debase the mind." A letter from
Lieutenant Colonel William Percy M. Ashley published in the
Rome *Courier* charged that two "faro banks" were "in full blast"
every night at Camp Wilson where the 29th Georgia was stationed. When the good name of that regiment was hotly defended
by one of its officers, the accuser modified his charges—the banks
were not faro, they were *"Chuckaluck."* [19]

"I think our Chaplain—Mr. Weaver, is trying to get up a re-
vival of religion among the soldiers here, but I think he has began
a hard task," a private wrote from camp near Savannah in 1862.
Alfred Hartridge attributed irreligiousness in the Army to the fact
that "the parents of the generation have neglected their duty—the
sacred duty of teaching their children how to meet death & not how
to waste life." Not every parent was delinquent. From "the
trenches" near Atlanta in 1864 Lieutenant John D. Hopkins wrote

to his daughter on the occasion of her fourth birthday to tell her how she could please him. "Your dear mama has taught you about God and your dear Lord Jesus Christ and your papa wants you to keep praying every day and asking God to make you a good girl and to bless little brother and papa and mama." [20]

Godlessness did not reign absolutely in the camps. A private stationed at Savannah assured his aunt that his own company was the best behaved in the regiment. "Out of 60 men there is only 1 man that will gamble, & but few that take the name of God in vain," he reported. "I am trying to serve my God yet." [21] At Fort Pulaski Father Peter Whelan, as pure of soul as he was careless of dress, regularly held mass in the casemates for the Catholic soldiers. Of this chaplain Olmstead wrote in his Memoirs, "I followed this good old man to his grave with a sense of exhultation as I thought of the welcome that awaited him from the Master whose spirit he had caught and made the rule of his life."

Letters of soldiers contain frequent references to attending "preachings." In 1862 the chaplain of a Georgia regiment reported that nearly one-third of a large congregation came forward after a sermon to acknowledge "their allegiance to the Lord." Enemy gunboats in Wassaw Sound were in view from the big canvas tent where the services were held, and the chaplain trusted "to the Lord to deliver us from their evil intentions." From time to time Captain Hanleiter would lecture the members of the Joe Thompson Artillery on the subject of Temperance and Morality. "There are many *very* bad women in Savannah. I saw several specimens of them today," this Atlanta officer wrote in April, 1862. A soldier who was stationed at Fort Pulaski in the fall of '61 reported that the only sickness in his company was venereal disease. "Our country men," he explained, "got badly stuck while we were encamped in the park." [22]

A more serious problem than bad women was the worship of what Captain Hanleiter called "the fiery God." In December, 1861, he reported that Private Delvin appeared in the ranks on parade under the influence of alcohol. His fondness for the stuff probably had something to do with his being badly cut a few weeks later in what was described as "an Irish wedding." In March of that year Charles C. Jones, Jr., told his parents, "Could we but rid our armies of the presence of this prime evil (Alcoholic drinks) there is no estimating the amount of sickness, immorality, neglect of duty and false courage which could be removed."

During the same month William Duncan expressed the opinion that a recent order closing bar rooms in Savannah at certain hours would do much towards improving the morale of the Army in the vicinity. There were other places to drink, however. "The crew of the Ram Savannah seem to be having a rowdy time on board of her," wrote Colonel Anderson on Christmas Eve, 1863. Some of the sailors were having quite a celebration. Lieutenant Graves was mixing an eggnog in his quarters aboard the ironclad when he was suddenly called on deck. There he found about twenty men who were behaving like "so many wild beasts" after breaking into the surgeon's supply room and taking several gallons of whiskey.[23] It was 2 a.m. before the guard got all of them in irons.

Existence on the Confederate ram was not easy. There was much growling and the food was poor. The men believed that the rice diet was causing them to go blind. Going ashore could be something of an occasion. In March, 1864, a sailor named Robert Watson and a shipmate visited Savannah. In Watson's words, they "got most gloriously drunk." Meeting up with some friends, each of them spent about $55 before the night was over, mostly on whiskey. A contrite young man, Watson was "heartily ashamed of myself for making such an ass of myself." [24]

Drinking to excess was not confined to the ranks. Relaxing on a Sunday in October, 1864, from the trials of command of the District, Major General Lafayette McLaws went across the Savannah River to spend the day with a friend. Returning by water, they were arrested by naval guards and brought to the city. On the way to the barracks they were taken by Josiah Tattnall's residence. The Commodore identified them and they were released. Edward Anderson (whose choicest invectives were usually reserved for this hero of Sharpsburg) commented in his diary that McLaws was "represented to have behaved before the Comd with a want of dignity, arising from its utter absence in his nature and in the present instance from too free an indulgence in liquor."

At Fort Pulaski there were high times during the early occupation by Savannah troops. "Wines and liquors were as free as water, and the cuisine of the messes would have done credit to any table, private or public," attested Captain Wheaton of the Chathams. "The well fed Artilleryman," wrote another member, "enjoying his champagne punch within the comfortable casemates, little thought of the coming day when even a glass of Confederate whiskey could not be obtained. . . ." [25]

Even while Fort Pulaski was besieged by the Union forces there was gaiety of a sort. On Christmas Day, 1861, a private noted in his diary, "Fine day here. Plenty of fighting and whiskey drinking." Another member of the garrison reported that the "Dixie Mess" and the "Hades Mess" had "an Egg Nog party in the casemate" to which officers were invited, everything passing off pleasantly amid songs and jokes.[26]

In the evenings after the day's routine there was singing at Pulaski. "In imagination," wrote Olmstead in his Memoirs, "I can yet hear Charles Umbach's fine voice trolling out 'Bonnie Eloise' or old Capt John McMahon giving us 'The Cruiskeen Lawn' . . . or perhaps Bill Sims in some rollocking song with a lively chorus in which all would join most heartily."

Apparently the music a Yankee band made across the river at Tybee induced one soldier in the garrison of Pulaski to desert. Among the regiments assigned to duty on Tybee during the siege of the Fort was the 46th New York. It was composed entirely of Germans. According to Horace Porter, "We were at this time very anxious to get some information about the construction of the interior arrangements for the defense of the fort, and one morning a strapping fellow in the regiment, who looked as if he might have been a lineal descendant of Frederick the Great's Potsdam Guards, became enthusiastic in the belief that if there was any son of Germany in the fort the playing of the strains of the Vaterland within hearing of the enemy would bring him promptly into camp." The plan was put into execution. "Sure enough," related

Porter, "one dark night a German came floating over on a log from Cockspur to Tybee Island. We got from him some very useful information."[27]

In after years a member of the Chatham Artillery could lyricize over its bugler—"old Hetterick" whose "sweet bugle" filled the night air at Camp Claghorn on the Isle of Hope, bringing to the men alternating thoughts of "joy and sadness, love and pleasure, peace and war." The Chathams possessed another musical genius in the person of Robert M. Charlton. By whistling through his fingers he could imitate the notes of a mocking bird almost perfectly. After the Confederate victory at Olustee General Colquitt was serenaded by a regimental band. When it played "the Mocking Bird," Charlton whistled an accompaniment that caused some of the spectators to look up in the trees.[28]

Comical incidents on the drill field were plentiful. They included the captain who gave the order, "Gentlemen of the Banks County Guards, *please* shoulder arms." There was also the officer whose men had had so much trouble distinguishing between their left and right feet that he required them to attach a sheaf of hay to the right and a sheaf of straw to the left. He then kept his men in step by calling out, "hay foot, straw foot, hay foot, straw foot." And, of course, there was the inevitable colonel who, walking backward while drilling the regiment, fell into a mud hole. When General Lee inspected the battery on Green Island in the fall of 1861, he reviewed the Savannah Volunteer Guards who were then garrisoning Fort Screven. As the review drew to a close, the men in column of platoons in two ranks marched by at double quick time. Among the soldiers in the lead platoon was a stout, clumsy volunteer. On a turning movement he stumbled and fell, tripping men to his right and left. The platoon behind could not stop quickly enough. The two became a confused heap of soldiers rolling on the ground. In spite of this malaccident which evoked "inextinguishable laughter" from everyone, Lee was impressed enough to tell the commander of the Guards, "If I had ten thousand such troops, I would not hesitate to meet a very much greater force of the enemy."[29]

Much mischief went on in the camps at Savannah. A more sadistic version of the "hot foot" was practiced. While an Augusta company was encamped at Thunderbolt two of its members greased a strip of paper and placed it between the toes of a sleeping companion. It was unnecessary for the historian of the company to add that after setting fire to the ends of the paper they "made themselves scarce in that locality." Near one camp, Judge Levi D'Lyon owned a farm on which he kept many goats. Much to the owner's wrath, the herd began to supplement the diet of certain members of the 30th Georgia Regiment. The defense interposed by the errant soldiers (a standard plea of the times) was not calculated to mollify old Judge D'Lyon. The animals had tried to run over them and they had acted merely in self-defense, pleaded the accused.[30]

False alarms were frequent. An officer describing an alarm for a reported landing of Federal troops on Skidaway in April, 1862, explained that green pickets had probably confused "the blowing of porpoises in the water for the sound of boats, & in the dense fog mistook them for the boats themselves." The error was compounded by a report that the enemy was crossing the bridge from Skidaway to Isle of Hope. Apparently other pickets mistook the posts along the causeway for an advancing column.[31] On February 2 of the same year Cornelius Hanleiter reported that the Chestatee Artillery had a "spirited engagement last night with an empty boat which had broken loose from its moorings . . . Brilliant exploit!" In May, '62, Hanleiter dryly noted in his journal that some heavy cannonading at Thunderbolt was directed "at an object in the River which proved to be a log."

A member of the 31st Georgia described a night alarm staged by its colonel for the purpose of detecting absentees in the regiment which was then encamped at Camp Wilson on the White Bluff road. The drums sounded, followed by orders to "Fall in!" In the excitement some of the men seemed to lose all control. One soldier tried to get in his blanket instead of his trousers. The old French bandmaster rushed up and down the camp street shouting, "Where de capitan? Where de capitan? I die by de capitan!"

When the commander of the 30th Georgia Regiment staged a similar alarm similar chaos resulted. Two or three of the men fell into an old well.[32]

Of camp life at Thunderbolt among the Savannah Volunteer Guards a soldier wrote in June, 1861, "A jollier crowd couldn't be found any where in this country." The observation did not apply to the members on their return from a false alarm one night. It seems that a sentinel reported seeing a man skulking in the marsh. "The captain ordered us to charge into it & bring the fellow out," related the same soldier, adding, "We went into the mud until we were stuck so fast that we couldn't get out." [33]

The tidewater section offered a pleasant novelty to soldiers from the interior—at least for a time. Lieutenant Montfort considered Cockspur Island "the prettiest place in the world." The Macon County officer was impressed by the good fishing there and by the oysters which were to be had "by the waggon load" only a few hundred yards from the Fort. "I catch enough any day for my mess & in a short time will catch enough for the entire garrison," he wrote in March, '62.[34] Beaulieu was prettier than Cockspur despite the cutting down of some of the great live oaks to give the guns a better sweep of the Vernon River. "A beautiful place, and as healthy as any in the world," Hanleiter described it. Not only was there "good water, good fishing, good prospect" but it was "far enough from the city and grogeries to make it just the place for comfort and pleasure."

But the novelty soon wore off. An Atlantan who signed his pieces "H.R.W." wrote from Pulaski in April, 1861, that "the lashing of the waves, the hum of the wild birds, and the leaping into the air of the fish, have become too familiar to awaken any but a passing notice from the cooped up *regulars*." A soldier writing that year from Camp Jasper declared that "the everlasting rat-a-dub-dub of the drums and the measured tramp of soldiers on drill, proclaims monotony more intolerable to the citizen soldier than the grim solitude of the never-changing pine flats." [35]

Soon, the refrain of nearly all comment was monotony and boredom. "I never was so tired of staying in a place in all my life," complained a north Georgia private in the winter of 1862. "Times are growing dul & we are all gitting in low Spirits," a soldier from Berrien County in south Georgia wrote the same year from Whitemarsh Island. A lieutenant promised himself, "When this war is over, if I outlast it, I purpose putting up my uniform in tobacco in a tight box, & that in the darkest and least frequented closet I can find." In June, 1862, he expressed the fear that the war would end before he got away from Savannah. "I get terribly tired of this tent here of mine sometimes," wrote the young officer who wanted action. He would be glad to defend the city if it were "really attacked" but "didn't enlist to do nothing but dig dirt." [36]

The volunteers are "literally rusting from inaction," observed Mercer in January, 1862. "These long pauses of inactivity are very unfortunate, they depress the spirits and enthusiasm of our troops, and insinuate the idea that their services are not necessary, and that they are wasting the public money & their own time to no purpose." At no other period did fractiousness at Savannah reach the level it did in the summer of '62. "There is a spirit of disaffection & mutiny among all the Troops of this District which if not promptly checked by some severe examples," said an officer, "will become the means of ruining all if not the loss of this part of the State." [37]

When General Hugh Mercer ordered soldiers detached from their commands in order to form a battalion of sharpshooters, two companies of the 54th Georgia openly disobeyed. Some of the officers sided with the mutineers. Major Basinger of the Guards was ordered to march with his battalion and disarm the recalcitrants. Leaving his men out of sight, he walked into the camp alone. After talking with the officers the men came to terms. Bloodshed that was otherwise probable was avoided, said Basinger who considered the episode "one of my best services to the Confederacy."

During the summer of '62 the terms of enlistment of many Confederate volunteers expired. General Mercer's orders to hold all of the twelve-months men for an additional period of ninety days created what John W. Hagan, in badly spelled understatement, called "a grateal of dissatisfactsin." When the volunteers were held in service, they brought habeas corpus actions. In July, '62, General Mercer informed the President that "nothing but the immediate declaration of martial law will save the service from injury of the gravest nature." Davis declined to issue such a proclamation on the ground that the situation was not covered by the terms of the statute.[38]

Command of the Georgia District was, as Hugh Wheedon Mercer could well attest, a thankless task. A grandson of the Revolutionary hero mortally wounded at Princeton, General Mercer had succeeded General Lawton in command at Savannah. He exemplified the saying about prophets in their own houses. "So you were amazed to learn that the quiet gentleman formerly with the planters B[ank] is the *Brigadier Genl Mercer*. It is even so," William Duncan informed a friend in June, '62. "I would not have you say it, but I think he is about as fit for a Genl. as you or I would be for a pulpit."

His critic overlooked that he was a graduate of West Point, had served for several years in the regular Army and had been an aide to General Winfield Scott. Writing in 1862, a Savannahian who was in better position to evaluate his qualities as a soldier declared that he had "more confidence in General Mercer than in any of our officers." [39]

He was at least more mercifully treated than his predecessor. "This community," complained Lawton's wife in 1861, "has exerted itself for his [General Lawton's] benefit in every form of fault finding and abuse—some the result of envy—some of ignorance and misconception—some pure malice." Sarah Alexander Lawton was not averse to faultfinding herself. With some derogatory comments about a Savannah naval personage, she wrote, "The Governor is expected here today. *I* have determined to show him no attention for I do not esteem him—but my husband must accompany him down the coast." [40]

What Alexander R. Lawton's failings were as a soldier (William Basinger said he possessed "common sense" to a degree amounting to "genius") is hard to discover. That people found fault with him cannot be denied. "General Lawton may be an excellent politician but he is certainly a poor general," reported a young soldier. "He don't seem to know anything about his business." [41]

The burden of complaint related to preparations for defending the coast of Georgia. "There has been a wonderful lack of energy in this matter on the part of our General & the complaints are loud and universal," William Duncan wrote in the summer of 1861. In the fall Mrs. George W. Anderson expressed the hope that some energy could be infused in the military leaders. "I do wish," she added, "we could send Genl Lawton to Brunswick, & have your Uncle [Hugh] Mercer transferred to us." In February, 1862, Charles C. Jones, Jr., after mentioning that Lawton was being defended on the ground that he had done all he could, observed, "That is not a proper answer. If he could do no more, then he should have abdicated. . . ." [42]

The command of the Confederate troops at Savannah was not made any easier by Joseph E. Brown. The Governor was "contentious" by nature, according to Henry C. Wayne who privately informed Hugh Mercer that he was ignorant of military matters and did not "choose to see" what he did not know about the relations and connections of military rank. "The crotchets of our disputatious Governor" (the words are General Mercer's) created many difficulties. [43] The dual military establishment at Savannah was not a happy one. The troubles foreseen by General Lawton in sending State troops to defend the coast and expressed by him to Judah P. Benjamin in November, 1861, came to pass.

The tact of the Confederate and the State Commanding Generals at Savannah made the situation at least tolerable. When Lawton was commissioned a Brigadier in the Provisional Army of the Confederacy he informed the Governor, "A Georgian myself, I shall ever studiously avoid any conflict with the constituted authorities of Georgia. . . ." Writing to General Lee in December, 1861, Henry R. Jackson, commanding the State forces at Savannah, assured the Virginian that "my personal relations with General Lawton are of such a character as to insure between us a perfect harmony of action." With truth Lawton could inform Jackson in April, 1862, that he had "used every effort to prevent collisions between the two forces here for a common purpose." [44]

Henry R. Jackson had attracted General Lee's attention in western Virginia in the summer of '61. The Savannahian later resigned his commission in the Confederate Provisional Army at the behest of Governor Brown to accept the State command. "I deeply regretted your resignation," Lee told Jackson at Savannah. "At the date of it I was negotiating for you with the department of war. I asked for but two men, and you were one of them." Others were less impressed by the Commander-in-Chief of the Army of Georgia. "In trying to emulate his great namesake," said Alfred L. Hartridge, he was making "an ass of himself." Possibly the comment was inspired by Jackson's promise that if Savannah were attacked, the history of its defense would be as "famous as that of the success at New Orleans under the veritable Old Hickory." [45]

Savannahians of high rank in the Confederate Navy fared as badly as general officers in the Army from jibing tongues. "The Commodore looks old and broken," wrote Sarah Alexander Lawton concerning Josiah Tattnall in 1861. "Surely it is no blessing to live to be old," she commented after pointing out that the naval authorities at Savannah were doing nothing that she could see "in the way of preparation."

11.

Webb Attacks the Monitors

≈ NO SEAPORT in the Confederacy turned out more or larger war vessels than Savannah. The work of naval construction was more energetic and on a larger scale there than in any other Confederate coast city, as attested by the Confederate naval historian, John Thomas Scharf. The lack of results from all this effort was attributed by him to the "oft-told tale" of there being only enough money and materials to build one good ship at a time.[1]

Three ironclads were constructed. They were the *Georgia, Atlanta* and *Savannah.* When William T. Sherman's Army arrived, two armored vessels were on the ways, the machinery partially installed in one of them. In addition to those vessels, three wooden gunboats were constructed at Savannah. The side-wheeler *Isondiga* was launched at Krenson & Hawkes' shipyard and the propeller *Macon* at Willink's. The *Macon,* which was 156 feet long with a draft of seven feet, had the "long, low hull and rakish build of a modern gunboat."[2] The other gunboat, the *Milledgeville,* was in the water but was not yet commissioned when the city fell. At least two torpedo ("cigar") boats were also under construction at that time.

The first of the Savannah ironclads, the *Georgia,* was launched in May, 1862, and placed in service that fall. Five hundred tons of railroad iron were used to provide her with an armor plate four inches thick. A Northern correspondent who saw the vessel from a distance called her a "nondescript marine monster" covered with long slabs or strips of railroad iron with a box on top of the deck that also seemed to be armored. There was one trouble with the ironclad. The engine was not capable of propelling her against the tide. She had to be moved by means of tow boats. Minor defects included a piece of timber from the ways that had stuck fast in her bottom when she was launched. She leaked so badly on one occasion that her officers held a conference on the advisability of throwing the coal overboard to keep her afloat. The *Georgia* leaked from above as well as below. Following a very heavy rain there was not a dry spot below, including the bunks. "A splendid failure!" a Savannahian called her.[3]

The *CSS Savannah,* an ironclad steam sloop, was commissioned in the summer of 1863. Built at the yard of Henry F. Willink, Jr., she was described by Commodore Tattnall as a "well-constructed and a very fine ship."[4] On her trial run she steamed at six and a half knots under fifteen pounds pressure of steam. One hundred and fifty feet in length, the *Savannah* had a draft of twelve and a half feet. She carried an armament of four Brooke rifles and a complement of twenty-seven officers and 154 men.

The most powerful of the Confederate Navy's armored vessels was the *Atlanta,* formerly the *Fingal.* The contract for converting the blockade runner into an ironclad was awarded to Nelson and Asa F. Tift. A high priority project, Richmond refused to permit the commanding naval officer at Savannah any say as to her construction. When Willink, one of the leading shipbuilders at the port, was asked by the Navy to put his men to work on the *Fingal* at another yard, he protested that the Department seemed to think all other naval construction at Savannah was secondary to her. "I consider the vessels I contracted to build, second to no others," he declared. Willink claimed that most of his employees would not work on the *Fingal.*[5]

Labor was obtained, however, and during the summer of '62 the river-front reverberated with the sound of tools. All week, Sunday included and sometimes at night, work on the *Fingal* proceeded. After the carpenters got through little was left of the original vessel except her lower hull and her powerful British-made engine. The sides were cut down to about two feet above the waterline and a new deck was built extending six feet beyond the hull. An overlay of timber from the deck to below the waterline strengthened the hull. The decking supported a casemate made of fifteen inches of pine and three inches of oak. Over the sloping casemate and upper hull a four-inch thickness of rolled railroad iron was laid. A solid iron beak projected twenty feet from the bow of the vessel. Four Brooke rifled guns manufactured at Richmond in 1862 comprised the armament of the 204-foot vessel.

Such was the *Atlanta,* as the Confederates renamed her. Despite her ponderousness (she weighed over a thousand tons) the ram had a trial trip speed of seven knots. She was, according to Anderson, "a pretty craft to look at." He pointed out, however, that the massive superstructure was a venturesome experiment upon the frail hull. A fatal drawback was her draft of nearly sixteen feet, making it difficult to navigate Savannah waters even during spring tides. Her unventilated hold was foul. One of her crew reported that a person carried below blindfolded would imagine himself in a swamp because of the dampness and steady trickle of water.[6] Her crew slept on a tender.

Ignoring her shortcomings, Southerners considered the *Atlanta* the last word in naval might. There were those who thought her "competent to almost any achievement."[7] She was feared in the North, Admiral Du Pont regarding her as "more formidable than *Merrimack* because of her stronger engine." Gideon Welles described her as "one of the most powerful ironclads afloat."

The *Atlanta* was placed in service early in 1863, but week after week went by without action. Impatience grew and grumbling came from both Savannah and Richmond. "The old naval officers, now provided with some formidable vessels, lie quietly in our harbors and rivers, and make no effort to injure the foe," complained a Savannahian, attributing the inactivity to their education under the old system. "They are brave men," he allowed, "but they have been accustomed to men of war, to Jack Tars, and to a certain equipment and routine which they now look for in vain."[8]

Tattnall was leery of the monitors and preferred to await an opportunity to strike when they were not in the vicinity. A Confederate deserter reported that one day while he was in a boat pulling up the Wilmington River he heard the Commodore say that he would move against Port Royal when the ironclads moved on Charleston. Another deserter overheard him make the remark that he was going to attack the wooden gunboats in Wassaw after the monitors had left.[9]

These reports agree with Tattnall's official explanation of his conduct. "I considered the *Atlanta* no match for the monitor class of vessels at close quarters, and in shoal water particularly," he informed the Secretary of the Navy on April 24, 1863. To still the "ignorant" clamor of what he called an "angry and excited public," he proposed an attack on the wooden gunboats engaged in the operations at Fort McAllister when the *Montauk* was not near. The arrival of other Federal ironclads caused the abandonment of the idea. A Savannahian who was afraid that Tattnall would "be goaded on, to do something desperate" reported that the community was drawing invidious comparisons between him and officers elsewhere.[10]

On one occasion he took the *Atlanta* round to Thunderbolt with the idea of getting to sea if the monitors should concentrate at Charleston. He contemplated either an attack on Port Royal or a cruise to Key West in the hope of surprising the enemy shipping there. At this point two Federal ironclads anchored at the mouth of the Savannah. The Confederate ram returned to bolster the harbor defenses.

According to a contemporary, Josiah Tattnall was "a man out of the common" and if given "suitable opportunities" would have "set his name among the great naval worthies." He would have no suitable opportunities in this war. His reputation had been unfairly clouded by his destroying the *Virginia* to keep her out of enemy hands in 1862. "He will be tried & probably acquitted but not, in the judgment of the people," William Duncan had said at the time.[11]

Tattnall was admired, even revered. But the feeling was general that he was too advanced in years for active service. Secretary of the

Navy Mallory apparently believed that a younger, more aggressive commander was needed at Savannah. In March, '63, he abruptly relieved Tattnall of command afloat, assigning him to shore duty. It was bitter medicine for the old naval hero and he swallowed it with strenuous protest. "Poor Cousin Josiah is very much depressed," reported a relative.[12]

Mallory found the same fault with the successor, R. L. Page. "Can you not strike the enemy a blow in Ossabaw while his ironclads are off Charleston?" the Secretary of the Navy telegraphed him on April 6.[13] Evidently Commander Page could not. Shortly he went the way of Tattnall and William A. Webb was given command of the station.

Webb was "a clever and spirited officer," according to Bulloch. Apparently he possessed just the derring-do Richmond was looking for. Because of some part he had played in the engagement of the ironclads in Hampton Roads he had achieved a reputation of being "a very reckless young officer, full of pluck and energy" and the very man to "demolish the Yankee fleet."

Colonel Anderson's pen may have been responsible for the communication signed "Georgian" that appeared in the Savannah *Republican* on May 16 and warned of overconfidence in "high quarters." The writer said that nothing less was expected of the *Atlanta* than the sinking of the monitors at Port Royal, the raising of the blockade and the occupation of the City of New York, all of which was to be topped off by rounding Cape Horn and making a dash for California. Balancing expectation against reality, the correspondent warned of "the known weakness of her hull, her scarcity of experienced young officers, and last, though not least, her crew of genuine *land lubbers,* who would be rendered seasick at their guns in a 'reef topsail breeze' or thrown into *mental asphyxia* at sight of a whale." The piece elicited a prompt defense by one of the crew of the *Atlanta.* "Some of our brave boys," he replied, "have thrown the harpoon and fatal lance into a sperm." Seven-eighths of the crew were seamen, in every sense of the word, continued the writer, and could reef, knot and splice with as much ease as their critic could misrepresent.

Whatever might be said about Commander Webb, he lacked neither boldness nor confidence. Within a week after taking over he informed Richmond that during the spring tides in early June he proposed to undertake "such attack on the enemy at such places as circumstances may determine." After the *Atlanta* came around to Thunderbolt he elaborated on his plans. His program was not quite as ambitious as the one outlined by the correspondent in the *Republican*. However, it included the raising of the blockade between Savannah and Charleston, an attack on the shipping at Port Royal, and a return to base by way of the Savannah River so as to cut off Fort Pulaski from its supplies.

Mallory suggested that he might wait for the assistance of the ironclad *Savannah* which was nearly ready for service. Anderson begged Webb not to be carried away by the clamor of the people but to act in concert with the new vessel. As a matter of fact, by the next spring tides the *Savannah* would make a successful trial run under Lieutenant Pembroke Jones who reported her in serviceable condition. But Commander Webb was impatient and boastful, said Anderson, and was "disinclined to listen to the counsels of older and wiser heads." He would like to have the assistance of the *Savannah* but "the whole abolition fleet has no terror for me," he assured Richmond.[14]

The presence of the *Atlanta* at Thunderbolt and the intention to come out was divulged to the enemy by several Confederate deserters. "In all haste" Du Pont dispatched the ironclads *Weehawken* and *Nahant* to Wassaw. The arrival of the monitors there on June 15 caused a revision of Webb's plans. He decided not to take the *Atlanta* beyond the sound. There would be enough on his hands inside. He would fight the Union ironclads. "Folly" was Du Pont's opinion of his trying to take on two monitors when Tattnall was afraid of one. But Webb and his officers were confident of success. One of the enemy ironclads was to be blown up by the percussion torpedo at the end of the spar projecting from the ram of the *Atlanta*. That accomplished, the other vessel would be dealt with.

During the night of June 16 the *Atlanta* took on more coal—

something that served only to increase her draft. Hoping to catch the enemy by surprise, she got under way down the river on the incoming tide early the next morning. . . . At 4:10 a.m. she was sighted by the watch on the *Weehawken*. Slipping cable and signalling the *Nahant* to follow, the *Weehawken* headed for the Confederate ram. According to a member of the crew of the *Atlanta,* Webb made a "stirring" address. "Boys, all I ask of you is, don't say stop too soon." Above his vessel flew the flag recently approved by the Confederate Congress, the first time the new colors had flown in combat.[15] A right gallant sight the pride of the Confederate Navy made as she came out of the Wilmington River. She was in Wassaw now—the biggest water some of her crew had ever seen. The channel ahead seemed deep enough to the pilots. Full steam, the *Atlanta* entered the sound.

Suddenly the ironclad was moving no longer. She had run on a bank that made southeastwardly from Cabbage Island. Reversing the engine, she got free. More trouble quickly followed. Due to the shallow water and the flooding tide against her bow she refused to obey the helm. The ram was forced back upon the spit. There, helpless and hapless, she sat.

A shot was fired from her bow gun in the hope of making the enemy engage at a distance. The *Weehawken* continued to close, with *Nahant* in her wake. When the former was three or four hundred yards from the stranded ram, she let go with her fifteen-inch gun. The four-hundred-pound cored ball struck the casemate of the *Atlanta,* splinters from the pine interior and the concussion of the blow disabling thirty or forty men within it. Another of the four shells that went home carried away the top of the pilot house, wounding both pilots and both helmsmen. "The first shot took away the desire to fight and the second the ability to get away," said Union Captain Rodgers.[16]

The plight of the Confederate vessel was hopeless after she ran aground. Her guns could not be trained with accuracy. "We missed two splendid shots from our bow gun in consequence of the cartridges not fitting," reported a member of her crew. He was stretching things a bit when he added that the *Atlanta* "gave the enemy shot for shot" and that it was "very exciting and close fighting, sometimes within fifty and seventy-five yards. Sometimes bow on, sometimes broadsides, and then about, and so on." [17] The engagement was more one-sided than that. As Bulloch remarked, Webb was not fighting his ship, he was enduring the fire of the enemy.

After twenty minutes Commander Webb surrendered his vessel and her complement of 137 men. "You all know that if we had not run aground the result would have been different," he explained to his crew. A small boat was sent over and Lieutenant Commander David B. Harmony came to receive his sword. "For God's sake, Captain, don't cast off these anchors, we have a torpedo underneath the bow," the Confederate officer admonished him. "With the utmost *nonchalance*" (according to the Philadelphia *Inquirer*) Harmony replied, "I don't care anything about your torpedoes, I can stand them, if you can, and if you don't wish to be blown up with me, you had better tell me how to raise the torpedo." [18]

The colors of the *Atlanta* had been lowered but a short time when the *Nahant* ranged near. Disappointed that he had not gotten in a shot, Commander Downes called over complainingly to know why she had surrendered so quickly. Later he would have something to say about Rodgers getting all the credit for the victory. The Supreme Court of the United States had the final say in 1866 on the controversy between these sons and namesakes of two naval immortals of the War of 1812. Upon the question of distribution of the prize money it ruled that the *Nahant* was one of the capturing vessels. It also held that the *Weehawken* was inferior in strength to the *Atlanta* but that she and the other monitor were together superior to the Confederate ironclad. [19]

The *Atlanta's* capture "startled" the community, declared the *Morning News*. "Oh! how provoking!" was Josephine C. Habersham's reaction. Everyone had anticipated a brilliant triumph and her sad termination had produced "general gloom," said George Mercer. "We think our government had as well give up the ship building business," declared the Athens *Southern Banner*.

According to John Thomas Scharf who had served as a midshipman at Savannah, the exaggerated reports of the *Atlanta's* fighting capacity deluded thousands into the opinion that nothing but treachery or incompetency could prevent her from vanquishing the Federal monitors. For instance, Lieutenant Joel Kennard, CSN, after watching the engagement from a tender, reported that there were two possible explanations for the disaster—loss of locomotion and mutiny of the crew. To Kennard the latter seemed the more probable.[20]

The rumor of mutiny was on many tongues for a few days. For Savannahians there was no other logical explanation. "It is supposed that the crew—mostly vagabond Irishmen . . . mutinied, and forced the Officers of the illfated 'Atlanta' to surrender," Captain Hanleiter commented in his journal. The *Morning News* published an anonymous letter from a naval officer on June 18 in which he said, "Now sir, my opinion is that the Atlanta has been betrayed to the enemy by base treachery." Rumor was carried even further by the Richmond *Examiner.* "Nor is the pain alleviated," lamented that paper, "by learning that the unhappy commander, after making a brief address to his crew of Georgians, in which he advised them to be resigned, fainted away upon his quarter-deck." [21]

Writing home two days after his capture, one of the *Atlanta's* crew attested to Webb's gallantry in the engagement. For his own part, the commander of the Confederate ship could not "speak too highly" of his crew which "displayed all the courage inherent in brave men." Most of them were from the mountains and had only a limited idea of a ship of war but they had "combined coolness with perfect obedience." [22]

Relieved that "every man stood nobly to his post," the *Republican* took its local contemporary to task on June 27 for "inferring treason against brave Southern men" and for indulging in "unjust and horrible suspicions about their countrymen." The *News* defended itself the following day. The suspicions were justified, it retorted, by the fact that on a previous occasion several members of the crew of the *Atlanta* had deserted after overpowering Midshipman Bevil.[23] Quite a change had come over the editor of the

Republican, it added, "since about a year ago when he suggested, through his paper, that the native Georgians, the 'brave Southern men' who manned our batteries and city defenses, should be required to take an oath of fealty."

In the North Captain Rodgers (who shortly became Commodore Rodgers) was hailed as a hero. His feat was described by a naval officer as "the most important naval capture of the war." [24] Secretary of the Navy Welles was delighted. The recent and rankling failure of his pet monitors at Charleston had been redeemed.

12.

Ladies at War

✧ "THE LADIES of Savannah are setting an example of patriotism and liberality that is worthy of all imitation," declared the *Morning News* on April 27, 1861. "Thousands of fair hands are daily employed in preparing clothing, bandages, lint, and numerous articles of convenience and comfort in camp life." Mercer paid tribute to them in these glowing terms: "God bless our patriotic women; what champions of liberty they are! They make the soldier's uniform and accoutrements, they inspire him with courage and chivalry, they give him the flag he would die rather than disgrace, they pray for him in the field, shelter and nurse him when sick, surround him with comforts and kindness when he lies wounded and dying." [1]

As the war wore on women's activities greatly increased. "How the women of Savannah rose to the demand that was made upon them is something for which her people have reason to thank God," declared Olmstead. Another Savannahian believed "the record of the patriotism, the heroic sufferings, the noble acts of the women of the Confederate revolution, is the brightest and the holiest in the annals of this world's history." [2]

When it came to hatred, the Confederate female was probably more ardent than the male. She hated with a passion mere man can not always muster. Her letters abound with references to "vile creatures" and "vile wretches." If the particular adjective had been a deadly missile, the struggle would have ended soon in Southern victory. An Indiana clergyman who came to Savannah under flag of truce to look up an invalid sister reported on his return to Hilton Head that there was "intense resentment at his presence." He was "an especial object of hate" among the women.[3]

Writing in the *Morning News* on August 23, 1861, a young lady who had heard that Virginia could not take care of all the Northern prisoners suggested that they be put to work making clothes and knitting socks for the Confederates. "As they seem to be unfit for fighting, probably such effeminate occupations would suit the state of their nerves better." The bitterness of this "Savannah Girl," as she signed herself, was well-nigh universal. When Josephine Habersham read an article by an English writer who said he had never heard Robert E. Lee speak *"harshly"* of the enemy, her tart comment was, "A little hate would not hurt his Lordship, I *think!*" On hearing what she called the "gratifying news that Lee was taking his army into Yankeedoodledom!" the same diarist wrote, "God grant that we may be enabled to teach these wretches the bitter lesson of experience in warfare on their own soil!" A rumor that the Confederates had taken forty thousand prisoners in Pennsylvania drew from the gentle Mrs. Habersham the observation, "Pity they hadn't just *happened to chance* to get killed instead." [4]

George Mercer wrote in his diary in September, 1861, that the women of the South were bravely supporting the "revolution" that they had "pioneered." There were others, too, who credited them with bringing on the sectional struggle. "Then the women were as eager as the men for the war?" a Northern war correspondent asked the colored sexton of the Independent Presbyterian Church at Savannah. "Yes, sir,—more," replied the latter. "They were crazy about fighting the Yankees. If it hadn't been for the ladies I reckon we wouldn't have had the war." [5]

"You women are the toughest set I ever knew," William T. Sherman is reputed to have said at Savannah. "The men would have given up long ago but for you. I believe you would have kept up this war for thirty years." [6] During the Union occupation of the city an harassed officer told the wife of a Confederate soldier, "Oh you Southern women how true you are to the cause!" "Because we know it is a just one," Mrs. Mary Drummond promptly rejoined. The militant spirit of women is reflected in a poem by one identified only as "a lady of Savannah." In the opening lines of "Boy-Soldier" she wrote:

> Oh! I wish my blue eyed
>   Were but twenty summers old!
> I would speed him to the battle—
>   I would arm him for the fight;
> I would give him to his country,
>   For his country's wrong and right.

Nothing was too good for the soldier. "Our brave boys were fighting for our homes and firesides," wrote a Savannah woman, "and we felt that we must do all in our power to help the cause along." [7] Carrie Bell Sinclair said in the columns of the *Republican*, "Would to God we could do all that our heart prompts us to do." Whether as president of the Ladies' Knitting Society or the author of such sentimental favorites as "The Soldier's Suit of Grey" and "The Homespun Dress," young Miss Sinclair did much to promote the cause on the home front.

Women threw themselves body and soul into the South's struggle. When William H. Russell of the London *Times* was in the city in 1861, General Lawton took him by his residence. The halls and parlors were filled with flannel bags. "There," his host explained to him, "are cartridges for cannon of various calibres, made by the ladies of Mrs. Lawton's cartridge class." [8] A group which met at the residence of Mrs. Emma P. Hopkins turned out more than four thousand cartridges in five days. "When our ladies thus lend their assistance to our cause," an appreciative soldier had written in the *Morning News* on May 11, 1861, "we need not be apprehensive of the result." In April of that year Mercer related, "Only this morning I was in our drill room assisting a number of ladies to make cartridges; among them were my sweet-heart, my sister and six cousins; there they were patiently cleaning the greased balls, filling the paper caps with powder, and tieing up the missles of death."

Knitting and sewing circles abounded. Among them were the Ladies' Knitting Society, the Monterey Square Knitting Society and the Rebel Sock Society. A member of the latter organization informed the *Republican* in January, 1864, "We are enlisted for the war, not to fight but to knit" and "we intend to work till the last gun is fired." Impressed by gifts in the way of havelocks, pincushions and a medicine chest, a scribe of the Troup Artillery informed the Athens *Southern Banner* in June, 1861, "Among no class in the Confederacy do the fires of patriotism burn more gloriously than [in] its noble daughters and those of Savannah are in the van—first among the foremost."

One of the most important women's activities was the Wayside Home which furnished food, lodging and other services to transient soldiers. During a period of seven months in 1863 it served 5,136 men. Many women were employed in war-time industry, and a department of the Wayside Home was set up to provide employment to wives and daughters of soldiers and to other needy females. During a single week it supplied twenty-five thousand garments of various sorts to the Quartermaster Department. The *Morning News* reported on May 6, 1861, that Lathrop & Company was seeking one hundred additional tailoresses to the seventy-five to eighty already hired in making military garments. Twenty-three women were employed as seamstresses and as cartridge makers by the Confederate ordnance depot at Savannah in February, 1864, according to its roster for that month.[9]

Bazaars, lectures, concerts and similar activities were sponsored by women in aid of the Confederate cause. The Ladies' Gunboat Association collected more than $115,000 throughout Georgia for the purpose of building a warship. "The Ladies' Gunboat," she was named when built.

The presence of enemy vessels in Georgia waters preyed so much on the mind of one upstate lady that she evolved a plan to "expell the Yankees from our coast." Writing to Governor Brown in 1862, she outlined a stratagem which in the realm of warfare by fire involved genius of rare order. Boats loaded with five hundred to a thousand barrels of turpentine were to be sent down the river at night to "within a mile of the fleet." The turpentine was to be emptied at the right distance from the ships so that it would not mix with the water before the tide bore it to the objective. At the proper moment fire was to be set to the combustible. She thought it would "do them much damage if not entirely rout them." [10]

Housewives stripped their homes of carpets for use as army blankets. They also stripped themselves in other ways, including silk petticoats which they contributed to the manufacture of the first balloon used in battle by the Confederates. Made at Savannah under the direction of Captain Langdon Cheves, it was successfully employed during the fighting in the Peninsular Campaign.[11]

Many women went into hospital work. The St. John's Hospital was established by the ladies of the Church of the same name. Madame M. C. Cazier was prominent in the establishment of the Bartow Hospital. In January, 1862, some members of Wright's Legion presented her with a woman's uniform of gray trimmed with gold braid in the style of a Confederate captain's. In April of that year she received another gray outfit from appreciative soldiers. "Though it distinguishes me, the first of my sex, as a soldier," she would proudly wear, she said, the *"belle habit* of gray." No higher honor could come to her than to know she had "smoothed the pillow of the sick, suffering soldiers." Of Madame Cazier a volunteer attested, "She nursed me and devoted on me a motherly care, for which I shall always remain thankful." [12]

Describing this phase of women's activities, Olmstead wrote, "They nursed the wounded with tender sympathy; they soothed the last hours of the dying; they brightened the days of convalescence." When three thousand Confederate soldiers were brought to Savannah in November, 1864, after their exchange as prisoners of war, nearly every woman in the city went to the wharves to meet them, "each one eager to aid these poor tortured wrecks of humanity." [13]

A soldier's death in a hospital in Savannah is said to have inspired the well-known poem by Marie Le Coste which begins with
the lines:

> Into a ward of the whitewashed walls
>   Where the dead and the dying lay—
> Wounded by bayonets, shells, and balls—
>   Somebody's darling was borne one day.[14]

Though women became angels of mercy it was too much to hope
that war would wholly transform the female character. For all their
good works they remained human—quite human. "I hear, Mrs.
Gordon, that your brother is an officer in the Union Army, and all I
have to say is, that I hope the first shot fired will kill him dead," a
Savannah woman remarked to the Chicago-born wife of William W. Gordon, CSA. "Thank you," young Mrs. Gordon replied,
letting the subject drop for the moment.

Nellie Kinzie Gordon had her troubles in Confederate Georgia
despite what she described as her "violent Southern sentiments."
Her uncle by marriage was General David Hunter who had issued
the proclamation emancipating all slaves in Georgia, South Carolina and Florida. Her father and two of her brothers were serving
in the Union Army while a third brother was in the Navy. Mrs.
Gordon, however, was quite able to take care of herself amid the
alien corn. Some weeks after, a brother of the lady who had
wished Mrs. Gordon ill was wounded in the back by a fragment of
bursting shell. When the two women next saw each other, Mrs.
Gordon remarked pleasantly but loud enough for the company
present to hear, "By the way, Mrs. ———; I hear that your
brother has been shot in the back; mine is very well, thank you!" [15]

The mental torture of anxiety for loved ones was well described
by a lady whose young son was stationed at Savannah in December, 1864, when Sherman's troops were preparing to storm the
lines. "I was wild with apprehension," she wrote. "What would be
the fate of my child, in whom every hope of my heart was centered,
and to whom I looked in later years for comfort, happiness, and

protection? At one moment I pictured him wounded, bleeding, dying. . . ." [16]

"And oh, those cruel lists of killed and wounded!" said Olmstead. "Towards the end, the prevalence of the garb of mourning told too plainly of the desolation that war had brought to almost every family in the community." Moved by the military funerals she witnessed, Alethea S. Burroughs wrote in "Savannah Fallen":

> Slowly, ah! mournfully, slowly they go,
>   Bearing the young and the brave,
> Fair as the summer, but white as the snow
>   Bearing them down to the grave.
> Some in the morning, and some in the noon,
>   Some in the hey-day of life;
> Bower nor blossom, nor summer nor June,
>   Wooing them back to the strife.

With a valor equal to that displayed on the battlefield women bore their sorrows. In a sermon preached by Stephen Elliott in 1862 he praised the spirit of the Southern woman who "bears it all and bows submissive to the stroke." Her daily language, according to the Bishop, was, "He perished for his country. I would not have it otherwise, but I should like to have given the dying boy my blessing, the expiring husband my last kiss of affection, the bleeding lover the comfort of knowing that I kneeled beside him."

Bishop Elliott had a notable exemplar in Josephine C. Habersham. "Oh! how glorious to die for one's Country. I can imagine no higher destiny for a noble minded man!" she wrote in October, 1863. A year later when a soldier consoled her upon the death of two of her sons in battle on the same day, she replied, "God is wise and just and good—infinitely good. . . . Believe me, young friend, that the true secret of Life's happiness is to be able to say 'Thy Will, not mine, be done!' "

13.

The Taking of the Water Witch

◁ COMMANDING THE *USS Cimmaron* in Wassaw Sound in the summer of 1863, Lieutenant Alfred T. Mahan, Annapolis, '59, had plenty of time to mull over the theory of the influence of sea-power upon history that was to bring him fame in later years. "Blockading was desperately tedious work, make the best one could of it," he wrote. "Day after day, roll, roll." [1] Even the largest fund of anecdotes soon ran dry, said Mahan, recounting that when two renowned story tellers were pitted against each other one night one of them was driven to recitation of "Mary had a little lamb."

Over in Ossabaw Sound it was the same story with Lieutenant Commander Austin Pendergrast of the *Water Witch*. For months during 1864 this 378-ton sidewheel gunboat had been on blockade duty without a consort vessel. Pendergrast had been attached to the *Congress* when she surrendered to the *Virginia* and had escaped under circumstances that gave him questionable status as a combatant in some Confederate eyes. It was probably with this in mind that he frequently remarked to friends that he would "never be taken."

Little chance of that fate on the Ossabaw station! To the likes of that post Admiral Dahlgren referred when he said, "As far as the eye can reach, not a living soul is to be seen for months that looks like an enemy." In these forsaken waters the idea of danger had become as remote as the rest of the world. Daniel Ammen related a small, but to him, significant incident involving Pendergrast that occurred while he was on blockade duty in Ossabaw Sound in 1863. A vessel tentatively identified as *USS Water Witch* approached from the outside. Nevertheless, related Ammen, "we beat to quarters for action, spread fires, unshackled the chain to slip it, and awaited her coming." As soon as the ship was definitely identified he dismissed the crew from their stations. "You seem to have been somewhat afraid of the Water-Witch," Pendergrast commented dryly when he came aboard. Ammen replied in polite reproof that he was not afraid but the "people on the Water-Witch would have been had she fallen into the hands of an enemy who was endeavoring to effect an entrance." [2]

If blockading was unexciting business, it was far less tedious than duty in the Confederate Navy at Savannah. At least blockaders had the satisfaction of knowing that *something* was being accomplished. And there was also the incentive of prize money. The feeling of frustration ran especially high at Savannah during the spring of '64. "This station is so dull and we have so little chance of a fight that all the officers are getting orders," reported a Marine attached to the *CSS Savannah*. The only action the ironclad had seen was occasional firing on her by Confederate pickets as she passed up the river, a practice that was very irritating to her commander. In May, 1864, a piece appeared in the *Republican* urging the local naval forces to stir up their strength against the enemy. Professing to be uninfluenced by the article, a lieutenant proposed to Flag Officer William W. Hunter that the *Savannah* proceed down to Wassaw Sound and "pounce down on them unawares." Nothing came of his "confidential" communication save a reprimand for making his proposal in writing. [3]

No one chafed more than Thomas Postell Pelot, formerly of the United States Navy and now executive officer of *CSS Georgia*. Ship! The description was enough to make one laugh. The "mud tub," Anderson called the floating battery. From this immobile hulk Pelot had gazed month after month over the waters of the Savannah River where nothing of greater interest had ever oc-

curred than the raising and lowering of the Union colors at Fort
Pulaski. In a letter home in August, 1863, Lieutenant Henry
Graves put it less prosaically. "Even as the glassy surface of the
Savannah which rolls around me and beneath me, flows on change-
less and monotonously day after day, so seems to flow the current
of events in these parts." There was hardly a naval officer on the
Savannah station who would not gladly have exchanged places
with Signal Quartermaster Adolphus F. Marmelstein and Midshipman Edward Maffitt Anderson, both of the *Alabama*. The
former had hoisted the Confederate flag for the first time aboard
the cruiser when she was commissioned in the Azores. From off
Martinique in November, 1862, the other Savannahian on the
Confederate raider had written home a ship-by-ship account of
chase and destruction in the Atlantic. Of her first victim Midshipman Anderson reported that they left her ablaze "in her lonely
position, filling the wide ocean with smoke, and standing as still to
her fate as though she was calling down curses on the head of Abe
Lincon and his cabinet, the disturber of peace and quietness, and
the principle cause of all our trouble. . . ." [4]

Back on the muddy Savannah a good deal of the time of Lieutenant Pelot had been taken up trying to persuade the crew of the
floating battery *Georgia* to re-enlist when their terms expired. His
luck was poor. Believing "an experienced and intelligent officer"
might have succeeded where he had failed, Flag Officer Hunter
recommended that the South Carolinian could be "more appropriately placed elsewhere." [5] Weary of the whole business, Pelot in
the spring of '64 requested permission to try a plan.

Capture of enemy ships by boarding parties is as old as naval
warfare. Richmond had even given thought to the problem in
relation to monitors. The Confederate Navy Department had entertained such suggestions as wedging the turret; placing wet
blankets over the pilot house; throwing powder down the stack;
using kerosene, etc. On at least one occasion the North had wres-
tled with the same problem. During the investment of Fort Pulaski
a report reached headquarters that an ironclad was in commission
at Savannah and that a plan was afoot to run her down the Savan-

nah River to open communications with the besieged fortress. A special detail was formed in the 48th New York to capture the ironclad if she so ventured. After boarding her, grenades were to be thrown through her portholes. Meanwhile, the iron roof was to be cut through by means of cold chisels in order to get at the crew below. Captain John Hamilton, USA, when consulted about these measures, jumped at a bright suggestion advanced by someone which eliminated much of the proposed procedure. The boarders would simply cut a hole in the smoke stack so that a bomb could be tossed into the engine room. When General David Hunter learned about the "Cold-chisel Brigade," as it was called, he disbanded it with the curt comment, "What fool got up that plan?" [6]

The taking of a wooden gunboat was not so complicated. All it required was courage, cutlasses and a careless enemy. This was Pelot's objective and Flag Officer Hunter approved it. Late in May, '64, the South Carolinian found himself in command of an "expedition designed to surprise and capture a vessel of the enemy now at anchor at the mouth of Little Ogeechee River." For the purpose of this mission Lieutenant Pelot was assigned fifty men from the *Georgia,* forty from the *Savannah,* twenty-five from the *Sampson* and twelve officers from the various vessels in the squadron. "I should judge from the excellent appearance of the men that they were carefully selected for the enterprise," reported an officer attached to the Union gunboat. [7]

The party reached Beaulieu on the afternoon of June 1. Captain Hanleiter who commanded there always regretted the loss of the portions of his diary dealing with the "thrilling incidents" connected with Pelot's expedition. Hanleiter's family was living with him at Beaulieu and one of his daughters was to recall the "charming and graceful manners" and "handsome and most military bearing" of the young South Carolinian. Wishing Lieutenant Pelot success, another daughter pinned a cape jasmine on his coat. [8]

The night Pelot arrived at Beaulieu he went out in search of the quarry. After looking for hours he concluded that "the bird had flown." Begging for more time, he informed Flag Officer Hunter that he had "every reason to suppose that I will find some game for tomorrow night." His men were "anxious for a brush" and would be discouraged if withdrawn. An extra day was granted him.

The following night was dark and squally. The seven barges pulled away from Beaulieu at 9 p.m. in two columns. Touching at Raccoon Key around midnight, Pelot received a report from scouts he had posted there. In Ossabaw Sound a half-mile due north of Bradley's Creek a Union gunboat had anchored for the night.

"We rowed quietly along with muffled oars," reminisced Master's Mate Arthur C. Freeman who commanded one of the barges. He quoted Pelot as telling them, "Now men, the hour has come! . . . the eyes of your country are on you! Mark well what record you leave to history tonight!" In Freeman's words, "The lightning flashed luridly in the distance . . . again it flits across the cloudy sky, and now the undefined form of some black mass rising from the water's surface is seen for an instant . . . all await in breathless silence the next flash." When it came it revealed unmistakably "the lofty sides of an enemy ship." [9]

In anchoring the *Water Witch* Commander Pendergrast had followed his usual routine. The crew was inspected at quarters, fires were banked, chains prepared for slipping and ammunition brought up for the guns. The deck watch was posted. . . . At 2 a.m. a strange craft was sighted thirty or forty yards away. "Boat ahoy! who goes there?" hailed the watch. "Runaway negroes," answered Moses Dallas, the colored pilot who a few minutes later was to give his life to the Confederate cause. The barges were now alongside the gunboat, port and starboard. "We are rebels!" shouted Pelot. "Give way, boys! Three cheers and board her."

The rattle on the *Water Witch* was sprung. "Call all hands to repel boarders, slip the chain, and start the engine," ordered Pendergrast rushing to the deck. A hail of bullets from the gunboat caused several casualties in one of the barges and it drifted off, returning to Beaulieu where the occupants reported the expedition to be a disastrous failure. Shouting like fiends, the boarders cut through the protective netting and swarmed upon the deck. Flashes of lightning illumined a wild melee from one end of the ship to the other. Powder in pistols had become wet from rain.

Sabres, cutlasses and pikes were almost the only weapons used. The officers resisted desperately. Seven were wounded, including Pendergrast who was knocked unconscious and would have been killed had the cutlass that struck him been sharper. With certain exceptions, the crew offered little resistance. A boarder related later that he and Tom Muller stood at the head of a hatchway and hollered, "Stay down there, or I'll cut your d—— noses off." Nobody came up, he said.[10]

The bravest man among the crew proved to be a colored hand who was in charge of the small arms rack. He stood his ground, according to the *Republican,* firing revolver after revolver until he fell with six or eight bullets in his body. Jeremiah Sills was killed while those who "despised him were cowering near with idle cutlasses in the racks jogging their elbows." The watch below showed no desire to resist and the engineers acted in a "most cowardly" manner, said Pendergrast. The men seemed "paralyzed with fear," he reported. One of them testified later that he went to his station on the hurricane deck but that "they was a'firing at me—for the balls was a-coming all around me." He blandly added, "I then looked which way I should go down again." [11]

Within twenty minutes after Pelot reached her deck the *Water Witch* was in Confederate possession. But the young lieutenant did not live to enjoy the victory. He was shot through the heart early in the fight.

"For desperate daring," said Arthur C. Freeman, the capture of the *Water Witch* had "hardly its parallel." Savannahians who for so long had possessed so little to cheer about on the local battle front were rhapsodic. Their hero was buried at Laurel Grove following funeral services at Christ Church, his cap, jacket, sword and the signal book of the captured gunboat on the lid of the flower-banked coffin. The day after Pelot was killed Mary E. Bulloch wrote some lines which included the stanza:

> How nobly he has won it—
>   The martyred hero's crown!
> Place on his grave a chaplet
>   Of glory and renown.[12]

The rest of the story is an anticlimax to glory. Anticipating the enemy would come after her ("The *Water Witch*," Admiral Dahlgren had immediately ordered, "is to be recaptured if possible, or destroyed"), the Confederate prize was taken up the Vernon River to the sleepy riverside resort known as White Bluff. There was to be fighting again on her quarterdeck late one night —fisticuffs between Engineer Fabian and John Thomas Scharf.* The commander of the steamer was too short-handed to discipline the combatants. Seldom has a naval officer had a more frustrating command than that of this marooned gunboat—"a command that can result in nothing as far as I am concerned," wrote Commander Warley in requesting a transfer. For a time Lieutenant George W. Gift, CSN, was second in command. "When you get command of the *Water Witch* let's run away with it and give our allegiance to Maximillian, and be Count and Countess Somebody," his wife playfully suggested.[14]

The *Water Witch* was not destined to go to Mexico or anywhere else. The Confederate authorities were unable to get her to Savannah where there was much need of her service. Consideration was given to cutting off two points in Skidaway Narrows so she could navigate that channel. But nothing came of the suggestion except extended correspondence between Savannah and Richmond.

---

* One day while the *Water Witch* was at White Bluff the future historian of the Confederate Navy ("so handsome, with his blue pants and navy jacket") asked the hand of Anna Wylly Habersham whose family lived near the anchorage. After an appropriate delay, the young lady replied, "Mr. Scharf. The subject of your note surprised me greatly. I can answer you only as a true friend. By not referring to this again you will oblige Yours truly, AWH. Do not let this answer mar our 'Friendship.' "[13]

14.

"A general deep-felt weariness of war"

"IT IS a simple proposition that if these undecisive battles continue we, in the end, must be overcome," George Mercer gloomily prophesied in the spring of 1863. Voicing the fear that the Confederacy would be gradually destroyed, he declared that the people were eating the "bitter fruits" of some grave errors. Summer brought a deeper gloom. "We cannot otherwise but feel despondent," wrote Elisha Wylly of Savannah in chronicling the reverses the South was sustaining on all fronts.[1]

"It is impossible to disguise the fact that a great calamity has befallen our arms," wrote a correspondent in the *Republican* on August 14 of that year. "Since the fall of Vicksburg and the battle of Gettysburg serious apprehensions are felt for our future destinies." The writer sounded an ominous note: "A desire for reconstruction" was maturing in the South.

Where the road led which the Confederacy was travelling was becoming plain to all who would look. Apparently there was no other route to take. "We seem to stand appalled, and know not where to look for a guiding hand, or which way to escape," wrote "One Whose Heart has Bled by this War" in the *Republican* on September 14, 1863. There was one road, however, that he was determined not to take. "Come war, come famine, come extortion, come anything but the wrath of God rather than reunion with the North."

That seems to have been the prevailing mood at Savannah. *"Reconstruct the Union!"* Such was possible, declared the *Morning News* on February 4, 1863, "when light has learned to dwell with darkness; truth with falsehood; honor with dishonor; justice with fraud." "No, my countrymen, dismiss all thoughts of reconstruction, for that is impossible," admonished a citizen in the *Republican* in August. Only when the last Southern soldier had fallen and women applied torch to the last habitation "then and not until then let us think of submission."

In his Annual Report for the year 1863 Mayor Thomas Holcombe declared that the alternative of submission was equality of the Negro and the white. "Never! No, never," he protested. "Annihilation rather than to submit to such an alternative." Urging no talk of peace, a contributor to the *Republican* on October 2 of that year declared that heavy blows, thickly laid on, were the best arguments to convince the enemy of the "true measure of our rights." That paper declared on January 3, 1864, "There is but one way to build up a peace party at the North, and that is by establishing to their satisfaction the utter hopelessness of their efforts to subjugate us."

Peace became an issue in the congressional race in the First District in 1863. A voter confronted the three candidates with the question, "Are you in favor of settling the present difficulty with our enemy, by a continuation of the war, or will you . . . advocate an immediate cessation of hostilities for the purpose of negotiation with a view of obtaining an honorable peace?"

Congressman Hartridge replied that he favored only that peace which recognized the South's independence. The sole hope for the end of the war, he said, lay in the "triumph of our noble arms in the field." T. Butler King took a somewhat similar line. He declared himself in favor of "an amicable and *satisfactory* adjustment with the United States, by the acknowledgment of our independence by that Power." The third candidate, C. H. Hopkins, was regarded as being for peace at any price. However, on the record he confined himself to unqualified endorsement of any plan that would bring "to our bleeding and distracted country an early, permanent and honorable peace." His only reservation was that the measure must be supported by the people at the ballot box, concurred in by the Senate and approved by the President. The *Republican* professed to be able to make neither heads nor tails of Hopkins' position. Its own policy as expressed on September 21, 1863, was that "we should send no whipped men to the Legislature—malcontents, croakers, petitioners for peace who would dishonor their country."

The peace movement as represented by Hopkins took a bad beating at the polls in Chatham County. In the congressional election of 1863 Hartridge received 1,320 votes, King 176, and Hopkins 17.

It was not hard for people to identify those responsible for the unhappy state of affairs. Faultfinding was a universal pastime in the Confederacy. Captain Hanleiter described a discussion that took place among certain officers in Wright's Legion concerning the situation in June, 1862. Some of the men manifested a disposition to depose President Davis or, as Hanleiter expressed it, "to get up another Revolution ourselves." The Atlanta officer informed the complaining parties that he had "enlisted in defence of the new Government, and would defend it against all usurpers of every degree." [2]

The tendency at Savannah was to sustain the President. Castigating those who would destroy the government, Bishop Elliott declared in a sermon in November, 1861, that Davis's defensive strategy "demands a high degree of moral courage." Agreeing with some of the criticisms of the President, William Duncan nevertheless wrote in 1862, "Now is the time to *sustain* him, & not to criticize him." During the same year this Savannahian wrote, "I regret to find you so severe on Mr. Davis, I hardly think he is quite as blamable as you seem to think him." [3]

The President was royally welcomed at Savannah in the fall of 1863. Arriving at the Central depot on a special train, he was greeted by Mayor Arnold with an "eloquent" address. During the day Davis took a trip down the Savannah River to inspect the fortifications. That evening he addressed a large assemblage from the portico of the Pulaski House. His speech, according to the *Morning News,* "thrilled every heart within the sound of his clear, earnest voice." Chaplain Lee who heard the talk called it "good every way." [4]

The reception at Masonic Hall that night was densely crowded. People filled the street trying to get in, said Henry Graves who soon gave up the struggle. "I concluded I had had enough of the President and so put about, and making a safe escape from the crowd, I wound up the evening by calling on a pretty sweetheart of mine here, which was far more to my taste I assure you than to form one of the crowd who with open mouths and strained eye-balls, gape after the coat-tails of the President." [5]

Others, less impatient, gained entrance. Among them was Josephine Habersham. Pleased by Mr. Davis' affability, she wrote in her diary, "He has a good, mild, pleasant face, not very re-markable, but thoughtful and, altogether, looks as a President of our struggling Country *should* look, care worn and thoughtful, and firm, and quiet." [6] Chaplain Lee, who also succeeded in edging his way through the mass of people, reported that he "gave his Excellency a hearty shake of the hand" and said to him, "May God sustain you in your course." He received in return from Davis "an earnest 'Thank you, Thank you.' "

There were other scapegoats than Jefferson Davis. No country at war ever found more. Gazaway B. Lamar, who praised the President and absolved him from any degree of blame for failure, thought the fault rested mostly with the Confederate Congress. That body had attempted, said the Savannah banker, to conduct a gigantic war entirely on credit and when faced with the necessity of heavy taxation had imposed the burden inequally and partially. [7]

Other whipping-boys were the German Jews. They were "a most noxious element," said George Mercer. They "escape service as Aliens, owe no allegiance to our Govnt. think only of accumulating wealth, and are always ready to persue any course that will save it." On another occasion he complained, "They are all growing rich while the brave soldier gets poorer and his family starve." Writing in September, 1863, Mercer philosophized about the social changes that accompany a revolution. They were wonderful and many, he said, "the rich are ruined, the poor grow rich." The recipe for success was simple—"buy, keep, and re-sell at a profit . . . vide the Israelites." From time to time letters defending the Jews appeared in Savannah newspapers. A contributor to the *Morning News* on February 23, 1863, took exception to the "unjust flings" against them. "I believe," said the writer, "they are true patriots and have given and are giving as much toward supporting the Government, clothing the troops, administering comforts for the sick and wounded, etc., as any other class of citizens."

Mercer also believed that the slaves were a source of great weakness to the Confederacy. It was true that "in no single instance (and this speaks volumes!) have they voluntarily armed against their masters" but they frequently served as guides to the invaders and for money would give all the information sought, he said. To others there was no question where Negro sympathies lay. "The colored people are nearly all in sympathy with us," reported W. H. Pierson, the Union surgeon captured with the *Water Witch*.[8] As a whole the slave was a positive factor in the South's military effort. "The negro is performing an important part in the great work of our redemption," wrote Peter W. Alexander, the war correspondent. "At one of the factories today I saw a number of blacks engaged upon the monster shells of parrot balls. At another place several were at work upon a species of machinery which must be nameless." The success of the North would be the ruin of the black man; "it is for himself that he works," argued Alexander.

It is unlikely that many slaves would have believed this had it been explained to them. "You see, boss, Ise bin laborin' for forty years and I aint got nuffin to show for it. I jus' thought I'd cum down and breave free." Thus a runaway from Savannah explained on reaching Hilton Head. A more literate refugee from slavery was Susie King Taylor who left the city shortly after the war commenced and became a laundress for a Negro regiment. "I remember, as if it were yesterday," wrote this colored authoress, "seeing droves of negroes going to be sold, and I often went to look at them, and I could hear the auctioneer very plainly from my house, auctioning these poor people off." [9] The voices of auctioneers continued to be a familiar sound in war-time Savannah. The increasing precariousness of the right of property in human beings did not affect the market for slaves—at least able-bodied ones.

Unhappy as was the slave's lot in life, probably more Confederate soldiers and sailors deserted around Savannah than Negroes ran off to the enemy. "They are, by all odds, the happiest-looking folks in the Confederacy. They sing, while the whites curse and pray," said W. H. Pierson of the *Water Witch*. On May 30, 1863, the *Morning News* described the annual parade of the Savannah Fire Department and reported, "We have no recollection of having seen the negroes enjoy themselves more heartily." Occasionally they enjoyed themselves too much. A week before, a citizen wrote a letter of complaint in the same paper. "It is almost impossible to walk the streets," said the contributor, "without meeting some negro with a segar stuck in his mouth, puffing its smoke in the face of persons passing . . . and endeavoring to keep the inside walk."

Defection of soldiers and sailors was a problem of some proportion at Savannah. There was a steady trickle of desertions from fort, camp and vessel. For the most part they occurred among the sizeable foreign-born element serving there. In August, 1861, George Mercer wrote that the Irish soldiers were embracing the cause with "great spirit and ardor." No religious group at Savannah embraced it more warmly than the Catholics. On St. Patrick's Day in 1862 Corporal Landershine recorded in his diary that the Sisters of Mercy presented the Wise Guards with a handsomely worked silk flag, bearing on one side a cross and the language, "In hoc signo vinces." There were some, however, among the Irish who did not wish the Confederacy to conquer by that or any other sign. "I find that no reliance whatever can be placed on the shipped men of foreign birth who are in this squadron," reported Flag Officer Hunter in November, '63. [10] In every case of

THE CHRONICLERS, 1:

GEORGE ANDERSON MERCER

(Photograph taken probably while he was at Princeton.)

THE CHRONICLERS, 2:

WILLIAM STARR BASINGER

Memoirist and Historian of the Savannah Volunteer Guards

THE CHRONICLERS, 3:

CHARLES H. OLMSTEAD

Author of "Memoirs" and War-Time Reminiscences

THE CHRONICLERS, 4:

CHARLES C. JONES, JR.
Historian and Mayor of Savannah, 1860–1861
(Photograph taken probably in 1859 shows First Lieutenant
Jones in the dress uniform of the Chatham Artillery.)

Georgia Historical Society

FRANCIS S. BARTOW
Lawyer, Orator and Soldier

National Archives

THE RIVERFRONT AT SAVANNAH, 1865

View looking east from the City Exchange, showing the Claghorn and Cunningham Groceries and Ship Chandlery.

Georgia Historical Society

WILLIAM JOSEPH HARDEE
Lieutenant General, Confederate States Army
(Photograph shows Hardee in United States Army uniform.)

Library of Congress

WILLIAM TECUMSEH SHERMAN
Major General, United States Army

Frederick Hill Meserve Collection

JOSIAH TATTNALL
Commodore, Confederate States Navy
(Photograph shows Tattnall in United States Navy uniform.)

Peabody Museum of Salem

Destruction of the *Harvey Birch* by the *CSS Nashville*.

Library of Congress

JOHN WHITE GEARY
Brigadier General, United States Army

Boston Public Library

THE RAMPARTS OF FORT PULASKI

(Photograph taken during the Union occupation of the Fort.)

National Archives

WILLIAM BABCOCK HAZEN
Brigadier General, United States Army

National Archives

The Confederate Ram *Atlanta* on the James River after its capture by Union forces.

National Archives

PIERRE GUSTAVE TOUTANT BEAUREGARD
General, Confederate States Army

U. S. Navy

The two hundred-foot Federal ironclad, *Montauk* (left), moored alongside an unidentified sister ship long after the war had ended.

"mutinous conduct" the personnel involved, he said, were either Irish or English.

An instance of mass desertion occurred on January 12, 1864. "About three a.m. in the morning," related Anderson, "I was roused from sleep by Lt. Murphy who came over to inform me that the Sergt of the Guard at Battery Cheves, with the corporal, the sentinel on post and seven men—making 10 in all—had stolen the Battery boat and deserted to the enemy taking with them their ammo and clothing." According to Mercer, they were all Irishmen. On the Union side of the same picture, the commander of *USS Unadilla* had the "pleasure" to report the arrival of "ten deserters from the rebel army, all of whom have been for many years residents in the South." They informed the Union authorities that Confederate rule was "an evil only to be endured because of the inability of the people to oppose or escape from it." [11]

The despondency in ranks is reflected in the correspondence of Celathiel Helms. In August, 1863, this south Georgia private wrote from Thunderbolt, "I believe that nearly all the people here think that we are whipped and I think that we are whipped." In January, 1864, Helms reported that "the men is a deserting from all quarters and is going home and a going to the Yankees too . . . all the men nearly says that they cant stand things much longer." It was "the notions of every body here," he added, that the war would soon end. Asked to re-enlist by the authorities, Helms told his wife that "most of us have come to the conclusion that we have inlisted one time too often for our good." [12]

"The present," wrote George Mercer in the winter of 1864, "is the gloomiest period that we have yet reached; for the first time since this struggle commenced signs of disaffection are exhibited in the Army." There was reason to fear "that great weariness of the war, and an absorbing desire to go home, are prevalent among many of our men." [13] His observations were prompted by a near mutiny at Rose Dhu a few days before. A corporal revealed a conspiracy among the troops posted there. A large part of three companies had planned to desert with their arms, win over the troops at Beaulieu and then march to the camp of the 57th Georgia Regiment. They seemed to rely upon the latter outfit "as ready to join them," reported General Colston. They then planned to make their way to the interior of the country. Tired of the war, they evidently figured that one way to end it was to set an example that troops elsewhere would follow.

The disaffection in the 57th Georgia stemmed in part from a claim by some of the men that they had not been properly exchanged after their capture at Vicksburg. Among the grievances were deficient food, family hardship and inability to obtain furloughs. "They are demoralized by the influence of home, to which they are too near, their friends and relatives persuading them that they ought to be at home," said General Colston. He recommended that the troops immediately involved in the plot be transferred elsewhere and that the 57th Georgia be sent on duty in the "presence of the enemy." [14]

The presence of the enemy was the last place some men in that outfit wanted to be. On February 22, 1864, a large Union force landed on Whitemarsh Island in two separate columns, one of which advanced to the bridge to Oatland Island in an effort to cut off Confederate communication with the mainland.* A light battery had recently been posted at that point and a small work was under construction. Hastily placing two guns in the embrasures, the Confederate artillerists forced the enemy back from the bridge. In retreating to Gibson's landing the column came upon a detachment of about fifty men from the 57th Georgia Regiment. When ordered to fire, only about half of the Confederates obeyed. They broke in "wild confusion" as soon as the enemy returned the fire and could not be rallied until they reached the picket near Turner's Rock. Their being "driven" from their position (to use what a correspondent in the *Republican* on March 4 called "a mild expression") gave the enemy a decided advantage. However, more stalwart units contained the Federals. The Confederates "came on like bees," according to a New Hampshire soldier.[15]

* Apparently this movement was a diversionary one, connected with the Federal expeditionary force then operating in Florida.

The Confederacy was dying but the idea of defeat was so terrible that many Southerners could not look that probability in the face. "Our cause is too holy to be in serious peril!" wrote Mercer. "We must prevail, so just, so noble a cause cannot perish . . . There is much in the dark future to make a patriot sad, but he should not despair . . . If we love liberty—if we are firm and true— we shall yet pluck independence from the dangers that beset us."

A deep faith was held by many Southerners that somehow disaster would be averted in the end. This belief was described in the *Republican* on September 9, 1863, as the "undefined idea that something will happen, a something supernatural and miraculous which will crown our efforts with success." In August of that year a Savannah lady wrote, "If God be for us, what have we to apprehend as a nation? Individual suffering we must expect, but I am sure that our Confederacy will yet come gloriously out of the fires." Writing about the state of affairs in the South, Mrs. William H. Stiles declared that the cause of the Confederacy was God's and he would "deliver the country in his own time." [16] In April, 1864, Bishop Elliott told a congregation that self-destruction was the only mode by which the South could be conquered. One of the great errors of the enemy was in supposing that numbers and material power were decisive and the "maintenance of a mighty principle was nothing." The Confederacy had seen its prayers answered so often, continued the Bishop, that "we come to-day boldly up to the throne of Grace, firmly believing that our prayers . . . will return to us laden with blessings from . . . the God of the armies of Israel."

The Bishop of the See of Savannah possessed equal faith in the efficacy of prayer, albeit more worldliness than Elliott in the matter of the South's salvation. Augustin Verot suggested sending a solemn embassy to Emperor Napoleon imploring him to intervene, and another such mission to the Emperor Maximilian of Mexico offering him an alliance, offensive and defensive. Gazaway Lamar of Savannah urged an alliance with France. When his son, Charles A. L. Lamar, was abroad in the summer of '63 he instructed him to call on Slidell in Paris. *"Tell him, from me,"* wrote Gazaway, *"to negotiate for the French Protectorate."* The people of the South would gladly accept it "in the last extremity," he predicted, and "with Mexico, France and the Confederacy in alliance, and free trade, we should eclipse the world." [17]

The events of the summer of 1864 increased the South's despondency. The fear expressed by a Savannahian almost two years before had materialized. "Suppose," he had written, "Chattanooga should after all become the battleground of the great battle of the west and suppose Bragg defeated—What comes of Georgia—Rome, *Marietta* & Atlanta?" The question was being answered by General William Tecumseh Sherman. "Over our country," wrote Carrie Bell Sinclair that fall, "hangs a dark, impending doom." From the Confederate lines at Atlanta late in July, 1864, Colonel Olmstead informed his wife that Georgia was in "great peril." For the first time, he confessed, he was "low spirited and despondent." If the Confederates allowed themselves to be quietly besieged in Atlanta, Sherman could detach a force and "carry desolation to every corner of the land. . . . May God grant us a deliverance out of our troubles." [18]

When a soldier named Hardy heard a rumor that the enemy was in possession of Atlanta, he wrote home from Beaulieu, "If they are we are in a right bad fix, but we will never give up, at that." Trying to put a good face on things when Atlanta fell, a marine stationed at Savannah informed his mother that he was not at all discouraged.* "We will whip them as sure as the sun shines," he assured her. By that time, however, Private Hardy had changed his tune. The war would be over in six months, he believed. "This," he added, "is my sincerest wishes." As for the Negroes running off with the Union Army, they could "go and be hanged." [19]

---

* A Southern newspaper (apparently one of the Savannah dailies) questioned, on September 12, 1864, the importance of the loss of Atlanta. "Whoever heard," the editor asked, "of such a fuss being made over the fall of a twenty year old town, three hundred miles in the interior of a State, as we and the Yankees are making over the *evacuation* of Atlanta." See Scrapbook of John Jacob Nevitt in the Georgia Historical Society.

"Rusting in idleness" at Savannah trying to maintain what he described as "a pageant called a navy," Lieutenant George W. Gift reflected bitterly upon President Davis. "A poor prejudiced narrow minded partisan," he had wantonly abandoned Georgia, South Carolina, Florida and Alabama. The fate of those states hinged on Atlanta, Gift thought. If Hood should now fail, he foresaw four more years of suffering and privation, all because "Jefferson Davis wished to frighten Abraham Lincoln [Early's demonstration before Washington] at a moment when a victory would probably have virtually ended the war." [20]

During the summer of 1864 a Northern prisoner of war kept a sharp eye about him while he was at Savannah and Macon. Upon his exchange that September he reported that he found "a general deep-felt weariness of war" and "a sort of expectation" that it would soon be over.[21]

15.

"I die in the best cause a man could fall in"

IN JULY, 1864, Joseph E. Johnston was relieved of command of the Army engaged in defending Atlanta. His removal came as a "terrible" piece of news to Colonel Olmstead. General Johnston was the idol of his troops and his dismissal took the heart out of them, he wrote. Everyone had "the blues," reported another Savannah soldier. "I beleaved at the time that it was the worst days work Jeff Davis ever done," wrote an officer in Mercer's Brigade. There would be "no more flanking," he quoted a war correspondent ("Genl P.W.A.") as having announced at the time. "The first lick Shearman made," complained the soldier, "he flanked him [Hood] 30 miles." [1]

On September 1, 1864, Hood evacuated Atlanta. In October General William T. Sherman obtained approval of his plan of cutting loose from his communications and marching to the sea, three hundred miles away.

The interval during which the Union Army was being reorganized and rested for the coming campaign through Georgia presents a favorable moment for a glance at Savannahians fighting on other fronts. To the scenes of low morale among some of the military elements stationed at Savannah the contrast is a stark one.

At the commencement of the Pennsylvania campaign the Georgia Hussars participated in an engagement in which a number of the enemy were captured. Lieutenant Robert Saussy of Savannah was ordered to escort the prisoners back. For this purpose he had a detail of four men besides himself. En route, he was informed that some enemy cavalry were along the road in front of him. Saussy decided to go ahead. Ordering his prisoners to lie down in a ditch with their faces to the ground, he left two guards with orders to kill the first man who even turned over. Lieutenant Saussy and two of his men crept forward through the underbrush. On reaching the road where the Federals had halted they opened fire accompanied by a loud shout to "charge the rascals." The enemy scattered. Saussy then resumed his mission, delivering the prisoners safely at Culpeper. "I hope we shall meet again in this war, sir," a Union officer remarked to him in rather bad spirit. "I hope we will but you won't see anything like this," replied the Georgian. "Like what?" asked the prisoner. "Why," answered Saussy, "five of your men take twenty or thirty Confederates to the rear through a debatable territory, meet and drive off a regiment of our men on the road." [2]

During the fighting at Kelly's Ford, Virginia, in November, '63, Lieutenant Joseph McLeod Turner of the Georgia Hussars carried out an assignment that took him to another part of the field. He then attached himself to an outfit that was being out-flanked by the enemy. "Riding leisurely and composedly up and down the line, uttering words of encouragement and good cheer," wrote the historian of the Hussars, "he was a conspicuous mark for the aim of the enemy not fifty yards away." Halting his horse in face of the foe, Turner drew his pistol and deliberately emptied every barrel. With the discharge of the fifth shot he was struck in the forehead.

A few days later a farm boy showed up at the Hussars' camp with a package addressed to the commanding officer. It contained all the effects found in Turner's pockets. A letter from a Federal cavalry officer accompanied the package. "Although I am upon the Union side, and nothing but a Yankee, still I admire bravery," he said, "even in an enemy." [3]

After hard service for nearly two years at Charleston the Chatham Artillery returned home in February, 1864. Scarcely had it encamped at White Bluff when it was ordered to report to the Atlantic and Gulf depot. The outfit arrived at Olustee, Florida, on February 17. In the victory that day the Chathams had a distinctive part. Ordered by General Colquitt to withdraw his guns from an advanced position, Captain Wheaton remonstrated, "General, I think we can hold on where we are for some time; it certainly can not be long before the ordnance wagons will be up, and their arrival will change the situation." Colquitt withdrew his order with the admonition, "Be sure you don't lose your pieces." [4] Wheaton did not. Reinforcements arrived in time and the day was gained.

Another artilleryman who disliked to pull back was Robert Falligant. Leaving the University of Virginia when the war commenced, he had won a senior second lieutenancy for gallant conduct at Sharpsburg. At Cold Harbor in 1864 the Savannahian made a name for himself when his single piece protected the right of the Confederate line for several hours. General Kershaw repeatedly praised his conduct. "I have no hesitation in saying," wrote an observer, "that in all my experience as a soldier I never witnessed more gallant action than this of Lieutenant Falligant and his dauntless cannoneers, nor do I believe that any officer of his rank made a more important contribution than he to the success of the Confederate arms in the great historic battle." [5]

G. Moxley Sorrel, private, Georgia Hussars, had soon tired of cavalry life on Skidaway Island in the summer of 1861. The spare-framed Savannahian went off to Virginia where he became one of the best staff officers the Confederacy produced. He was to have his day of glory as a line officer in 1864. In the fighting in the Wilderness in May, General Longstreet turned to Sorrel. "Colonel, there is a fine chance of a great attack by our right. If you will quickly get into those woods, some brigades will be found much scattered from the fight. Collect them and take charge. Hit hard when you start. . . ." He did. Sorrel's command rolled back the exposed left flank of Hancock's forces. "More conspicuous gallantry on the field I never saw," said a friend in describing his leadership that day. Later, when the members of the 12th Virginia recognized Sorrel at Marshall, Virginia, every man in the regiment took off his hat amid shouts of "Lead us, Sorrel! Lead us as you did in the Wilderness." [6]

In the original crew of the *Alabama* was Midshipman Edward Maffitt Anderson. The young Savannahian was aboard the raider when she was sunk by the *Kearsage* off Cherbourg. On July 5, 1864, his father recorded that the news of the loss of the *Alabama* had been confirmed. "My heart has sunk within me, for my fears tell me that my darling boy is lost." A few days later, after perusing a newspaper account, Edward C. Anderson wrote, "My worst fears are realised & my noble boy is no more." The newspaper had reported that young Anderson had been blown overboard by a shell, leaving a leg on deck. "The news came like an earthquake upon me," said his father. . . . A fortnight afterward, a happier entry appears in his diary. "About 10 ock Sally Anderson rushed in, pale & breathless" and announced that "Eddy was safe." Midshipman Anderson had been only slightly wounded and had managed to keep himself afloat until rescued.[7]

In the spring of 1864 General Hugh Mercer's Brigade was sent to the front in north Georgia from Savannah. The spic and span appearance of the men who had long been stationed on the coast gained for them from veterans such derogatory epithets as "New Issue" and "Silver Fork Brigade." The titles were forgotten in the trail of dead and wounded the outfit left from Dalton to Atlanta. In a single day's fighting outside the latter city it sustained 168 casualties. Among the Savannahians who fell at Atlanta on July 21 were two brothers. Before going into battle that day Joseph Habersham scribbled on the envelope of a letter in which he had thanked his mother for her "beautiful Prayer" the message, "Willie and I are well." A few hours later Lieutenant Habersham was mortally wounded. His last words were, "Tell my Mother I die happy. I died at my post fighting for my country." Learning of his brother's death William Habersham exposed himself so recklessly that he was warned to be more careful. "When I shoot these last ten cartridges I will take care, not before!" Willie replied. He was killed an hour after his brother fell.[8]

Among the outstanding officers Savannah contributed to the Confederacy was Edward S. Willis who had resigned from the U. S. Military Academy shortly after Georgia seceded. Better soldier than student (he ranked fifty-sixth in a class of fifty-seven his third year), Willis served ably on Stonewall Jackson's staff. Later he became colonel of the famed 12th Georgia Regiment. His account of his capture at Port Republic in June, 1862, and of his subsequent escape to the advancing Confederate column is a classic of that type of chronicle. "When I met the Twelfth Georgia regiment such a cheer greeted me as I never heard before," he wrote. The men jokingly informed Willis that they were coming after *him*.[9]

Major Robert Stiles vividly described his first meeting with the young Georgian whose tattered uniform, devoid of any insignia, and his long, tawny hair and face of commanding intelligence and force made an unforgettable impression. "Stiles," said a Virginian after Willis left, "there goes the only man I ever saw who, I think, by possibility, might make another Jackson!" [10]

"I put my trust," Willis told his mother, "in Him, who in the darkest hour, has never deserted me, and who, I believe, will carry me safely through the war." If he should fall, " 'tis His will, and no one should complain." Nor did Colonel Willis when his time came. On May 31, 1864, at Mechanicsville, he was "shot down," wrote Moxley Sorrel (who lived on the same street in Savannah), "mortally wounded—the gallant, fair-headed, white-skinned, slight young colonel . . . valiantly leading the brigade." [11] He was twenty-three. The day after his death his commission as a Brigadier General arrived.

Alexander S. Pendleton, an intimate friend, wrote a letter of consolation to Willis' father the day after the Savannahian's death.

> Dr. McGuire, Medical Director of the Corps, was with him, and as I came to the pallet where he lay, he said 'Willis, here's Sandy Pendleton come to see you.' Ned opened his eyes, and grasped my hand with both of his, and said, 'Sandy, the doctors won't tell me whether I am going to die. Am I mortally wounded?' I replied 'Yes Willis, I am afraid you are mortally wounded.' He said 'That's right old fellow, that's the way I like to hear a man talk. I am not afraid to die any more than I was afraid to go into battle.'. . . He then asked Dr. M. minutely as to the course of the ball, and seemed relieved when it was described. Hearing that he wished to see Lt. Col. Moxley Sorrel of Genl. Longstreet's Staff I told Ned he had been sent for. He thanked me, and I asked him if there was anyone else he wanted to see. He said 'Yes Moxley Sorrel's Sister to whom I am betrothed. I am not afraid to die. I don't mind it myself, but it will almost break her heart & my poor father's & mother's. Tell her not to be distressed. I die in the best cause a man could fall in.' [12]

16.

In Which Sherman Heads East

HAD IT been possible to look down over Georgia from a great height in late November, 1864, the hypothetical observer would have seen what appeared as four gigantic blue caterpillars, crawling slowly on innumerable legs across the country in the direction of the sea.

They lived off the fat of the land they destroyed, these four Army corps of General William T. Sherman, as they passed through this Confederate heartland. "While we have been on this march," said an Indiana soldier, "we went threw a rich country and we got plenty of sweet potatoes beef fresh pork molases honey and other things. We are giving georgey one of the gratest rakings ever it got. . . . We cut off all the raleroads and burnt as we went." An Ohio sergeant quipped, "I do not think the cars will run for a fieu days yet." [1]

To Lieutenant Colonel Charles Ewing the march was "one big picnick." A Wisconsin Indian recruit described it as a "big hunt." Captain Poe of Sherman's staff wrote his wife that "for forty miles in width, the country throughout our whole line of march is a desert." [2]

To General Henry W. Slocum the march to the sea was the romance of war. "We lived on the fat of the land," he wrote. "Turkies chickens ducks and sweet potatoes at every meal." As the Union columns passed through the towns and villages the darkies came out in groups, continued Slocum, and "welcomed us with delight . . . danced and howled—laughed cried and prayed all at the same time." [3]

Summing up the march through Georgia, a soldier in the 143rd New York informed a friend that they "subsisted almost entirely on the country which is much the finest I have seen in Jeffs Dominions. Destroyed all we could not eat, stole their niggers, burned their cotton & gins, spilled their Sorgum, burned & twisted their R Roads and raised Hell generally as you know an army can when 'turned loose.'" A member of the 15th Iowa wrote, "Didnt we live, those Georgians were clever people to have so many good things ready for us. . . . I dont suppose they liked to board us but I didnt ask." A Minnesota soldier, referring to the "black streak behind us about 50 miles wide," expressed the wish that he could for even a day be "out of the smoke of burning Houses & 'such like.'" [4]

Appeals to the populace from Southern leaders to rise up and smite the Philistines filled the crisp air of this Georgia November. "Assail the invader in front, flank, and rear, by night and by day," exhorted Congressman Hartridge and other colleagues in a circular addressed to the people of Georgia. "You can destroy the enemy by retarding his march. Georgians, be firm!" counselled Senator B. H. Hill. Governor Brown proclaimed, "Death is to be preferred to loss of liberty. All must rally to the field for the present emergency, or the state is overrun."

Bishop Stephen Elliott was more realistic in appealing to the patriotism of Georgians. In a sermon in September, 1864, he said there was nothing left but to follow the example of the Psalmist and "crying to God to 'Give us help from trouble,' to acknowledge that 'vain is the help of man.'"

Vain, indeed! The reservoir of manpower in Georgia was nearly dry. "You have not many men between 18 and 45 left," President Davis conceded in a speech at Macon that month. No troops could be spared from other fronts to oppose Sherman's fifteen infantry divisions. With Kilpatrick's cavalry added, the Union Army totalled approximately sixty-two thousand men. All that the State had was a tatterdemalion force under Adjutant General

Henry C. Wayne, consisting of about five hundred men—militia, released convicts and prison guards, a battery of artillery and the cadets of the Georgia Military Institute. The latter went "into a fight as cheerfully as they would enter a ball-room," Wayne said of them.[5] There was also Wheeler's cavalry to the number of around three thousand. They managed to terrify Georgians more than they did the enemy. "They are doing us little good and an immense amount of harm," protested the *Morning News* on December 1, claiming that General Joseph Wheeler had "demonstrated to every man in the Confederacy, except the President and Gen. Bragg, that he is not capable of commanding 10,000 cavalrymen in a war such as this. . . ."

A telegram Wayne dispatched from Oconee, Georgia, pleading for reinforcements ended on an unconsciously comic note. "The enemy are flanking me on the right," he wired McLaws. "Send me a map of the State of Georgia."[6] Needless to say, no reinforcements were available. Possibly Wayne received the map. Looking at it, there could be no real doubt, for all the speculation on that subject, where Sherman's roads led.

Savannahians had learned to live with the stubborn fact of the presence of enemy gunboats and troops at the city's doorstep. The threat of attack on the city was an old story. It was something to be shrugged off in a community that for more than three years had been beleaguered from the east. Westward, however, in the summer and fall of 1864, the clouds were of a different and uglier blackness—big with the portent of coming doom. The foundations of the Confederacy rocked with the tramp of Sherman's troops.

The dislocations caused by the enemy's presence in Georgia were severely felt at Savannah. "Everything was in a state of dissolution," wrote a Union prisoner. As Sherman's Army drew closer to the city the Negroes there became unruly and would work no more than they could help, related this prisoner.[7]

Other signs of dissolution were to be seen. There were outbound trains carrying refugees, bank specie and property to safer climes. There were incoming trains carrying thousands of prisoners from

Andersonville and other points. The burden of handling prisoners was a terrible one for an already overburdened city. The garrisons of the forts around Savannah, said General McLaws, were reduced "so low that it may be said with truth they are merely picketed." Stockades were hastily erected. Colonel Anderson's diary contains pathetic glimpses of the prisoners. "I visited the stockade this afternoon & was shocked to see the pitiable condition of the prisoners. They were dirty and half clad & altogether the most squalid gathering of humanity it has ever been my lot to look upon." Around the enclosure he observed "a large number of respectably dressed women, some of whom were throwing bread to the Yankees." Another officer called the prisoners "the most miserable, degraded, ragged, filthy wretches your eyes ever beheld." [8]

Where the prisoner of war controversy is involved there is a Southern side. In November, '64, a large batch of Confederate prisoners reached Savannah after being exchanged near Fort Pulaski. Jane Wallace Howard who helped nurse the men declared that their condition was "horrible to an extreme, scarcely looking human, nearly naked, covered with vermin and festering sores." At the same period a considerable number of Confederate officers were confined at Pulaski. Part of the so-called "Immortal Six Hundred," they were victims of Union retaliation for the policy of housing Federal prisoners at Charleston in order to discourage the bombardment of that city. During the winter of 1864–'65 the half-frozen officers existed at Pulaski on a semi-starvation diet of one-quarter pound of bread, ten ounces of cornmeal and one-half pint of pickles per day, all of which was supplemented by stray cats. [9]

If hate had been a weapon, Georgians would have been well-armed. "I have vowed," wrote Henry Graves in the fall of 1864, "that if I should ever have children, the first ingredient of the first principles of their education shall be uncompromising hatred and contempt of the Yankees." Similarly, George Mercer had recorded in his diary, "Vengeance is the Lord's; but we are men, with men's passions . . . shall we not swear our young Hannibals to eternal hatred!" George D. Smith of the Volunteer Guards

wrote to his aunt in 1863 to inquire about his grandfather's an-
tecedents, having heard that he was "connected with those people
in Yankeedom." He was determined not to believe that there was
a drop of "rascally *puritan* blood" in the family. If so, he expressed
the hope that "the leeches drew all the nasty stuff out" when he
was "a young'un." [10]

Not even the clergy was immune to this hatred. The North
was "a stink & a by-word among other nations," wrote a Ver-
mont-born chaplain in the Confederate Army who was stationed
at Savannah in the winter of '64. The same year he informed his
wife that "blinded by their own fanaticism they have elevated the
Negro above themselves." [11]

Even death did not insulate the North from hatred. Among the
prisoners who died at Savannah in September, 1864, was a lieutenant in the 3rd Maryland Infantry. A lady who had befriended the
Union officer during his last illness purchased a cemetery lot and
paid the expense of a decent burial for him at Laurel Grove. Learning of the interment of a Federal soldier where the Confederate
dead rested, the *Republican* called on the city authorities to put a
stop to such sacrileges and branded as outrageous "the polluting
of the sacred soil with the bodies of those who burn their houses,
orphan their children, and ravish their wives." The *Morning News*
apparently disagreed. It published a communication which called
the *Republican* article a "shocking want of civilized feeling" and
a "horrible misrepresentation of the noble Southern character." [12]

On one subject the rival newspapers saw eye to eye. When the
Republican advocated calling up the militia in the summer of
1864, one of the men affected wrote the *Morning News* on the
subject of *Republican* editor Sneed's own military service. "Mr.
Sneed now has a chance to show his patriotism," declared the
correspondent, assuring the editor they "would like to have his
company." "As a general rule," explained the *Republican* in November, "we believe that editors, if they do their duty, can effect
more for a struggling cause with the pen than they can with the
sword." This position, agreed the *News,* was a "sound" one.

Wishful thinking was the main contribution of the press to the

Confederate cause during these weeks. On November 23, after the Union Army had started toward the sea, the *Republican* referred to it as "the invading, or *fleeing* army of Sherman." When the enemy was momentarily slowed at the Oconee River, the *Morning News* reported, "The skies are brightening. Everything looks glorious. Ere long, Mr. Sherman will get a lashing that he little dreamed of." When Sherman reached the Ogeechee River ten days later, the *News* explained that the campaign could not help the Federal cause. "No progress is made toward the subjugation of any country by an army which can do nothing more than pass through," the editor insisted.

Not all the wishful thinking was supplied by the local press. The enemy's transportation was "sadly out of order," reported Colonel Jones. "At present our prospects appear more encouraging but as yet all is uncertainty," he added. A soldier stationed at Fort Lee was much more sanguine. "Our forces," he wrote, "have been pulling back to get him [Sherman] in the marshes, to prevent his having so good a chance to escape." At the proper time "the forces from Macon & Augusta which are hovering in his rear will close in." [13]

The forces in Sherman's rear were no stronger than those in front of him. "It is laughable," a Minnesota soldier commented, "to consider the nature of the opposition we have met on this campaign." The rebels were supposed "to annihilate Sherman's army certain," wrote an Ohio officer, "but as soon as we arrived within hailing distance they cut sticks and run." [14] Whatever "cut sticks" meant in the parlance of the Midwest, there was little the State troops could do but retire before one hundred regiments and five thousand cavalry.

In Savannah, women talked with each other in whispers of reported doings of Sherman's troops on the march through Georgia. As the days wore on the atmosphere became one of "expectant terror," reported a female resident. [15] Newspaper tales of robbery and rape did not allay apprehensions about the coming of Sherman to Savannah. That he was coming practical-minded people did not doubt. On December 3, 1864, a member of the 7th Georgia Cavalry wrote his mother from Virginia that he was "sorry to see that you speak of it as a foregone conclusion that Sherman can take Savannah at his convenience as if resignation was all that is left to you." He regretted that his father felt the same way she did. After the Union Army got past Millen and into the "desolate pine barrens & swamps" its difficulties would begin. "In these," he said, *a few* resolute men can hold him in check indefinitely." [16] It had not turned out that way. Sherman's Army continued to draw nearer.

The state of affairs in Georgia had its critics. Private Harden of the Confederate Signal Corps never forgot a disgruntled soldier who one day held forth on the subject of the march to the sea. Deploring Sherman's unchecked advance through Georgia, the old sergeant warned that without quick action the Confederacy would go "to the dogs." His concluding remarks were so eloquent that when he was through his audience, still under his spell, dispersed quietly. The theme of his oration was that somewhere in the Confederate Army, very probably in the ranks, was one man who if promoted immediately to high command could accomplish the overthrow of Sherman's Army and achieve independence for the South. [17] When Harden thought it over afterward, the identity of the soldier the sergeant had in mind became crystal clear.

Savannah had been almost stripped of troops that year. A report by General McLaws in the summer of 1864 showed only 1,800 men in his entire command. Strolling through the city that July at twilight, Lieutenant George Gift of the Confederate Navy found the squares on Bull Street crowded with ladies but saw scarcely a sign of a man. It made him feel quite out of place to realize that every male capable of bearing arms was off at the front.

Strenuous efforts were made to increase the defending force as Sherman approached. "Every available man at the South should now be sent to Savannah," counselled General Lee from Virginia. All who could shoulder muskets were called up. "The old can fight in the trenches as well as the young," declared the *Morning News;* "let no man refuse; and if any do, let us know his name." Extreme means of increasing the garrison were attempted. Men confined in the barracks (other than those charged with "repeated desertions or some more serious offence") were ordered released in order to rejoin their commands.

In spite of all this effort, the total force mustered at Savannah amounted to less than ten thousand men. The largest single accession to the garrison—in fact the only one greater than battalion strength—was approximately two thousand Georgia militia and State Line commanded by General Gustavus W. Smith. They consisted largely of mechanics from the shops at Macon and Augusta who were exempt from regular service because of their occupations. They deserve more than passing mention. Travelling by rail from Macon to Albany, they marched fifty-five miles across the country to Thomasville. The promised railroad transportation to Savannah was not ready there. Then Bob Toombs rode into the city. Threatening "dire vengeance on superintendents and road masters," he obtained the necessary engines and cars. "A man of extraordinary energy" was General Richard Taylor's opinion of Toombs.

As the train rattled northward across the pine barrens on the night of November 29, 1864, Gustavus Woodson Smith might well ponder the caprice of fortune that had taken him from the acting command of the Army of Northern Virginia in 1862 to that of these raw troops. Fate, however, had reserved for him and his Georgia militia a measure of glory on the morrow.

When the train pulled into Savannah at 2 a.m., a peremptory order from General Hardee was handed Smith. His troops were to proceed at once to Grahamville in South Carolina. "You know that the militia of this State cannot be legally ordered beyond its limits without a special act of the Legislature," protested General Smith. "But if you can satisfy me that it is absolutely necessary that my command shall go into South Carolina I will endeavor to carry out your orders."

Hardee had no difficulty in making that showing. More than five thousand enemy infantry and marines from Hilton Head had landed along the Broad River and were marching on the railroad that connected Savannah and Charleston. Few regular troops were available at the moment to oppose the thrust. Smith's militia were

badly needed. Should the enemy obtain a foothold on the railroad, the only corridor out of Savannah would be closed.[18] Upon
the security of this route depended the retention of the city.

Returning to the train, General Smith sent emissaries through
the cars to sound out the men about crossing the Georgia border.
Most of the officers were willing; some of the rank and file said no.
Had not the militia of South Carolina refused to cross the Savannah
River into Augusta to relieve the guard there for service against
Sherman? Smith then sent word to the troops that it was his order
that they go. He promised a "big fight before 12 o'clock—must
win it—and would be brought back to Georgia within forty eight
hours." Shortly, the trains pulled out of Savannah with laughter
ringing through every car.[19]

Such were the events that preceded the Confederate victory on
what the General Assembly of Georgia proudly referred to as the
"memorable and well-fought battle-field at Honey Hill in South
Carolina." The rebel yell that day was more "prominent than I
ever heard it," said a soldier in a Massachusetts Negro regiment.[20]
According to Gustavus Smith, repeated attacks over a six-hour
period by a largely superior force "failed to drive us an inch from
the position first assumed by us." He had never seen or known of
a battlefield upon which there was so little confusion and where
every order was so cheerfully and promptly obeyed.

Praise for the Georgia militia came from the regulars who took
part in the battle. An officer in the 47th Georgia attested that they
"did as good fighting as could be asked of troops." The road along
which the enemy retreated was "strewed for miles with knapsacks,
Canteens, Haversacks, ammunition, accoutrements and other camp
Equipage," said the same soldier who obtained for himself a "good
overcoat, India Rubber blanket, canteen, haversack, pipe, Tin cup
and as much provisions as I could well carry." According to General John K. Jackson, his entire Augusta battalion was re-equipped
with Enfield rifles left by the enemy.[21]

Within the allotted forty-eight-hour span Gustavus Smith and
the Georgia militia were back in Savannah. A few days later they
took position in the entrenchments outside the city.

17.

Sherman at the Gate

≈ UPON MAJOR General Lafayette McLaws fell the responsibility of selecting the line along which Sherman was to be resisted. The former West Pointer had rendered worthy service in the Virginia theatre in command of one of Longstreet's divisions. The bushy-bearded, thick-chested McLaws was one of the most dogged defensive fighters in the Confederate Army. But his star had waned after a bitter controversy with Longstreet over the carrying out of an order in Tennessee. In 1864 he had been transferred to Savannah. There McLaws had made a poor impression upon Edward Anderson who said that he was "very slow in his decisions & apparently very vacillating." The Augustan was either "very deep or very stupid," he added, suspecting the latter.[1]

Spending the war in command of river batteries the enemy never intended to attack perhaps warped Colonel Anderson's judgment of men. Be that as it may, the care and skill McLaws habitually brought to the selection of his position was to serve well at Savannah. The line adopted revealed a good eye for the possibilities the terrain afforded in the way of defensive warfare.

Southwest of the city the Little Ogeechee River and its branch known as Salt Creek afforded a good natural barrier as far northward as the rice fields of Silk Hope plantation. Between that point and the Savannah River lay a chain of swamps which Sherman's Chief Engineer, Orlando M. Poe, described as "ten-fold worse" than those along the Chickahominy. "This is a country of

awful swamps, with level flats, between which are rice fields,"
said a member of the 103rd Illinois. As an Ohio soldier put it,
"The country around Savannah is low and wet" and "cut up by
innumerable canals which were used to overflow the rice lands." [2]

By breaking a dyke on the Savannah River at Brampton plantation water was admitted at high tide flooding a large area in front
of the Confederate right. A strong earthwork known as Fort
Hardeman protected the dam by which this water was retained.
That work constituted the extreme right of the Confederate line.
Further south a similar inundation was effectuated. The water level
in the Ogeechee Canal being higher than some of the surrounding
country, it was possible to flood a considerable section in front
of the Confederate line by cutting locks and banks. A fairly continuous sheet of water, two to six feet deep, was thus introduced
in front of a large part of Hardee's line.

All of the communications of the city crossed swamps or
creeks along narrow causeways. Where railroads and highways
intersected the Confederate line causeways were cut and breastworks and batteries erected. At other strategic points earthworks
were constructed. They were connected in some instances by
trenches. Fifty-four heavy guns were mounted along the line.
These were augmented by eleven field batteries, totalling forty-
eight pieces.

The defensive line represented a great arc, some ten miles in
length, extending from Williamson's plantation on the Savannah
River near Pipemakers Creek around to the Gulf Railroad bridge
over the Little Ogeechee. The Confederate front actually was
nearly fifteen miles long since troops had to be stationed in the
stretch between the bridge and Coffee Bluff. At its nearest point to
Savannah the line was around three and a half miles distant; at its
furthest approximately nine.

Strong as the line was from the viewpoint of the terrain, nothing in the number or the caliber of the troops manning it promised
anything in the way of a successful defense, much less scaring
Sherman away by a show of strength at Savannah. Speculating as
to the Confederate forces there, an Illinois officer wrote in his diary

on December 7, "I do not know how many men Hardee has in the works there but it does not seem possible that he could raise more than 20,000 or 25,000 men. Admitting that $\frac{2}{3}$ are veterans which is hardly possible, he certainly cannot defend 15 miles of works with those men against 60,000 of our men, most all of whom are veterans." [3]

General Sherman's own estimate of the enemy was more accurate but still far from correct. "Some 5,000 or 6,000 infantry," he guessed, "and it may be a mongrel mass of 8,000 to 10,000 militia and fragments." The word "mongrel" well describes the hodgepodge Hardee had for the defense of Savannah. His forces "summed up," the Confederate General said, "land and water side, militia, reserves, dismounted cavalry, local and details, 9,089." Spread over a front running from the Savannah River to Rose Dhu on the Little Ogeechee, they constituted what Charles C. Jones, Jr., called "scarcely more than a skirmish line strengthened at intervals." [4] In one sector a brigade and a half confronted the entire 20th Army Corps. At Lieutenant Henry Graves' station there were not a hundred men where there ought, for successful resistance, to have been at least five hundred. "Of this small body," he said, "only the Marines (not half) were regulars."

The six-mile stretch from Shaw's Dam on the Ogeechee Canal to the Gulf Railroad bridge over the Little Ogeechee was manned by only 2,700 men. Among them was General Hugh Mercer's command consisting of about nine hundred troops. Made up largely of reserves, detailed men and dismounted cavalry, they defended a stretch of line two miles long. Small as was the force in that particular sector its strength proved even less than anticipated. Included among the troops was Brooks' Foreign Battalion, consisting of around four hundred fifty men. Officered by South Carolinians, the outfit was composed of Irishmen, Germans, Spaniards and Englishmen who had served in the Union Army before becoming prisoners. They had been released upon volunteering for service in the Confederate Army. "Galvanized rebels," people in the South called them. Marching into the works outside Savannah the battalion had presented a brave appearance. It was the façade of treachery. On the night of December 14 seventeen men went over to the enemy with their arms. It was obvious the Foreign Battalion could not be counted on. The commander obtained permission the next day to move the outfit to the rear. The men were notified to be ready to march at 8 p.m.

Many of Brooks' Battalion had different plans as to where they were to march that night. Shortly after the announcement was made one of the men informed an officer of whom he had become fond that he wanted to see him alone. Entering a tent, a huge German sergeant tremblingly revealed to Captain Martin a plot that was afoot. Two companies planned to overpower their officers and go over to the enemy lines in a body that evening. The mutiny was to take place when the men fell in to march.

Without rousing the suspicion of the plotters, two officers were dispatched to headquarters for help. To add weight to the appeal the commanding officer of the battalion later went himself. For an hour and a half Captain Martin and Captain Wardlaw, the only officers left in the camp, confronted two hundred mutinous soldiers. "Strange, weird, unreal," Martin described the scene in the woods near Savannah that evening. Donning an expensive military coat he had recently purchased, he remarked to the other officer, "Wardlaw, if I am saved I intend to save my new coat, and if I am killed, I intend to die, like Lord Nelson, in full feather." They exhausted every pretext for delay. Finally, with their backs to an oak tree and only a pistol and two swords as their weapons the two men awaited the approach of the mutineers.

At this point Georgia troops arrived on the scene. The conspirators were disarmed. At a drumhead court-martial that night the facts of the plot were established. At midnight the condemned men—the four sergeants who were ringleaders, a German barber and two soldiers of the battalion previously apprehended while attempting to desert—were shot. The marksmanship of the firing squad was poor. Two of the men were merely wounded and had to be shot again. Before they were put out of their misery, related Martin, "such wails and dismal cries" arose as "might have proceeded from the damned in Hades." [5]

On December 7 advance units of Sherman's 15th Corps had crossed the Ogeechee River at Jencks Bridge, about eighteen miles west of Savannah. A few miles to the north the 20th Corps passed by Ebenezer the following day. Stopping for a look at the ancient church where patriots had worshipped during the American Revolution a Union officer drew an unfriendly comparison between the men who helped win independence for the colonies and the traitors now trying to win independence for the South. "Follow the Example of those who bowed the knee in this house when Freedom was won and the Flag that they handed down to you will be borne safely through our nation's bitter trial," wrote Captain Peter Ege.[6]

In sombre mood the *Morning News* announced on December 7, "Not many days will elapse before the time to do our work. Let every man set his house in order, and be on hand at the tap of the drum." Two days later the same newspaper asked, "Did you forget it? Forget what? Why to carry your axe, spade and shovel to Maj. McCrady. If you have either, or all these articles, take them 'round.' " They were becoming more necessary by the hour.

On December 9 the First Division of the 20th Army Corps reached the vicinity of Monteith, fourteen miles from Savannah where Hardee had established an outer line of defense to protect the Charleston Railroad. Manned by a small force under Major Alfred L. Hartridge, it extended from the Augusta Road to the railroad bridge over the Savannah River. A redoubt had been thrown up by the Confederates across the road through Turkey Roost Swamp. A flanking movement by a Union brigade was commenced. As the soldiers advanced through the swamp a shot from a Confederate battery crashed through the trees. The commander ordered his men to lie down. "Lie down in a foot of water! H——l. If you will give orders to go ahead, I will," protested Colonel Hawley to Major Alfred Smith. "We both sung out together 'Forward, double quick,' " the latter related. After firing a volley or two the enemy "skedaddled," according to a member of the 102nd Illinois Regiment.[7]

By sundown on December 9 the western portion of Chatham

County swarmed with blue-clad regiments. The infantry spilled over into Bryan County on the right bank of the Ogeechee while Kilpatrick's cavalry ranged southward into Liberty County. There his men played a vandalic role. In the course of the next two days the Federals closed along the entire Confederate front. They were "now within sight of the spires of Savannah (i.e. we would see them if there were not so many trees in the way)," wrote a member of the 22nd Wisconsin on December 11. Another Wisconsin soldier noted in his diary that day, "General Sherman says the siege is laid at dark." [8]

In the investment of Savannah the Left Wing of the Union Army occupied the area opposite the Confederate line running from the Savannah River to a point on Lawton's plantation about six miles west of the city. This wing (Army of Georgia) was commanded by Major General Henry W. Slocum, a New York lawyer and a graduate of West Point. It was composed of the 14th Army Corps under command of Major General Jefferson C. Davis of Indiana and the 20th Corps commanded by Brigadier General Alpheus S. Williams of Detroit.

The Right Wing (Army of the Tennessee) was commanded by Major General Oliver O. Howard of New York. A West Point product, it was to him Robert E. Lee was alluding when he admonished his son in 1852, "You must 'crowd that boy Howard.' You must be No. 1." Because of his reputation for religiousness he was called "the Christian soldier of the United States Army"—a title puzzling to the white populace along the line of Sherman's march. Howard's two corps, the 17th and 15th, manned in that order the stretch from Lawton's plantation to the Gulf Railroad bridge over the Little Ogeechee. The 17th Corps was commanded by General Frank P. Blair, Jr., a St. Louis lawyer. On its right was the 15th Corps of General Peter J. Osterhaus, a former officer in the Prussian Army who had settled in Illinois where he was a dry goods clerk before the war.

The night of December 10 when two divisions of the 15th marched along the towpath of the Ogeechee Canal to take position in the line was long remembered by soldiers from the prairies. It was a scene of "poetic beauty," wrote one of them. "The spreading live oaks and the tall specter-pines" formed an arch over the smooth, dark green surface of the canal which reflected under the full moon the shadows of the marching men. The eerie solitude of the swamp was broken by thousands of voices joining in "Down on the Suwannee River," "Old Kentucky Home," "Just Before the Battle, Mother" and other familiar songs.[9]

As Sherman's Army closed upon the Confederate line its presence in the environs of Savannah was signalized by the capture of a railroad train and a steamer. The south-bound Gulf train carried refugees and invalid soldiers. Among the passengers was the president of the Georgia Central Railroad. The captors of Richard R. Cuyler made quite a fuss over their prisoner. "A regular old brick," Henry Hitchcock called this Savannah railroad executive, impressed by the philosophic resignation with which Cuyler had listened to Sherman's detailed account to him of how much of his railroad he had destroyed.[10]

The next day (December 10) a foraging party from the 150th New York captured the *Ida* on her way up the Savannah River, opposite Argyle Island. Apparently the little side-wheeler was carrying a dispatch. Confederate Flag Officer Hunter, who had been engaged in protecting the Charleston and Savannah Railroad bridge and in patrolling the river above it with two gunboats, was directed by Hardee to destroy the bridge and then to "return to the right of the line of land defence for Savannah, and give it all the strength and protection in your power."[11]

Anticipating the attempt by the flotilla to return to Savannah, Winegar's battery of rifled guns had taken station at the Potter plantation on the Savannah River. "I should be content to live in such a paradise as this all the rest of my life," wrote a Union chaplain of Colerain plantation.[12] It proved in any event a paradise for artillerists. Early on the morning of the 12th the gunboats *Sampson* and *Macon* and the tender *Resolute* headed back to the city. As they came downstream the Confederate vessels passed several places where Flag Officer Hunter reported seeing "smoking ruins," among them no doubt the former residence of General

Nathanael Greene at Mulberry Grove. It had gone up in smoke
with its rich memories of Greene and his gay wife Katy, of "Mad"
Anthony Wayne, George Washington and Eli Whitney. There in
1793 Whitney had devised the cotton ginning contraption that
helped bring on sectional conflict.

Winegar's battery opened at 2,500 yards from the bluff. Soon,
according to John T. Scharf who was in charge of the bow gun
on the *Sampson,* there was a "terrific fire" from both sides. The
Sampson was hit three times, the *Macon* twice and the *Resolute*
once. Unable to run the battery and observing the enemy trying to
move a gun further up the Savannah to cut off his retreat, Captain
Hunter gave orders to turn about.[13]

In the confusion of the turning movement the damaged *Resolute* collided with both the gunboats. She drifted helplessly upon
Argyle Island where she was captured by troops from the 3rd
Wisconsin Regiment. The *Macon* and *Sampson* did not stay to
assist her. "With the aid of a barrel of bacon in the furnaces,"
wrote Scharf, they "soon steamed from under fire"—steamed,
indeed, out of the war clear to Augusta, some two hundred miles
upstream.

The crew of the *Resolute* were "loud in their curses at the other
boats for thus deserting them," reported a Northern chaplain.
Even more outspoken was one of her officers, a former resident of
Buffalo. "He was d——d glad to be captured" as he was "tired
fighting for a country that was already gone to h——l." [14]

That was the way they liked to hear Southerners talk—not like
Hardee's aide, Duncan L. Clinch, who had been taken when the
Ida was captured. The Confederate officer tried to defend himself
(lamely enough Henry Hitchcock thought) after Sherman had
dressed him down about "Southern Gentlemen" allowing themselves to be dragged into rebellion by "rebel leaders." There was
no personal abuse but it was the "sharpest" talk yet heard from
the General on that subject.

The scene is not a pleasing one. It does little credit to Sherman,
this verbal assault on a prisoner of war. But Clinch was possibly
asking favors (he was a brother-in-law of General Robert Ander-

son who had surrendered Fort Sumter) and there were other reasons for Sherman's being out of sorts. A couple of days earlier one of his cavalry officers had had a leg blown off west of Pooler when he stepped on a torpedo—those "murderous instruments of assassination" (the phrase is Hitchcock's) which the barbarous Southerners were employing for no other reason than deterring the enemy from destroying their country.

Sherman almost had his own head shot off on December 10. "The general," as Major Van Duzer put it in his diary, "had a very narrow escape from a shell today." While he was walking toward the front down the railroad for a closer look, a shot from a cannon whizzed close by him. Sherman saw the ball coming in time to step aside. "It did not miss him over a foot," a soldier said.[15]

Apparently Hardee was not going to give up the city without a fight. Such, however, was not Sherman's problem at the moment. Food was the immediate concern. Thousands of cattle had been driven along to Savannah. His Army was "fat and happy," said the Union commander. But the coast country was not middle Georgia, concerning which an Ohio volunteer informed his parents, "By the way, does every body talk of starving out the rebel army up in that County yet? If so, I think if they had of been on this trip it would make converts of them."[16] After sixty thousand men had remained encamped around Savannah for a few days eating became something of a problem.

By December 11 foraging had nearly ceased on the Union left. "The men are now subsisting on rice and beef" and are "reduced to one cracker per day to a man," an Illinois soldier reported. "I am not in a very amiable state of mind," an Iowan wrote on December 18, "on account of my stomach calling for some thing to digest and it being impossible for me to furnish it." A private in Sherman's Army informed his wife, "I went off the other day in search of food and raised a sheep's head. . . . I would give 5 dollars for a small loaf of bread this morning."[17]

Except for rice for men and rice straw for horses there was little to eat in these parts. Plenty of rice was to be had on the plantations along the Savannah River where the slaves excited the

wonderment of the Northerners, especially the ones they saw on
Argyle Island. They had "great splay feet and hands" and grotesque
bodies and spoke what the soldiers called "plantation Latin." With
their help shifts of soldiers working day and night were soon
turning out hulled rice in quantity. Rude machines were used to
thresh it, after which a fanning mill threw the grain and the chaff
into a kettle of water where the grain sank to the bottom, the chaff
floating on top.[18]

Though rice proved to be, as one soldier called it, "salvation," it
lingered as an untender memory in the minds of Sherman's men.
Years were to pass before some of them could eat it again. "How
the Chinese and Japanese get along with it" was a puzzle to a
Wisconsin officer.[19]

"Unless we can very soon communicate with the fleet which is
awaiting us somewhere near on the coast, this large army will
begin to be pinched," Major Hitchcock had written on December
10. All that stood between it and ample rations (along with
twenty tons of accumulated mail) was an earthwork fort on the
Ogeechee River.

After a respite of twenty-one months the war was about to
touch Fort McAllister again.

18.

Fort McAllister Again

⫷ ON THE 8th of December, 1864, Sherman sent word that he wanted General Howard to try to get a message to the Navy announcing the arrival of the Army on the coast and his designs on Savannah. The following night a bateau left King's Bridge and disappeared down the winding Ogeechee River. In it was Captain William Duncan of the 15th Illinois Cavalry whose seeming fondness for the bottle did not impair his reputation as one of the most skillful of Sherman's scouts. With him were two other scouts. Howard's dispatch to the naval commander, written by pencil on a small piece of paper, was concealed in a plug of tobacco. "When I shook his hand that night and bade him good bye, I never expected to see him again," said Lieutenant Colonel Strong of Sherman's staff.[1]

The two-day trip to the sea was a small epic of daring and resourcefulness. After narrowly escaping capture while hiding ashore the first day out, the party drifted at night past Fort McAllister without being seen. Their worst troubles commenced on reaching rough water on the 11th. Sighting a gunboat in Ossabaw Sound, they made for her, nearly swamping on the way. Hope was fast ebbing for the Union scouts when a boat put out from *USS Flag*. The men were taken off just before their frail craft capsized.[2]

The following morning Howard's dispatch reached Port Royal. "The excitement, the exhileration, ay the rapture, created by this arrival, will never be forgotten by the officers and crews of the

Federal vessels who saw the beginning of the end of the war," said a member of Dahlgren's staff.[3] Three days later the Northern public, hungry for news from Sherman's "Lost Army," knew that it was safe and sound on the coast of Georgia.

Early on December 13 the tug *Dandelion* steamed up the Little Ogeechee. Aboard was Lieutenant George A. Fisher of the U. S. Signal Corps to whom the job was assigned of establishing communication with Sherman. Using a row boat he reached a small creek three miles southeast of a rice mill that stood on the north bank of the Great Ogeechee. The mill belonged to Dr. Cheves whose nearby residence at Grove Point had been ransacked, the wreckage of "his splendid furniture & library" being something about which "the darkies all seemed pleased enough," a Union soldier recorded in his diary.[4] Through his glass Fisher could see a flag of some sort hanging from the top of the mill. As he peered, a hand reached up through a hole in the roof and pulled the folds apart, revealing, in his words, "our own glorious Stars and Stripes."

Lieutenant Fisher returned at once to the tug which moved up in sight of the mill. Signal flags began to wag. Over at Cheves' Captain James McClintock, signal officer, had maintained a vigil for nearly three days. The signals from the *Dandelion* were immediately acknowledged. From the tug Fisher queried, "How can I get to you? What troops are at Fort McAllister?" The reply came back in General Howard's name, "We are now investing Fort McAllister with Hazen's division."[5] It was nearly 4:30 p.m., December 13, 1864.

Sitting on the roof of a shed at the rice mill, Sherman watched the drama unfolding over at Genesis Point. Across the marshes, "in plain view, two and half miles, sullen and silent, like a great lion at bay," said Colonel Strong, "stood Fort McAllister." Many Union officers watched the show that afternoon from Cheves' mill. "With the use of glass I could see the fort, rebel flag & even the men very distinctly," said Major Van Duzer. He arrived there, he wrote, when "affairs were evidently drawing to a focus rapidly as the Genl. was beginning to get somewhat excited."[6] Sherman was indeed, as he expressed it in his Memoirs, "dreadfully impatient."

He did not have long to wait now. "There they go grandly; not a waver. See that flag in advance, Howard; how steadily it moves; not a man falters. There they go still; see the roll of musketry. Grand, grand!" It is William T. Sherman talking. It will be better, however, to observe events at the Fort from a less windy vantage point than Cheves' mill and through a more reliable medium than Sherman's running commentary as reported by a war correspondent of the New York *Herald*.[7]

For five days the Fort had been isolated from what was left of the Confederate world. Before contact was lost rations sufficient to support two hundred men for about forty-five days had been brought in. To the dispatches to headquarters sent by its commander, Major George W. Anderson, neither order nor response had been received. Anderson had made his choice. "I determined," the Savannahian said, "to defend the fort to the last extremity." There was to be one alternative, "death or captivity."[8]

It was hopeless, of course, this idea of resisting a division with only one hundred fifty effective men. The garrison was brave enough, to be sure. "They were evidently among the best men the South could boast of," said Major Van Duzer who reported that "their manner, habits and language spoke much in their favor." Many had never been under fire, however, and a considerable number were mere boys, according to Major Anderson. They were wearied from days of toil in preparing to defend a work not designed against an attack from the west. Trees had been felled, buildings torn down, mines laid, abatis erected, new traverses constructed and gun locations changed.

Two or three days before the Union infantry reached Fort McAllister Judson Kilpatrick of the U. S. Cavalry had reconnoitered the area. Requesting permission to take it, he informed General Sherman that with the help of infantry he could capture "the little sand fort down there." Sherman does not seem to have entertained a great deal of respect for this cavalryman whom an officer described as "the most vain, conceited, egotistical little popinjay I ever saw."[9] At General Oliver Howard's suggestion

the honor of capturing the Fort had gone to the 2nd division of the
15th Corps commanded by General William B. Hazen. A thirty-
four-year-old graduate of West Point, he had frequently proven
his mettle in the war. Before many days Hazen would have a
Major General's commission, delivered personally by Secretary of
War Stanton.

Hazen's division was then at Judge Lloyd's place on the Little
Ogeechee—a paradise of "tropical beauty" the like of which he
had "never before or since been quartered in." There was to be
little opportunity to enjoy it. His troops had scarcely encamped in
paradise when orders were received to march. George Ward
Nichols watched the head of the column go by "with that steady
gait which was the certain sign of an expedition which meant
work." [10] That night (December 12) Hazen's troops halted at
King's Bridge which had been rebuilt by the engineers "in an
incredibly short time," according to Sherman.

Early the next morning they crossed the Ogeechee and swung
eastward down the road to Genesis Point. As they marched past the
farm houses on Bryan Neck that sunny December day the Negroes
flocked out in droves to watch, jabbering at the "top of their
voices in a jargon" that sounded to Hazen "like a mixture of
French, English, and the clatter of blackbirds."

A mounted picket captured a mile west of the Fort around noon
revealed that the causeway there was mined. A delay occurred
while the torpedoes were being removed. Leaving eight regiments
in reserve, the assault troops to the number of 1,500 men advanced toward the Fort. A few hundred yards from the works they
started deploying, an operation that lasted well into the afternoon
due to the difficult terrain. Hazen made no formal demand for
surrender, believing that it would merely advertise his intentions
and be met with a boastful refusal.

Meanwhile his sharpshooters, approaching as close as two
hundred yards to the works, kept up a steady fire from behind
stumps and the remains of the outer buildings. It was difficult for
the defenders to work their guns. In one instance six out of a crew
of eight cannoneers were picked off. "I shall never forget," remi-

nisced a Union soldier, "how Sergeant J. A. Saunier, when we reached a point near enough to fire, said, 'Watch me make the Johnnies get off the works' "—an anecdote duly recorded in the history of the 47th Ohio by regimental historian Joseph A. Saunier.[11]

Back at the mill Sherman became more and more impatient as the afternoon wore on. The assault must be made that day, he finally signalled. It was five minutes before five o'clock and the sun was low in the west ("one of the loveliest sun sets" Colonel Strong "ever looked upon") when the bugles sounded three times for assembly, followed by the command forward. The line advanced "as with a single impulse," said Hazen.[12] "Ye Gods! I never saw the like," wrote Strong. "Over the fallen trees that had been slashed for a thousand yards—over snares and pitfalls for tripping up the men—over three rows of abatis and two rows of chevaux-de-frise—over the ditch eight feet by twelve—over the huge 13 inch shells made into torpedoes which were sown among the obstructions . . . never wavering nor faltering for an instant —with a fierce and impetuous rush to the fort and with a gallantry almost unparallelled and with a wild cheer . . . away they went."

Soon they were struggling up the parapets. A flag appeared atop one and then disappeared. Another suffered a like fate. But soon a dozen were waving there. Savage hand-to-hand fighting with bayonet and rifle butt took place. An Ohio officer described it as "terrible for a short time . . . as we drove them from one bomb proof to the other." [13] The battle was "desperate and deadly," reported Hazen. The enemy succumbed only "as each man was individually overpowered." According to Major Anderson, *"The fort was never surrendered. It was captured by overwhelming numbers."*

Among the Confederates who fought that day was Captain N. B. Clinch. Already wounded twice, the Georgian responded to a captain's demand to surrender with a blow of his sword. A hand-to-hand duel ensued between the two. Soldiers came to the Federal officer's aid. Clinch battled them all until he fell, having sustained, according to Anderson, three sabre, six bayonet and two gunshot wounds.[14]

Fifteen minutes after the assault commenced it was all over. Sixteen of the garrison were killed and fifty-four wounded, nearly one half of its effective strength. On the Union side twenty-four officers and men were killed and one hundred ten wounded. Most of the Union casualties were caused by the explosion of torpedoes buried around the Fort.

Impressed by the spectacle he had witnessed that day, a Union surgeon recorded in his diary, "It seemed to me a great & important moment . . . that then was an epoch in time which would never be forgotten." Sherman was "almost beside himself," reported Major Van Duzer. "This nigger will have no sleep this night!" exulted the General, repeating the exclamation an elderly slave had used at Howell Cobb's plantation on first seeing him. One of his aides was scarcely less jubilant. "Take a good big drink, a long breath and then yell like the devil," Lewis Dayton advised General Slocum in reporting the fall of McAllister. "It was the handsomest thing I have seen in this war," reported Sherman.[15]

The General now got in a skiff and with William E. Strong and George W. Nichols at the oars pulled down to McAllister. "I never saw General Sherman in as good spirits as that night," declared Colonel Strong, relating how he joined in the chorus of many a familiar song as the boat made its way down the moonlit Ogeechee. He arrived in time to join Hazen and his prisoner, Major Anderson, for supper at the Middleton house near the Fort. The General was much amused, according to Hazen, at a colloquy between Anderson and a Negro who waited on the table that night. The servant in question belonged to the Anderson family. "Jim, what are you doing here?" asked the surprised Confederate officer. "I'se workin' for Mr. Hazen now," was the colored man's reply. A correspondent of the New York *World* passed along another anecdote. It seemed that among the spoils of the Union victory was a stock of Havanas that had been laid in by the Confederates. Knowing Sherman's fondness for cigars, Major Anderson asked to be excused for a moment. "I have some very good cigars; I would like you to try one," he said on his return. "Thank you, but I have some very good ones here. Permit me," replied Sherman, handing Anderson one of his own cheroots.

The prisoner could smile at the victorious General's little joke. Sherman's reaction to the torpedoes was another matter. He informed Anderson that "he had it in consideration to shut him up with a number of his men equal to the number of our men who were killed by torpedoes and blow them up by gunpowder." [16] General Sherman personally ordered a detail of prisoners to remove the unexploded torpedoes—an "unwarrantable and improper treatment of prisoners of war," Major Anderson maintained.

When news of the capture of the Fort reached the Union lines, there were waves of cheering. An Iowa private reported that the men "endulged in a great jollification, speech making and other demonstrations" continuing into the night. The rebels called over, said an Indiana officer, to find out what all the shouting was about. "Let fort McAllister go to hell," they yelled back. According to Henry Hitchcock, the Confederate pickets had been calling over earlier that day in a taunting tone, "Hello, Yanks,—don't you want some hard bread? Come over here and get something to eat." That night when they inquired about the cause of the elation, the reply came back, "Fort McAllister's taken—the *cracker line* is open—that's what's the matter—how are you, Johnny!" Spiteful firing all night from Confederate batteries was the only rejoinder, said Hitchcock. [17]

With the opening of the Ogeechee supplies started to flow to the Union depot established at King's Bridge. The troops began to receive hardtack—"Lincoln pies," the men called it. "Now that we have our base and communication with the sea, Savannah is doomed," opined Hitchcock. The enemy, he said, "might as well 'git up and dust.'" General Hardee was probably thinking along the same lines.

19.

The Plank Road

◁ IMPATIENT FOR news from the outside world, Sherman went down the Ogeechee the same night McAllister fell. Travelling in a yawl, he came upon a gunboat six miles downstream. From there he wrote several dispatches before returning to the Middleton house. He had not been long asleep when he was roused. General John G. Foster had reached the Ogeechee by steamer and wanted to see him. Sherman went back down the river at dawn. Aboard the *Nemaha* he conferred with Foster; he requested bread and forage and asked to have siege ordnance brought around from Port Royal.

Admiral Dahlgren was on his way to Ossabaw and Sherman wished to confer with him. The *Nemaha* cruised up the inland passage and met the flagship at Wassaw. An officer on Foster's staff memorably portrayed General Sherman as he observed him that day. "The most American looking man I ever saw," wrote John Chipman Gray. "Tall and lank, not very erect, with hair like a thatch, which he rubs up with his hands, a rusty beard trimmed close, a wrinkled face, sharp, prominent red nose, small, bright eyes" and "black felt hat slouched over the eyes."

Sherman talked incessantly using a great deal of slang, reported the young Bostonian. He told his listeners that Savannah was his "sure game." As he said it, wrote Gray, he stretched out his arm and clawed his bony fingers in the air to illustrate how he had his grip on the city. There was no hurry. He would take his own time.

The quarters on Dahlgren's flagship were excellent. "Luxurious rascals compared to us dwellers in tents" was Major Hitchcock's verdict of naval life, reporting a "capital time" while aboard.[1]

Sherman did not get back until the morning of the 15th. After showing the Admiral around McAllister he travelled in Dahlgren's barge to Cheves' rice mill where he had left his horse. From there he rode to Howard's headquarters at the plantation along the Darien Road known as Berwick. On his arrival there he sent instructions to the Commanding General of the Left Wing to place the siege guns (which could be expected shortly) "as near the heart of Savannah, as possible, ready to bombard." Meanwhile, if Slocum could get a force across the Savannah River so as to threaten any dirt road leading out of the city, the investment would be complete and there would be no escape.[2]

"The finest plantation I ever saw," was an Indiana officer's opinion of Berwick. He was impressed by the avenue leading off the Darien Road, "bordered by the finest spreading live oaks," as well as by the mansion, every room of which was "lavishly furnished with costly furniture."[3] The night of December 15, 1864, was one not readily forgotten by members of Sherman's staff. The moon was full, the air balmy, the japonicas in bloom, and Sherman in fine spirits. A group of about twenty-five officers sat around the fire singing songs, reminiscing about war experiences and listening to music of the headquarters band.

The war seemed further away that night than it actually was. Scarcely two miles from Berwick was the Confederate battery called Battery Jones. Manned by the Terrell Light Artillery, it protected the point where the highway to Darien crossed Salt Creek. The battery was one of Hardee's busiest during the siege. Sherman's prediction that the Confederates had some "good artillerists" was soon realized. He learned something of their marksmanship the day his forces closed on this part of the Confederate line. "We had just got settled," said a Northern soldier, "when the Captain of a couple of guns which were in the embrasures close at our right told us to lay low." He was going to wake up "the Johnnys. . . . He woke them up all right. . . . They replied, knocked the muzzle off the gun next to us, the wheel of the other, blew up the caisson . . . and threw one shell in the muck in front of us which exploded and covered us with about 20 tons of black mud." A Northern officer witnessed on December 17 what he described as "one of the most interesting artillery duels" he ever saw. Out of a hundred shells fired by the Confederates he counted only two that "didn't burst almost directly over our works." When an ambulance came dashing down the road to collect the wounded, the rebels put a solid shot after it, continued this officer. "Such scampering we never saw whereupon they set up a loud hurrah." [4]

The scampering was nothing compared to what occurred one afternoon at the headquarters of General John M. Corse. A rumor got abroad that he had secured two barrels of genuine old Monongahela whiskey. "It was marvelous to observe what a number of friends the general had," said George W. Nichols in telling the story in *Harpers Monthly*. A large number of thirsty Union officers congregated at his headquarters, located on a plantation in the fork of the Little Ogeechee. Many of them brought medical certificates attesting their need of alcoholic stimulant. It happened that the Confederate battery across the way was accustomed to open fire every day at 3 p.m., a schedule that coincided with the gathering of Corse's visitors. Shells suddenly began to crash near them as they lolled in the sunshine. One shot passed through Adjutant Leo Carper's tent, scattering his papers "without regard to red tape or military order." There were hurried adieus. In a few minutes all that remained of the "tea party," narrated Nichols, was a "cloud of golden dust which followed the heels of the fast-galloping steeds as they disappeared down the long avenue of oaks." [5]

From the "trenches before Savannah" a member of the 21st Minnesota described the sound of shells on December 16. "Whew," he wrote, "there goes a dose of grape for some one— here comes a Sixty four shell. I wish you could be here & see & smell & hear, them. I never knew what excitement was untill under fire. The musketry sometimes is such that you cannot hear yourself think & the wh-i-z, p-h-i-z of the bullets makes you think of your lost relations. A shell sounds like a steam engine starting w-h-e-w—w-h-e-w—w-h-e-w—commencing slow & gradualy growing faster & faster & finaly ends with a roar." [6]

The week that followed the fall of Fort McAllister was marked by heavy artillery fire and by probing of the defenses to test their strength. Day by day the Confederate line was more closely developed through construction of breastworks and rifle pits. The situation was calculated to make Hardee nervous. "I hope you will not fail to come here tonight. It is all important that I should confer with you," he telegraphed Beauregard on the 8th. The latter came over from Charleston the next morning.

Whether General Beauregard fully appreciated the enemy strength or his designs is not entirely clear in the light of Henry C. Wayne's version of a conversation with him at headquarters on December 9. The Adjutant General who had been in front of the Union Army for three weeks reported that Sherman had seventy thousand troops and that his objective was Savannah. "My God, Harry! what has come over you? You did not use to be so nervous!" Beauregard retorted. "General Bragg telegraphs me from Augusta that Sherman has not more than twenty-one thousand men with him . . . and is making a hasty retreat for his gunboats, either across Sister's Ferry to Port Royal, or to Ossabaw." Wayne responded, "Believe me that Savannah is his objective point, and that on Friday night he will invest the city." [7]

Before leaving, Beauregard reiterated in writing the instructions by which Hardee was to govern himself. They were clear enough: the responsibility was entirely his. He was to hold the city as long as it was advisable in *his* judgment to do so. If it came to a choice between Savannah and its garrison, the latter was to be preserved for operations elsewhere.

Hardee's anxiety increased in the next few days. "I have been obliged to extend my line," he telegraphed on the 11th. "It is impossible to hold it without immediate reinforcement." In a code telegram three days later he expressed the fear that he might find himself surrounded without the chance of escape. He requested instructions. The following day Hardee asked Beauregard to

"come here and give me the benefit of your advice." To President
Davis he telegraphed the same day, "Unless assured that force
sufficient to keep open my communications can be sent me, I shall
be compelled to evacuate Savannah." [8]

Beauregard returned on the night of the 16th, remaining there
for two busy days. Long consultations took place in the Oglethorpe
Barracks between the two West Point classmates of 1838—the
small, swarthy, quick-thinking Creole and the tall, broad-shoul-
dered Hardee who, though Georgia-born, looked as much like
a French officer as Beauregard. The important thing at the moment was to complete the pontoon bridge across the Savannah
River to Hutchinson Island and thence over Back River connecting with a road to Hardeeville. To Beauregard's surprise he
found the work only about a third completed. Renewed efforts
were made to collect rice flats and to complete the bridge. Floor-
ing was ripped up from the city wharves for planking; railroad
wheels were utilized as anchors. A thousand Negroes were put to
work on the roads.

By the morning of December 19 the bridge and temporary
roads that tracked the dykes across Hutchinson Island and Penny-
worth Island were practically ready for use. "The construction of
the pontoon bridge in the number of days which it occupied and
out of such material was truly astonishing and reflects credit
upon the head which directed it," wrote a North Carolina soldier. [9]

Meanwhile, on December 17 a letter came in to General
Hardee under flag of truce. Written personally by Sherman and
delivered by his brother-in-law, the communication stated that
he was now in contact with the Navy; that he possessed guns
that "can cast heavy and destructive shot as far as the heart of your
city" and that for some days he had "controlled every avenue by
which Savannah could be supplied." The surrender of the city was
demanded. Liberal terms would be granted in event of capitula-
tion. However, if forced to attack, Sherman promised little effort
on his part to restrain an Army "burning to avenge a great national wrong they attach to Savannah, and other large cities which
have been so prominent in dragging our country into civil war."

The innuendo of sacking calls to mind the summons sent into Savannah by another general. Eighty-five years before, Monsieur le Comte d'Estaing had made a similar threat in demanding the surrender of the town. The difference was that in 1779 British reinforcements were on the way to aid the town. There were to be no reinforcements and no obsidional awards for Confederate generals at Savannah in 1864.

In refusing to surrender the city Hardee took issue with two of Sherman's statements. The nearest position along the Union line to the heart of the city was, he claimed, four miles (out of artillery range). Furthermore, he was not cut off but was in free and constant communication with his Department. As for Sherman's threat of pillage, having always conducted his own military operations in accordance with rules of civilized warfare, Hardee said that he would "deeply regret" the adoption of any course that might force him to deviate from them in the future.[10]

The question of distances was not worth cavilling over. "By tomorrow morning," Sherman informed Grant, "I will have six 30-pounder Parrots in position." Hardee would then learn whether he was right or not. Sherman was right—he was sure of that. The same morning he sent the summons he had stood by the three-mile post on the Augusta Road and noted that the Confederate line lay not more than a quarter-mile to the east. No less an authority than R. R. Cuyler had informed him that the mile posts were measured from the courthouse.[11]

It was impossible to refute the statement about the Confederate communications still being open. By way of the "Union Causeway" which ran northward from Screven's Ferry across the Savannah River there was access to the Charleston and Savannah Railroad. Thanks to Honey Hill that route was still open. Why Sherman ignored this fact in the summons to surrender is not clear. Certainly, he was aware of the existence of the causeway. The explanation possibly lies in his statement to Grant on December 18 that the route in question was inadequate to feed an army and the populace of Savannah.

As already noted, Sherman suggested on December 15 that a

force be thrown across the Savannah River to threaten in flank any road located there. General Slocum needed no urging. "D—n it," he had remarked that day, "let us take this plank road and shut these fellows in." Turning to Colonel Ezra Carman, he directed him to get his whole brigade "ready to go over in the morning to the island [Argyle] and then to the South Carolina shore." Slocum preferred to send a whole division over so as to cut the escape route instead of threatening it. In fact, to do the job right he had suggested the use of even a larger body of troops. "I have no fear of placing a corps on that side," he informed Sherman, "and this done the fate of the city is sealed." There were boats enough to cross a brigade every hour, Carman assured him.[12]

But Sherman was determined to play things safe. He said later that he had to keep his Army together as he might have to transfer it by sea to Virginia. He made up his mind not to commit any considerable force to operations in the rugged terrain across the Savannah River. The difficulty of fighting in that low country was indisputable. "All this had been admirably provided for," argued Carman, by the making of fascines, ladders and stringers. Sherman temporized. Replying to Slocum's suggestion of sending a corps across, he limited him to one brigade for the operation. He also completely changed the main objective of the trans-Savannah movement. The force that was sent across the Savannah was not to threaten the escape route north but a road on the Carolina side that ran to Augusta.

Another reason Sherman assigned for not sending a larger body there was that it would be isolated by the broad river. The operation was "extra hazardous" as the communications, particularly any pontoons, would be endangered by the rebel gunboats.[13]

Confederate sea power had at last made itself felt in the war! It consisted in this instance of the little wooden gunboat *Isondiga* with her two guns. The ironclad *Savannah* could not get that far upstream because of her deep draft. In fact, the former could do so only when the tide was high and it was impossible, even on a flood tide, for the *Isondiga* to navigate the branch separating Argyle Island from Carolina. The Confederate gunboat shelled the enemy positions daily but with more sound and fury than damage. And always at a respectful distance.

The initial order to put a brigade over on the Carolina side at Izard's plantation had been soon countermanded. On the 19th the trans-Savannah operation, stalled by indecision for two days, was revived. Early that morning a brigade was sent across the river under orders to establish a "bold front." After considerable effort the fifteen hundred Union troops managed to establish a line nearly two miles long, extending from the rice mill at Izard's to an inlet of Clydesdale Creek.

Wheeler's cavalry on the Carolina side of the Savannah was reinforced by troops hastily withdrawn from Hardee's line. The enemy force was contained. After the war General Wheeler said that two brigades, fighting as well as the Federal troops did that day, would have driven him from his position. Carman's own opinion was that at any time between December 12 and 15 the causeway was "at the mercy of a brigade," that on the 15th or 16th the Confederate force could have been utterly demolished by one brigade, and that on the 18th or 19th the escape route could have been easily taken by two brigades.

However, no order to attack would come. On December 17 Carman had talked with Sherman, who was sitting under a fly tent, and assured him that the flanking movement was practicable. The General was not impressed. He was waiting for Hardee's reply to the summons to surrender. His demand might scare him out of Savannah. If not, he would attack.

Reconnaissances during the week since the investment of the Confederate line had disclosed a number of points where it was vulnerable. Howard reported that at least two of his division commanders were "perfectly confident" of success in the event of an attack upon the Confederate left. Jeff C. Davis, whose corps was positioned between the Charleston and Savannah Railroad and Doctor Lawton's plantation, stated that five points in that sector were available for an attack. Alpheus Williams reported that while there were very few assailable positions on the Confederate right the confidence of his men in taking them was "perfect and earnest." One of General Williams' brigade commanders believed that the works in the vicinity of the Augusta Road could be easily carried. Indeed, the opinion universally prevailed, reported Orlando Poe, that an attack would be successful.[14]

Confederate officers agreed. "If the Federals had massed their forces for a determined assault, they could, any day during the continuance of the siege, have carried it," declared Colonel Jones. General Gustavus Smith expressed the opinion that the enemy was "in position to prevent the escape of any portion of the garrison for two or three days before we gave up the place." [15]

When Hardee's answer to the summons reached Sherman on the 18th he immediately ordered preparations for an attack. A simultaneous assault was to be made at every accessible point along the line. It was tentatively set for December 21. Preparations were now accelerated. Fascines, ladders, foot bridges, even rafts, were constructed. Practice in laying pontoons was staged. Close reconnaissances of the front were undertaken. "In brief," said General Howard, "every possible preparation was made to assault the enemy's works."

Sherman's orders were scarcely issued before he changed his mind. He developed what appears to have been a bad case of vacillation. Perhaps he never really intended to make an assault. On December 16 he informed his wife that he would demand the surrender of Savannah but would not assault as a few days would suffice to starve out the garrison. He was reluctant to sacrifice men in a frontal attack. His experience had left him little stomach for that sort of warfare. Forcing a passage would be at the cost of many precious lives when the city was as good as gone. That was the way Sherman saw things. The General valued his reputation for conserving lives. "Men march to certain death without a murmur if I call on them, because they know I value their lives as much as my own." [16]

The view of the rank and file in his Army was summarized by an Iowa soldier. "We can easy take Savannah by storm but we would lose a good many men, and I for one, do not feel anxious at all to charge the large mud fort in front of our Division."

Private Upson felt more confident about an assault. "If we make a start we are going through and I think the Johnnys know it for they do not talk as saucy as they did at Vicksburg." [17]

On December 19 the Commanding Generals of the two wings were instructed that no assault was to be made until further orders from Sherman. Preparations were to proceed at "all possible speed" but they were not to move until he returned from a trip he decided to make. He would go to Hilton Head (after conferring with Admiral Dahlgren) to discuss with General Foster the matter of reviving the operation of cutting the railroad to Charleston. They would flush Hardee out of Savannah rather than capture him.

20.

Exit Hardee

⇐ THE FINAL days of Confederate occupation were long remembered by the inhabitants of Savannah. "How solemn and impressive was the Sabbath service the last in the Confederacy," said Mary Copp Wilbur. "Excitement prevailed everywhere." Rumors of outrages on the march through Georgia created wild apprehensions in female minds. Reports of Yankee doings elsewhere were "dreadful," wrote a Savannah woman. No one knew what to expect.[1]

Pierre Gustave Toutant Beauregard left Savannah early on the morning of December 19. Before departing he dictated a plan for the evacuation. The field batteries were to withdraw at dark with as little noise as possible and proceed to the city where they were to cross the pontoon bridge at eight. Ambrose R. Wright's division was to cross at 9 p.m., followed at eleven by the division of Lafayette McLaws and at midnight by that of Gustavus W. Smith. The garrisons of the various river batteries were to assemble at Fort Jackson from which transportation was to be provided to Screven's Ferry across the Savannah River.

Hardee accompanied General Beauregard as far as the head of the Union causeway on the Carolina side where they conferred with General Joe Wheeler. From that point they could see the movement of Union troops across the river to Izard's plantation. "Gentlemen," remarked Beauregard, "this is not a demonstration;

it is a real attack on our communications. You must get out of Savannah as soon as possible." [2] The same day confidential orders were circulated from Hardee's headquarters concerning the evacuation. The Mayor was informed of the plans.

All day on December 20 wagons loaded with Confederate Army baggage rumbled northward over the pontoon bridge. The sound of Confederate cannon was louder than usual that afternoon. "Neither did the night interfere with the noisy racket," declared a member of the 21st Wisconsin, "ten P.M. and still they were blowing away." At dark that evening Hardee's troops began to file out of the lines around the city, leaving spiked cannon, campfires and a few pickets behind. The garrisons of the river batteries crossed to Screven's Ferry in boats "without confusion or mishap," said Edward C. Anderson. He thought the enemy had discovered the movement from Pulaski as "a large, luminous rocket" was sent up near there which was answered by a similar one from Sherman's lines west of the city. "But there was no further demonstration." [3]

Some of the Confederate pickets did not remain long after the troops left. "As officer of the guard," wrote a Georgia officer, "I had orders to relieve the picket line, evacuate this post at 11 p.m. and make a hasty retreat." At the appointed time he repaired to the first sentinel post only to find that the guard had fled "to parts unknown." So had the sentinel at the next. At the third, however, he found one of his "old true and tried soldiers steady at his post as the boy that stood on the burning deck whence all but him had fled." [4]

Another soldier who stayed to the end was a young wagoner named McCollum. Volunteering to remain with a friend who was assigned to picket duty that night, he was given the job of keeping the fire going. The departing soldiers were throwing their corn meal away and he persuaded them to leave it in a pile. McCollum wiled away the long hours of the night by cooking an enormous corn meal cake in sheaves of rice.[5]

Berry Benson and a young officer were left in charge of the withdrawal of pickets in another sector. "About 8:00," related

Benson, "the Lieutenant began to get a little nervous and pretty soon he sent a man to camp to know what was going on." His fidgetiness increased by the minute. Before long the lieutenant sent another soldier back to the camp for information. Then a third was dispatched. "I don't know what in the hell to do!" he said. Finally, Benson could stand it no longer. "Lieutenant," he protested, "there's only one thing to do: obey orders, stay here till 11:00 & then go." One of the last soldiers to pass through Savannah, Benson would never forget what he called the "musical sound, in the dead of night, of the 'clink-clank, clink-clank' of the horses' iron feet as the troopers rode down the brick pavements." [6]

The night ineffaceably impressed itself on men's minds. Captain Woodbury Wheeler of the 10th North Carolina Battalion remembered as he marched down the Ogeechee Road toward Savannah how the waving moss on the live oaks seemed to personify the ghosts of departed hopes. "Played out! Played out!" Union pickets called back across the lines when a band struck up "Dixie." Another soldier who vividly recalled that night was Cornelius Hanleiter. Passing through the city, the Atlantan found no opportunity to "embrace with my dear wife and children, whom I had not seen in over a week, and whom I was about to abandon, in a comparatively strange land, to their fate among ruthless enemies." [7] He described in his diary the hectic scenes. Soldiers were discharging their fire-arms and "making the night hideous with their oaths and blasphemies"; horsemen were galloping about without any apparent object while women, apparently with an object ("nymphs of the pave," Hanleiter suspected), roamed "hither and thither."

The night was exceedingly dark, said the Atlanta officer, and "everything seemed to move on without system or direction." Along the roadside horses and men struggled in mud and water. Every time Hanleiter stopped to assist "some poor fellow, or horse, that seemed to have been abandoned to his fate" he found himself pushed onward by "the apparently endless mass of men and horses and mules and wagons and artillery behind me." Some of the wagons fell from the bridges, horses and drivers being lost with "scarcely a word of sympathy heard for either!" The evacuation was "horrible in the extreme."

A Spalding County soldier wrote that it was "the hardest march for some 17 miles that I nearly ever taken." Some of the men threw away everything but their blankets. "I can't describe my feelings when we had to leave," continued this Confederate, "desperate to think after 4 years service that I have to leave my native state to the mercy of a ruthless enemy." Similar reactions were experienced by Henry Graves who had spent twelve days and nights in the trenches and the mud. The idea of evacuation had not entered his head. They had been told, he wrote, that General Hardee had decided to hold the city "at all hazards." There were no words to picture the gloomy bitterness that filled his mind on the dreary march through mud and darkness. He tortured himself with many thoughts but above all with the regret that "some of the best and truest friends" he had were "about to be abandoned in their utter helplessness to the power of an enemy." Reaching Savannah around midnight, Graves obtained permission to stop by a house where he had been made to feel much at home during his stay in the city. He found the family sitting up waiting to bid him goodbye. Farewells said, Lieutenant Graves joined the "long line of silent men who were pouring in a continuous stream over a pontoon bridge." [8]

The stars that night were "veiled in clouds as if in sympathy," wrote a Savannahian. Her family sat around the fire, she related, talking of nothing but the events of the day and anticipations of the morrow. Remembering that a captured enemy sword was in the house, she took it to the front door and waited for some one to pass. Seeing a horseman approach, she called to him. He turned out to be a Confederate officer. The soldier rode on into the black night with the sabre. [9]

After passing through Callibogue Sound late that night, a Northern officer wrote in his diary that he noticed very large fires in the direction of Savannah and that he heard an explosion. [10] The Confederate Navy yard and warships were being destroyed. The new gunboat *Milledgeville* was burned in the channel opposite

Willink's shipyard east of the bluff. A ram was destroyed on the stocks at the Krenson & Hawkes shipyard west of the city. The *Isondiga* was burned after she grounded above the pontoon bridge while the floating battery *Georgia* was blown up at her moorings.

"A grand and fearful sight met the eye, fire, fire everywhere," reported a Confederate who left aboard the little *Swan*. Thirty-six years later George Blount vividly recalled the scenes he witnessed that morning. One that particularly impressed itself on him was the farewell between Captain William M. Davidson and a slave who had come down to the waterfront to say goodbye to him. As he left, the Confederate officer admonished him, "Take care of my wife," something which the colored man, amid sobs and tears, promised to do.

On the trip to Screven's Ferry the men on the steamer were subdued in spirit and sad in heart, narrated Blount. Flames from burning vessels rose vertically in the dawn, warming the cheeks and smarting the eyes of those aboard vessels still plying the stream. Around them drifted the barges from the dismantled pontoon bridge, some of them burning "like torches." [11]

As Blount disembarked at Screven's Ferry he saw the *CSS Savannah*, her colors still flying, out in the stream. A day of grace though not of grandeur was left the ironclad. Commander Thomas Brent had been unable to get her to sea. It was "better," read his orders from Richmond, "for our cause and country" that the squadron should "fall in the conflict of battle" than "tamely surrendered to the enemy or destroyed by their own officers." The *Savannah* was trapped in the harbor by the Confederate Navy's own torpedoes. The channel of the Savannah River being impracticable because of the obstructions, Lieutenant McAdam was sent down to Turner's Rock to remove the torpedoes in the Wilmington in order that the ironclad might escape by way of Wassaw. He was unable to do the job with the equipment at hand; the anchors had become too deeply imbedded in the mud. [12] The torpedoes and the *Savannah* had to stay. It was just as well, for two monitors were waiting in the sound for the Confederate man-of-war.

Throughout the day following the evacuation the ironclad remained near Screven's Ferry covering the removal of stores still in progress there. She fired on Fort Jackson when the Stars and Stripes appeared on its walls on the morning of the 21st—the only time that fortification ever experienced hostile fire. During the day the *Savannah* was shelled from the foot of Bay Street by Captain Winegar's battery. Commander Brent reported that the enemy "opened upon the ship a well-directed fire of field artillery from the bluff near the gas works." [13] It was, indeed, well-directed even though no damage was done. According to a member of the crew, nearly every shot struck her sides and one (which did not explode) went down the smokestack and came to rest on the grating.

"We were not slow in returning the compliment but with what effect I cannot say," wrote the same seaman. [14] According to Brent, he was unable to give his guns sufficient elevation to reach the enemy when he returned the fire. On January 7 the Chicago *Tribune* reported that "many of the shots fired by the ram went into the city, entering dwellings and storehouses, and unsettling chimneys, to the infinite disgust of the citizens." The truth seems to be more nearly approximated in the *Morning News* on March 9, 1872. An article described the damage to the only house in the city struck during the siege, a wooden building at the northwest corner of Lincoln and Broughton Streets. "The officers of the Savannah," said this account, "received the fire some time in silence, but it was, finally, though reluctantly, on account of the danger to their beloved city, decided to return the compliment. One of her heavy guns was made ready for action, and sent on their winged way three successive shells, which, however, passed over the battery without doing any injury . . . one of these shells, passing over the battery, and the house tops of the vicinity, exploded directly in front of the old house, mentioned above, a fragment of which struck the side of the house, tearing off a long strip of the weatherboarding."

About 7:30 on the evening of the 21st the crew of the *Savannah* abandoned ship. Four hours later, from near Fort Pulaski, John Chipman Gray saw a dull red glow in the west suddenly become "a

tall fiery column with a ball of thick black smoke at its sum-
mit." [15] The explosion rattled windows as far away as Hilton
Head. According to Robert Watson, a member of the crew, it lit
the skies so brightly he "could see to pick up a pin" eight miles
from the site.

A Marine attached to the Confederate ironclad heard the explosion some time after he reached the Carolina shore. "You have
no idea what a sad blow it was to me," Iverson Graves informed
his mother. "Thinks I, there goes my pleasant quarters, my good
clothes, my good warm overcoat, and I am forever cut off from
Savh. and the hope of ever making myself agreeable to the Savannah girls; my heart sank within me. My limbs ached, my load was
terribly heavy, and my eyelids had a mutual attraction for each
other." He thought of his canteen which he had been "provident
enough to fill with whiskey." Taking a good swig, the young
Marine "felt the generous fluid to course through every vein and
fill me with fresh strength and spirit." [16]

This lugubrious end to the annals of the Confederate Navy at
Savannah seems appropriately completed with the glimpse of stout-
hearted old Josiah Tattnall, who had seen to the destruction of the
vessels, trudging at the head of his sailors along the road that led
northward from Screven's Ferry. General Hardee took the same
route on the 21st after crossing on the *Swan* with such stragglers
as he could collect.

Satisfied with what he had accomplished at Savannah, Hardee
declared that the safe withdrawal of his Army from the lines was
one of the most satisfactory exploits in his career. "There is no
part of my military life," he said, "to which I look back with so
much satisfaction." Writing from Hardeeville a day after the evacuation a North Carolina soldier, who called the loss of Savannah
a "severe blow," predicted that "Sherman will be applauded and
Hardee will be censured." But, he added, "to all who speak ill of
Hardee say that it is to his skill and indomitable energy that the
South owes the rescue of ten thousand of his troops." [17]

Sherman was by no means happy about things. He was "somewhat disappointed" at Hardee's escape, but he was "not to

blame," he informed General Halleck. He had moved as quickly as possible to close up the "Union Causeway." But the intervening obstacles were such "that before I could get my troops on the road Hardee had slipped out." This is something less than the straight of the matter. The escape of the garrison was a sore disappointment to Secretary of War Stanton. "It looks like protracting the war while their armies continue to escape," he complained.[18]

As a participant in these scenes Charles C. Jones, Jr., CSA, may be subject to disqualification for bias. *"Audi alteram partem,"* he wrote in the preface to his account of the siege. His views are at least interesting. "All the balderdash which has been written and spoken about this vaunted 'march to the sea' can never in the clear light of history," he claimed, "cover up or excuse the lack of dash and the want of ordinary military skill and precaution . . . in permitting the Confederate garrison to retire unmolested by a route so precarious in its character, and by a flank movement which could have been easily frustrated by a single division." [19]

Writing in his diary concerning Hardee's escape, a Northern officer said, "I do not find fault with Genl. Sherman for this mistake for I know there must be a reason for it yet I cannot but feel that in the end it will prove disastrous to us." One can hardly call it disastrous. But the fact remained, as a Confederate officer was to point out, that Hardee's little Army would comprise "the bulk of the only force afterward interposed between Sherman and Grant." [20]

If mistakes were made at Savannah (and the capture of Hardee was entirely possible), they could be forgotten in the broader aspect of Sherman's accomplishment in Georgia. "He is a great General," wrote Henry Slocum. "Few there were who made no mistakes, and let us rather overlook those that were made," said Ezra Carman.[21] Apparently that was the way Sherman, deep down in his heart, looked at the thing. "Well, Carman," the conquering General remarked after the war, "we didn't catch Hardee, did we? But it is all right, anyhow; the war ended all right and just as it ought."

21.

Enter Sherman

  EARLY ON December 20 General John Geary notified headquarters that the enemy had completed a pontoon bridge across the Savannah River. From the loft of a barn on Izard's plantation Colonel Carman watched the movement across the bridge that day of "wagons, family carriages, men and women on foot, singly and in groups." He sent a staff officer to headquarters. It was still not too late to prevent the evacuation, reported Carman.[1] Nothing came of his suggestion.

  That night, from seven on, the movement of troops and wagons across the pontoon bridge could be distinctly heard on the Union left. To Colonel Henry Barnum it was clear that the Confederates were pulling out and he ordered his pickets to observe the enemy closely. About 9 p.m. another Federal officer reported that the troops opposite him seemed to be moving out of the works.[2]

  All along the line it was a similar story. Hardee was obviously leaving. But no one did anything about it. An Indiana private thought that the officers knew they were going and did not try to stop them. "What do you think about investigating the matter?" a fellow officer asked Lieutenant John Henry Otto when the outposts were relieved around midnight. For several hours they had been convinced the enemy was leaving. Crossing a causeway leading toward the Confederate line, the two officers crept forward on hands and knees to an earthwork. "All was quiet as in a grave," related Otto. He put his cap aside, drew himself up and looked over the top. The guns were still in place. Small heaps of dimly glimmering coals were the only other thing he could see. Otto felt for the vent of the cannon. It was spiked. "The birds had flown," he said. Another of Sherman's soldiers expressed it more strongly. They had "ignominiously skedaddled like thieves and scoundrels they are." [3]

Meanwhile, the evacuation had been discovered on the Union left. With ten picked men, Colonel Barnum had crossed the flooded rice fields in front of the Confederate works. It was not an easy reconnaissance for this New York officer who was still handicapped by the wound he had received at Malvern Hill.* In the advance positions campfires glowed but no enemy was to be seen. Barnum and his men then crept forward to the main works. [4]

Meanwhile, Mayor Richard Arnold and the aldermen had remained at the Exchange throughout the night awaiting the completion of Hardee's withdrawal before going out to surrender the city. At their invitation several prominent citizens were present to discuss the existing state of affairs. One of the decisions reached was to oppose unanimously the plan made known by Josiah Tattnall concerning the burning of a warship on the stocks, a step that would endanger that part of the city. The Commodore left with assurances to the group that he would try to obtain fifty men to throw the ship off the ways and, failing that, to burn her only if the direction of the wind was right.

Arrangements had been made for hacks to transport the city officials out to the lines. However, Wheeler's men went off with the horses. Only one buggy was available and the city fathers became separated on the way. As Aldermen O'Byrne and Lachlison walked down the Augusta Road they were halted by a Union picket. They were escorted to General Geary whose division was

---

* A medical history of his wound, regarded by doctors as an extraordinary one, is contained in *The Medical and Surgical History of the War of the Rebellion* (Washington, D. C., 1875), II, 213. At the time of the Savannah campaign Barnum still carried a linen seton in his body, running the course of the ball through his stomach and tied together outside at its ends.

already in motion toward Savannah. After questioning the two aldermen for some time he unceremoniously accepted the surrender
of the city. A short time afterward, Savannah was formally surrendered by Dr. Arnold in person. "I respectfully request your protection of the lives and private property of the citizens and of our
women and children," Geary quoted the "worthy Mayor" as saying.[5] The request was promptly granted. Any violation of orders
would be punished by death, and Geary seemed to mean it.

It was the end of the Confederate road for Savannah. For the
North, it was strong evidence that the struggle was nearly over.
The city had been won at a cost in killed and wounded (inclusive
of the casualties at Fort McAllister) of not more than two hundred
and fifty.

To one of Sherman's soldiers it was "the greatest victory of
the war & one that will prove a greater benefit to our country &
cause." The Federals had proved that the South was but a hollow
shell. An Indiana surgeon expressed the view that the "old rotten
concern" would not be able to stand "more than two or three more
of Sherman's crazy spells." As a Minnesota volunteer put it, they
had marched "through the very heart of a self-styled powerful nation" which should "have swallowed up a force like ours reckless
enough to make the venture," yet so far from destroying them, the
whole resources of the Confederacy had availed "only to burn a few
bridges and cut a few pine trees across the road." [6]

The first sound Elizabeth Basinger heard on the morning of
December 21, 1864, came from the little colored maid in her
house. "Oh, Miss! Oh Miss Lizzie!" she exclaimed, "de Yankees is
come, dey is as tick as bees, dey is so many on horses and de horse's
tails is stannin out right straight, you just come look out de win-
der." [7] A great tramping outside awakened Mrs. Mary Drummond
who had slept late after spending a large part of the night burning
papers of importance. Looking out, her heart seemed to stand still
on seeing a great line of blue-coats marching around the square. It
was impossible, she said, to describe her feelings.

With Mayor Arnold as a guide, Barnum's Brigade, the men

cheering all the way, had reached the City Exchange at 6 a.m. There the Union flag was raised and Geary made a "fine speech" complimenting his men on their accomplishments. He was followed by Colonel Barnum who delivered some "neat and appropriate" remarks, according to an officer.[8]

When it came to eulogizing the feats of Sherman's Army, it is unlikely that either of these two lawyer-soldiers matched the simple eloquence of an Indiana private named Essington. "We stand here at Savannah," he rhapsodized, "Master of over a Hundread fields which was bought and Paid with Freemans Blood here we have ended what I think will go down to History and be told over and over again as one of the greatest acheevements on Record   here we will Rest awhile then where to God onley knows but by his mercy and Love he has guided us safe so far for the Past 36 days   we have had no communacation with the wourld we only new we were alive and day by day closeing in and around the enemys lines and felt confident the time was near when they would say enough go home we are wroung you are Right." [9]

While General Geary was addressing the troops in front of the Exchange Colonel Barnum observed a sergeant step out of the ranks and enter a store from which he emerged wearing a fireman's hat. When the ceremony was over, the New York officer went over to the soldier. Slashing the pilfered hat with his sword, he proceeded to rip the chevrons from his sleeves.

The sergeant was only doing what a lot of civilians were up to around town. Even as the ceremonies at the Exchange were proceeding riotous crowds were "sacking stores and store-houses," declared Geary. According to a correspondent of the New York *Herald,* mobs composed of "Irish and Dutch women, negroes and the thievish soldiers" were breaking open and robbing shops when the Federals entered the city. "It was a fearful time. I almost grew gray. I never suffered such fear in my life," wrote a Savannah resident. Warned that Confederate soldiers might search the Telfair mansion on St. James Square for gold and silver, William B. Hodgson, the distinguished Oriental scholar, and the other occupants armed themselves and, dividing into watches, maintained an all-night vigil. The only things the Confederates made off with were a horse and three mules.[10]

The disorder had been going on most of the night of the 20th. According to a Confederate soldier named Turrentine, one riot had to be suppressed by force. He blamed the trouble on "the meanest set of men that ever lived"—Wheeler's cavalry who had "stolen and destroyed more than the enemy." Most of the blame, however, belonged elsewhere. Another soldier who had a better opportunity to see what went on that night attributed the disorders to the "white scum of the city" which "came out of their dens like nocturnal beasts to the work of pillage." [11]

Geary immediately sent patrols through the streets to break up the lawlessness. Among other places, a guard was posted at the Masonic Hall, a favor the members of Solomon's Lodge remembered with gratitude since this prompt action had dispersed "the plunderers" and saved the valuable mementoes of the lodge. General Geary was able to report that "in a few hours this city, in which I found a lawless mob of low whites and negroes pillaging and setting fire to property, was reduced to order." [12]

Where was General Sherman all this time? The Union commander had spent all of December 20 at Port Royal conferring with Foster about a joint movement of their troops up the Broad River to cut Hardee's escape route. It was not until early the next morning that the *Harvest Moon* left for the Ogeechee River. On account of heavy weather her pilot was forced to take the inside route. While navigating the channel through Romerly Marsh opposite Wassaw Island Dahlgren's flagship stuck fast on a mud bank. After some delay, General Sherman and his staff piled aboard the Admiral's barge and the oarsmen pulled for the Ogeechee. It was not a particularly comfortable trip. A strong northwester was blowing and it was freezing. "They never before had such cold weather here," people in Savannah told a Union soldier, accusing the Northerners of bringing it with them.[13]

Toward evening on the 21st a tug came alongside the barge with the news that Hardee had evacuated the city. Sherman got aboard, according to Dahlgren, and eagerly pushed on. If he was somewhat put out over events, he could console himself in his knowledge that had he been given two more days, "the garrison would have been hemmed in completely." Other than General Hardee's escape, the only mite of consolation Confederate sympathizers could draw from the events of that bleak December day was this historical sidelight of the conqueror stuck in the mud up a creek while his troops were making a triumphant entrance.

On his arrival at Savannah the morning after the occupation Sherman repaired to the Pulaski House where as a young lieutenant he once had stayed. In recapitulation of his accomplishment, he would tell a friend, *"I knocked daylight through Georgia,* and in retreating to the south like a sensible man I gathered up some plunder and walked into this beautiful city. . . ."[14] At the Pulaski he received a number of callers, among them Mayor Arnold. Others who came to call were Hardee's brother and the wife of Gustavus Smith, each bearing a letter from the Confederate Generals requesting Sherman's protection. During the day the Union commander sent his well-known message to President Lincoln presenting him as a Christmas present the City of Savannah, numerous heavy guns, considerable ammunition and "about 25,000 bales of cotton"—a bit of whimsey for which General Sherman credited A. G. Browne of the Treasury Department.

Possibly the captured cotton (it turned out to be 38,500 bales) had something to do with the handsome quarters on Madison Square in which Sherman found himself installed before the day was out. Among those who had called at the hotel was Charles Green, a wealthy British subject who was the owner of one of the finest houses in town. He had insisted that the General use it as his headquarters. Wagging tongues in Savannah attributed his invitation to the motive of salvaging the cotton seized by the military. Green explained later that he proffered his house because he wished to spare some other Savannahian the embarrassment of having to give up his home. At all events, Sherman and the members of his staff liked their host whom they found "extremely pleasant and courteous." At an elegant dinner party in the house on Christmas night the General offered a toast to Green who responded with "as happy a little after-dinner speech" as one of the guests ever heard.[15]

Mr. Green did not get his cotton back, nor did anyone else. The Army held on to it. Sherman was ordered not to turn over the cotton to owners or to agents of the Treasury Department without orders from the War Department. When a representative of Edmund Molyneux, his Britannic Majesty's late consul at Savannah, approached the General about restoration of his cotton, he was informed by him that British subjects would be treated the same as Americans and that he was "unwilling to fight for cotton for the benefit of Englishmen openly engaged in smuggling arms and instruments of war to kill us." Sherman told William B. Hodgson at Savannah that there was not a man in his Army who would not eagerly join in an invasion of England and that he hoped when the rebellion was over North and South would unite in such a war. He would be happy to lead the American forces, he said.[16]

Molyneux's status as a British subject did not prevent his handsome residence on Bull Street from being appropriated by General Howard as his headquarters. One would have thought that its contents were safe in the hands of this "Havelock of the Army," as Howard was known. "There is but little use of liquor, and a most gratifying absence of profanity, about his headquarters," it was said. Profanity possibly there was not, but other vices evidently existed there. "Oh mem, the Yankees is in the house, and they're the most accomplished thaves and robbers that iver ware," complained the Molyneux housekeeper. A claim was later filed against the United States on the owner's behalf for $11,000 damages to the contents during the Union occupation. The losses included expensive wines and brandy and much of the library. Possibly Howard was not to blame. According to a Union officer, the General handed him the keys to the wine cellar and to a room where valuables were stored under instructions not to let anything be taken out. "Whether the General relented, or whether I myself was to blame, I do not know; yet both the liquors and the books, together with the other articles, found their way into our Headquarters," confessed Captain Bedford. "We had no respect for the English Government, and hence none for its flag." [17]

Quarters for the rank and file presented less of a problem. Squares became camps. "The lovely square in front of our house soon became a village with streets its parade ground," said Mrs. Mary Copp Wilbur. Venturing out of her house shortly after the Union troops arrived, Confederate-minded Fanny Cohen was "surprised to see what these wretches had done in the way of making themselves comfortable." All of the squares were so built up with wooden houses she scarcely recognized the streets. [18]

The city was divided into two principal military districts and they, in turn, into a total of five sub-districts. Each was placed in charge of an officer enjoined to exert the most strenuous effort to establish and maintain perfect order and subordination. An 8 p.m. curfew was ordered for enlisted men. Soldiers coming into town from the camps outside were required to have passes. Men were not to enter private houses. The strictness with which the provost guard enforced the pass regulations proved "very annoying," complained a Union chaplain. [19] The Mayor and aldermen were permitted to continue their civil functions. Acting in concert with the military, they were to see that the water works was operated, the fire companies maintained, the streets cleaned and lighted, and a good understanding between citizens and soldiers established.

The Union Army put its best foot forward at Savannah. "Notwithstanding the habits begotten during our rather vandalic march, its behavior . . . has excited the wonder and admiration of all," Sherman informed Halleck. "You would think it Sunday," he told Grant, "so quiet is everything in the city day and night." A Confederate officer was pleased to learn of the good order maintained in the city. "I am rejoiced," Colonel Anderson informed his wife in a letter he got through the lines, "to hear that Genl Shermans policy toward our people is marked with humanity and kindness. After so brilliant a campaign as he has made he cannot afford to stain it with an unsoldierly course." [20]

Sherman could boast that "women and children of a hostile people walked the streets with as much security as they do in

Philadelphia." In view of the number of sentinels posted around the city this was hardly surprising. "We found the officers in charge very willing to station guards wherever there were complaints," said a Savannahian. "Whenever a chicken would cackle, one would see one or two or more Yankee soldiers' heads pop up over the fence." Sentinels were placed everywhere. The diary of an Illinois soldier reveals that he was stationed at such divers places as the theatre, "Don Pulaski's Monument," the river and the "Nunnery." If virtue was to be protected, so must vice be. "I am on duty every other day, but the reason of it is because there are so many hore houses in town which must have a sentinel at each door for to keep them straight," wrote a Pennsylvania soldier. "There is the most hoars here that I saw in my life both black and white," said a Northern soldier identified as Jake. "I thought that Washington had enough but this beats that." [21]

John W. Geary was appointed military commander of the city. Six feet five inches tall with a formidable beard and piercing eyes, the former territorial Governor of Kansas and the first Mayor of San Francisco was well qualified for that post. Geary possessed executive ability and the right mixture of firmness and tact. "The citizens are delighted with him, and they may well be so; for no city was ever kept in better order," declared a member of Sherman's staff. A New York *Times* correspondent at Savannah reported in January, '65, that there was universal regret at his departure. General Geary would "not be forgotten here in the present generation," predicted the writer. He would always be held in remembrance as the "embodiment of the high toned gentleman and the chivalric Soldier," said a resolution adopted by City Council. "The noble Geary," Mayor Arnold called him. For his own part the General explained that he was "activated by no motives but which were in every respect compatible with those of a soldier, dictated by the true principles of charity and humanity." [22]

The military dictatorship proved a benevolent one. Sherman had stated at first that he was not going to feed hungry rebels. However, on the same day that he wrote General Joseph Wheeler to that effect he charged his chief of commissary with the duty of supplying needy Savannah families. It was a hard choice to be thus classified. "Some of the ladies refused to accept aid from the enemy," wrote Mary Wragg Bond. She, however, as housekeeper, decided that it would be "cutting our noses to spite our faces," so she marched down with an old Negro man who carried the basket and got her share.

Four years of war had left the city in a dilapidated condition. "Fences are broken down, sidewalks and wharves are going to ruin and Sherman's dead horses are laying about the streets by the dozen," wrote a Bostonian who visited Savannah in January, 1865. "The fact is, this is a most miserable hole." Improvement was noticeable after Captain Albert Stearns took charge of the street department following the departure of the main Army. In two months 568 carcasses of animals were removed by the military, together with 8,311 cart loads of garbage and 7,219 loads of manure. Repairs were made to streets broken up to provide ballast for the cribs sunk in the Savannah River by the Confederates. A coating of whitewash was applied to the entire row of warehouses along the bay, producing "quite a tidy contrast with their moss covered condition," according to Captain Stearns. He proudly reported that in one month 6,200 trees were whitewashed to a height of seven feet.[23]

Freedom of the press was granted as long as a paper was pro-Union. There was nothing to worry about from Confederate editors. William T. Thompson of the *News* and James R. Sneed of the *Republican* had departed with General Hardee. Before leaving Savannah the editor of the *Republican* arranged for the newspaper to appear on December 21, the day of the Army's entrance. "Under the fortunes of war we today pass under the authority of the Federal military forces," announced a piece directed "To the Citizens of Savannah." It counselled the inhabitants to keep indoors and to conduct themselves in such a manner as to win the admiration of a "magnanimous foe." The author rivalled in humility, commented a Northern correspondent, "the humblest protestations of Uriah Heep himself."[24]

The offices and equipment of both newspapers were seized. Four days after the troops arrived Captain Moses Summers began the publication of the *Daily Loyal Georgian*. It lasted only four issues. The paper had an immediate successor, however. John E. Hayes, a New York *Tribune* correspondent who had come in with Sherman's Army, forcibly entered the offices of the *Republican* on December 26. "I take possession, sir, upon my individual responsibility and by military authority," he declared.[25] The first issue of Hayes' paper (published under the name *Republican*) appeared on December 29. The editor explained that its former editors had fled the city "to escape the wrath of an insulted army, whom they took delight in villifying, while safely ensconced in a city beyond range of their guns."

The new *Republican* was followed within two weeks by another newspaper, the Savannah *Herald*. It was edited by S. W. Mason who until recently had been publisher of a war-time paper at Port Royal. The first issue of the *Herald* announced that it was "established on the ruins of the old *Savannah News,* a fire-eating sheet with a worm-eaten office."

Certain restrictions on the press at Savannah were imposed by Sherman. There were to be no comments whatever upon the acts of the constituted authorities and the publishers were held to strict accountability for libelous or mischievous publications and exaggerated statements. General Sherman had not forgotten that early in the war some Northern newspapers had questioned his mental stability.

The masthead of the *Daily Loyal Georgian,* "The Union, It Must and Shall be Preserved! Redeemed, Regenerated and Disenthralled!" had given that unregenerate rebel, Fanny Cohen, her "first hearty laugh since the Goths had been among us." In the seclusion of their homes Savannahians abused the Yankees to their hearts' content, she said. There was, however, an almost unanimous desire to see an early end of a war that was now over for the city. The inhabitants were "very mild on Secessionism," reported an Ohio soldier-editor named Robinson. The leading men were saying, he added, that the South had been "fairly conquered, and unless hostilities cease, will soon be *subjugated.*" Savannahians already were. "The white people here are the most whipped and subjugated you ever saw," said Sherman.[26]

Considerable Union sentiment in Savannah was reported by some Northerners. Chaplain Pepper said that the people were "generally Union," particularly the Irish and German to whom "the old flag is an emblem of hope and a signal of salvation." Another Northern chaplain found "more Unionism in Savannah, than in any place we have been in yet." An Ohio private reported that when he asked a resident "how he liked the Yanks," the Savannahian replied that he would "rather we hold the city than their own men." According to a Wisconsin soldier the "citizens clapped their hands and fairly danced with joy when the Stars & stripes" were seen flying from the first Union vessel to enter the harbor in four years.[27]

Skepticism about the genuineness of this feeling was expressed by others. "The real Union sentiment in this city, I fear, is small," said a Bostonian named Glidden. "The people look upon the Confederate cause as lost, and therefore come forward and take the oath of allegiance to the United States." They had no love for the Union, he added. A correspondent whose letter was printed in the Cincinnati *Daily Commercial* on February 16, 1865, expressed the opinion that there were not twenty respectable whites in the whole city who really favored the Union. He believed that if they could, "the majority of the people would cut all our throats tomorrow." During a hearing of charges against Henry F. Willink, Jr., builder of the warships *Savannah, Georgia, Macon* and *Milledgeville,* Willink denied nothing, freely admitting his Southern sympathies and his activities. Impressed by this frankness, the presiding naval officer recommended his release. "He was the only rebel and secessionist left in Savannah," the officer sardonically commented. He had found everybody else there "strong Union men." [28]

But a more friendly feeling toward the enemy did exist at Savannah than in most places in the South. "None of the rank bitterness found in Nashville, Memphis, Vicksburg and New Orleans" had been discovered by a correspondent whose piece appeared in the Cincinnati *Gazette* on January 2, 1865. Soldiers' letters teem with such observations. Lieutenant John Henry Otto noted the absence in Savannah of what he called "that defiant, proud, hatefull mien [and] the insulting remarks which we had to endure everywhere before." According to Captain Eli J. Sherlock, "There don't seem to be much of a rebel spirit in Savannah compared with Atlanta." A Wisconsin officer reported a sociability "we did not usually encounter in the South." The Lodge of the Freemasons was a center of fraternizing between Sherman's soldiers and Savannahians. "Rebels and Union men mingled," wrote a Northern Mason, "as if no war was going on, and I doubt not each prayed that the clangor of arms might soon cease." [29]

Lieutenant Colonel Robert P. York, who served as Provost Marshal at Savannah after Sherman's departure, could say amen to all this. At Vicksburg the women had thrown garbage on him as he rode through the streets. *"Garbage,* madam!" he emphasized in telling his experience to a Savannahian. To epitomize the contrast at Savannah, he received from the appreciative wife of a Confederate officer (apparently he had done her the favor of allowing a letter to her husband to go through the lines) a note which said, "I have heard that you have a family of your own. May Gods blessings rest on you & yours is the sincere prayers of Emma P. Hopkins." [30]

Discounting the fact that some people were prone to tell the Union soldiers what the latter wanted to hear, most Savannahians were convinced that the Confederacy was beaten. They were sick of the war. The presence of the Union Army of occupation crystallized the latent peace sentiment in the city. During the week that followed the arrival of Sherman's Army Mayor Arnold had been thinking hard about these things. In his opinion, continued expenditure of blood was not only criminal but served to strengthen the hands of those prepared for the harshest measures against the South. [31]

Dr. Arnold now took a step that possessed ominous implications for the Confederate cause. In response to a petition signed by about seventy-five citizens he called a public meeting to discuss the present and future welfare of the city. Some of the names that appeared on it were a matter of "deep mortification," Howell Cobb informed Jefferson Davis.[32] According to the New York *Times,* no one who was present at the meeting estimated the attendance at less than seven hundred.

Congressman Hartridge had recently expressed the opinion at Richmond that his constituents were in a condition where "a little bad influence would make them forsake the Confederate cause & make what peace they can with the Yankee government." His fears were now realized. In opening the proceedings Mayor Arnold said he had weighed the matter anxiously and had arrived at a positive conclusion. In his opinion, there was but one course to pursue. There could be no doubt in anyone's mind what that course was. Resolutions were presented and unanimously adopted. "Burying bygones in the grave of the past," the citizens voted to submit to the "national authority under the Constitution," in accordance with Lincoln's amnesty proclamation.

Savannah was at peace with the United States of America.

As may be imagined, bitter reaction in the Confederate South followed this withdrawal from the war. "Savannah has gone down on her knees and humbly begged pardon of Father Abraham, gratefully acknowledging Sherman's clemency in burning and laying waste their State! Oh it is a crying shame, such poltroonery!" exclaimed Emma Le Conte. "Most disgraceful," wrote a Savannah soldier.[33]

The resolutions did not represent the views of a majority in the city, declared the Richmond *Examiner.* Their purport, it said, was that every man "must curse all that he blessed, and bless all that he cursed." Sherman's supposed magnanimity was "treacherous bait to deaden the spirit of resistance in other places," warned the editor. "These miserable Sycophants," the Augusta *Constitutionalist* called Savannahians on March 1, 1865. "If there is one sink lower than any other in the abyss of degradation the people of Savannah have reached it."

A strain of pathos appears in letters from soldiers written after their home town had given up the fight. "I am in good Spirits, keep in the same yourself. Things look dark, but I hope the cloud will soon blow over," Captain Joseph Thompson wrote his father from the field in Carolina. In February, 1865, Basinger wrote his sister from the trenches in Virginia that he was glad that the women in Savannah, unlike some of the men, had treated the enemy "as becomes them. . . . Undying hostility, in peace as well as war, in defeat as well as in success." George D. Smith wrote from Virginia concerning the efforts of the Confederate Peace Commissioners, "If I could prevent it no communication at all should be held with the Yankees except at the muzzle of a gun." [34] A greater peace than any on earth would soon descend upon this young officer out of the muzzle of a Yankee gun.

Irrespective of what the rest of the South thought about Savannah, the city reaped some immediate benefits from re-adherence to the old government. The assistance came opportunely as the populace was beyond self-help. In his remarks at the public meeting on December 28 Mayor Arnold pointed out that the people were "without food, without fuel, without any remunerative industrial pursuits." Overnight, he said on a later occasion, everyone was reduced to "one dead level of poverty." For example, there were the Telfairs, probably the richest family in Savannah. "With our pockets charged with Confederate money," wrote the husband of one of the sisters, "we have not a sixpence with which to buy the most ordinary articles." [35]

It was no mere coincidence that shortly after the meeting of citizens Sherman turned over to the civil authorities the food supplies left at Savannah by the Confederates, passing along the suggestion that the rice which thus came into their hands could be used as the medium of payment for needed provisions in the North. A somewhat remarkable individual now appeared on the stage as Savannah's benefactor. Julian Allen of New York had arrived shortly after Sherman. A Polish-American, he apparently became attached to the city because of Casimir Pulaski's association with it. Observing its plight and convinced of the sincerity of the inhabitants in their allegiance to the Federal government, he turned crusader. With the blessings of General Sherman and Mayor Arnold he sailed northward on a mission of selling the rice and raising funds for relief.

Eloquent appeals were made by Allen in New York on behalf of a city in which "it would awaken pity in almost any one to see the pale emaciated faces of the women and children." The general committee of the Chamber of Commerce in New York endorsed his plan although at the first meeting several members expressed dissent. One of them declared that "this milk-and-water business" was no way to coax the Southerners back into the Union as they never expected to return "except through the medium of sharp steel and hot lead." [36] There was, however, a generous response in New York and Boston. In Faneuil Hall Edward Everett appeared on the platform with Allen and made an appeal that was not only "one of the most touching which ever fell from his lips" but the last public utterance of his life. The meeting adjourned with "three cheers for Savannah and Sherman."

Three weeks after Allen left on his mission to the North the *Rebecca Clyde, Daniel Webster* and *Greyhound* entered Savannah harbor freighted with food. "All the staterooms unoccupied by the committee and the commissioner were crowded with layers of dressed turkeys, geese, ducks, and chickens," according to a Northerner named Chittenden who was sent along to report on actual conditions in the city.

Amidst this demonstration of good will a discordant note came from Sherman's chief of commissary. When a committee of Savannahians called on Colonel Beckwith to ask for military labor and for wagons to discharge the ships, the Vermonter interrupted the portly cotton factor who acted as chairman. "No! A hundred times no!" fumed Colonel Beckwith. "What lazy, miserable curs slavery made of men! A few years more of it and you would have had a nigger to open your eyes in the morning and to work your jaws at breakfast. . . . Now get out, all of you!" [37] Local labor unloaded the ships of mercy.

A correspondent of the New York *Times* colorfully described the scene at one of the distribution points for the supplies. He saw several hundred Savannahians, tickets in hand, standing in line awaiting their turn. "A motley crowd," he called it—"both sexes, all ages, sizes, complexions, costumes, gray haired old men . . . old 'Uncle Neds' . . . well-dressed women wearing crepe for their husbands and sons . . . women in linsey-woolsey, demi-white women wearing negro cloth, negro women dressed in gunny cloth; men with Confederate uniforms." It was "the ragman's fair," summarized the writer—the day of jubilee when "Charity, like a kind angel, has suddenly stepped in to ward off the wolf which is howling at their doors." [38]

On Allen's return to Savannah near the end of January he was praised by the *Daily Herald*. Christian generosity had never been more "liberal and munificent," declared the editor. The city's Northern benefactors were warmly thanked by a Savannah committee. "The hand of sympathy so generously extended to us ought to carry conviction to every unprejudiced mind," said a resolution, "that there is but one course to pursue, and that is to aim at a speedy termination of the unfortunate strife which has been devastating the country for nearly four years."

22.

In Occupied Savannah

⮑ A HARD core of rugged Confederatism did survive at Savannah. It was concentrated largely among the lady-folk. "They think they are so liberal giving us food & they stole more from one plantation than the whole of N Y subscribed," wrote an embittered Savannahian. Having seen Sherman's Army with her own eyes, she had to concede its strength. "Still with Gen Lee at our head & with the blessing of the Almighty," said Mrs. William H. Stiles, "we shall not be made slaves to these wretches." [1]

The bitterness of women was no more than to be expected. "On the street, at church, or in the drawing-room nearly every lady you meet is dressed in black," wrote a correspondent of the Cincinnati *Daily Commercial* on January 1, 1865. "I really pity the poor women," said Orlando Poe, reporting that they were all in mourning. "They suffer for the cause they adopted and have no right to complain." [2]

The feeling and the spirit of many women was exemplified by the widow Saussy who had five sons in the Confederate Army, two still in service, two in Northern prisons and one on crutches as a result of a wound. The thing that troubled her most was the fear that her two sons in the field might leave their commands and come home to Savannah to see her. This idea haunted her so, she confided to one of them, that she made it a special object of prayer. "I had rather that each of you had given his life for his country and been buried in an unknown grave than to have such a thing happen with one of my boys," Mrs. Saussy said. [3]

An attractive young die-harder who talked to a Boston war correspondent politely informed him, "I hate you of the North." In her opinion, the two sections could never live together in peace again. To have one's friends killed, one's servants taken away and then to know that you had failed was too much. "What we are to do I don't know," she confessed, but she for one hoped to leave the country.[4]

Women could not very well leave the country but they could at least leave sidewalks to avoid walking beneath the American flag. According to Mary Wragg Bond, one of the "many things that seemed hard for us to bear was the suspending of flags across the streets so as to compel us to walk beneath." The Savannah *Republican* published a letter in January complaining of the "childish" behavior of some females in refusing to show respect for the colors. The same paper became exercised itself when the city authorities failed to fly the American flag over the City Exchange on Washington's Birthday.

A paragon of devotion to the Confederate cause was pretty Fanny Cohen. Her only pleasurable moment on December 25, 1864, was in "looking forward to spending my next Christmas in the Confederacy." She saw no reason why enemies should be received as friends. "I shall never do it as long as I live," Miss Cohen promised herself. She was never so embarrassed in her life, she reported, as the day Captain Poe called in answer to a request from her father for assistance in preventing the appropriation by the military of his Lafayette Square residence. "My hatred for the Army in which he was an officer and my desire to be polite made me almost speechless," she said.

What Poe's own thoughts were can be surmised from a letter he had written to his wife a few days before. "The belles of the city," he said, "have signified their willingness to walk upon the street with the 'vile' Yankee officers—which is a great coming down from their lofty pride of three years ago." There was little coming down by Fanny Cohen. When another Union officer who came by her house expressed a desire to meet her father, she merely held the front door open. "He walked out," she satisfiedly recorded, "like a well bred dog."[5]

It is possible that the "bright little Jewess living on one of the great squares" who conversed with a Union naval officer a few days after the evacuation was a sister of Fanny Cohen. In an unguarded moment he referred to Savannah as having been "captured." The "dark-eyed daughter of Abraham" indignantly rejoined, "Our city has not been captured, Sir. Your General Sherman only came here to save himself from being captured by General Hood. Our army was short of stores, and General Hardee, who is a personal friend of mine, has merely gone away for supplies." [6] Another naval officer had a somewhat similar experience. Calling at the house of an old friend of his mother to convey a message, Lieutenant Alfred Mahan found her polite enough but obviously agitated. That she was trying hard to keep a stiff upper lip was "touchingly apparent," he said. "I don't admit yet that you have beaten us," the Savannahian blurted out at one point. "At the moment," Mahan confessed, "I could almost have wished that we had not." [7]

Commander Daniel Ammen called upon the wife of the old friend of his naval days and reported that Mrs. Edward Anderson acted "a little stiff." "This is a nice business you are engaged in, coming along our coasts to rob us of our slaves," she reproved. Later, however, she accepted a loan of several hundred dollars. On his return North Ammen wrote to her that he had arranged to send a monthly allowance until her husband got home ("his marching around the country as a soldier under Hardee was pure nonsense," he thought). [8]

People with strong Confederate ties did not seem to mind consorting with the enemy. Major Hitchcock described a gay party at Sherman's headquarters on the night of January 5 attended by a number of prominent Savannahians, including Francis Sorrel, the father of General Moxley Sorrel. The latter's sister was also present. While the ladies did not disguise their sympathy, reported Hitchcock, they showed none of the "vile rebel vindictive spirit you find elsewhere." [9] While his father was fraternizing with Sherman and conceding that the South's cause was utterly hopeless, Moxley was recovering from a painful leg wound he had recently received in Virginia. A few weeks later at Hatcher's Run a bullet pierced his lung, breaking the ribs on both sides. The wound hardly mended,

Sorrel was on his way to rejoin his command when he learned of Lee's surrender.

Nellie Kinzie Gordon could smile at herself in recalling her initial fear of the Federal soldier. When she ventured down Bull Street the day after the occupation, she concealed a small pistol in her belt beneath her coat in case anyone gave her any "sass." The soldiers most politely stepped out of her way, she reported. Born and bred in Chicago, Mrs. Gordon had acquaintances of high rank in Sherman's Army. She had the reputation in Union circles of being among the "rabid 'southrons.'" Some officers, including General Alpheus Williams, did not call on her for that reason.[10] But others did. Colonel William P. Carlin of Illinois became a guest in her house. Mrs. Gordon tried to ease the burdens of Savannahians through these associations. Her efforts were sometimes misunderstood. "If I had refused," she said, "they would only have said 'damned little Yankee, she will get everything she wants for herself, and won't do a thing to help anybody else,' whereas, now I have the satisfaction of having been of use to people, and I don't care a fig what any of them said or thought of me."

Sherman visited the Gordon house more than once, the occasion of his first call being to bring some "home letters." The General roared in laughter at the Confederate sympathies of the little children, especially Juliette Gordon. In a satisfied tone she informed General Howard who had lost an arm at Seven Pines, "I shouldn't wonder if my papa *did it!* He has shot lots of Yankees."[11] Less ingenuous than this future founder of the Girl Scouts of America, urchins would sing to the soldiers, according to a correspondent of the Cincinnati *Daily Commercial:*

> Jeff Davis rides a very fine horse,
>   And Lincoln rides a mule.
> Jeff Davis is a gentleman,
>   And Lincoln is a fool! *

---

* Colored children had their own songs. Jane Wallace Howard recorded in her diary on February 15, 1865, "To-day a little negro amused herself

One youngster, however, never got over his fear of the Yankees sufficiently to talk to them, much less sing derisive songs. The morning the enemy entered town George Pritchard was on his way to market. Espying the blue-clad soldiers, he ran home as fast as his legs would carry him, "bolted the doors, barred the windows and waited for something terrible to happen." One day when this thirteen-year-old youth passed the Green mansion he saw a tall, red-haired officer out in the garden. "Sonny," the soldier said, "I am General Sherman but that need not frighten you." It did, nevertheless. "I flew home," said Pritchard. At least one Savannahian who talked to the Union commander found him pleasant. William B. Hodgson came away believing that Sherman's true character was marked by "innate benevolence." His mind was "quickly perceptive," he was "genial" and he particularly liked to talk about Savannah families he knew.[12]

Some women in Savannah, it was thought, associated with the enemy for what they could get out of them. One day after looking in at the house of a neighbor whose husband was a Confederate officer, Fanny Cohen recorded in her journal, "She was entertaining Genl Davis and his Staff, buttering them well for her own ends. She is certainly a fascinating woman and will get all that she wants of these Yankees." *

Miss Cohen's disapproval of consortion with the enemy was perhaps more pronounced where the motivation was flirtation.

---

by jumping up and down under my window, and singing at the top of her voice:

'All de rebel gone to h——
Now Par Sherman come.' "

* The lady in question and Jefferson Columbus Davis of Indiana were perhaps kindred spirits. The General was a Democrat; indeed, "an infernal copperhead," a Union officer, Major James A. Connolly, thought. The latter was so incensed at Davis' treatment of the Negroes who followed the Army that he wrote a complaining letter from the lines outside Savannah to his congressman-elect. Furthermore, Davis had posted guards over the property of wealthy rebels and had courted the smiles of rebel women, tattled Connolly.[13]

"Just between you and I," young Captain Charles W. Wills confided to his sister, "I have found the sweetest girl, here that ever
man looked at. She is just your size & form, with large very deep
brown eyes, almost black, that sparkle like stars. I swear I was
never so bewitched before." When the Illinois officer departed, his
"fair Ladye-Love" drove out in a carriage to Thunderbolt for what
he described as a "few fond farewells & c's." [14] Needless to say,
there were Northern counterparts of Southern Fanny Cohens.
Forty years later, when Wills' sister published his letters and
diaries, she deleted all references to the girl her brother had
courted in Savannah.

The problem of supporting themselves brought many Savannah
women into commercial relations with the conquerors. The people
were terribly hard up. "What things they have they are obliged to
sell in many cases for the necessities of life," reported a New York
visitor. [15] The thousands of troops in and around Savannah constituted a ready market. The Yankees were a blessing in disguise,
confessed a Confederate. "The soldiers had plenty of money to buy
whatever the citizens had, and paid well for it." Most Savannah
housekeepers had a knack for making cakes and pastries. "Come,"
said one of them shortly after Sherman arrived, "let us up and be
doing! These Yankees all want something sweet and we want
some greenbacks." [16]

The basements of fine residences became pastry shops. "How
are the mighty fallen!" jeered *Frank Leslie's Illustrated Newspaper* in February, 1865. "If ever God chastened a rebellious people, he has visited our erring brethren." It asked its readers to try
to imagine the Astors, Belmonts, etc. "turning cake vendors here
to gain a little Confederate script." Vending cakes was, however,
a hardly less respectable calling than that of charging exorbitant
rents or interest rates. At least it was more genteel than the occupation of some Savannah females; an old Irish lady, for instance, sold
to soldiers whiskey described by the *Republican* as able to "kill in
forty minutes at fifty yards."

The same ladies who vended sweetmeats to the Union soldiers
probably turned their backs when the Yankees paraded through

Savannah. There were plenty of opportunities to watch them. "General Sherman appears proud of his army and is determined that the citizens of Savannah shall see it in its best trim," wrote a Northern officer. One of the first orders issued by him after reaching the city was for a review of the 15th Army Corps on Christmas Eve. "It was a beautiful day, bright and sunny," recalled a member of the 3rd Wisconsin. "For several hours the stream of troops filled the broad handsome avenue, marching one column north and one south, all moving, swaying to cadence step, in unison with martial music that filled the air with joy and gladness to the Union cause." [17] During the following week the other three corps were reviewed. Looking at the bronzed veterans of the 14th march by with "proud firm tread, their tattered flags fluttering in the Atlantic breeze," Major Connolly could scarcely refrain from shedding tears of joy. The review of the 20th Army Corps on December 30 with the "prancing steeds, gaily caparisoned," the "battle scarred colors" and "superb bands" presented "a kaleidoscopic picture which words cannot paint," reported the *Republican*. General Alpheus Williams was proud of the showing his corps made that day. "Hundreds of officers have told me it was the finest and most splendid review they ever saw. Gen. Sherman confesses it was the best of all."

The troops marched past many homes where blinds were drawn. "Every ones' shutters were tightly closed," wrote Nellie Gordon. A colored servant never forgot what Mayor Arnold replied when he was requested to order the women and children to turn out for a review. Despite his desire to make peace with the Union, Arnold felt he must point out that fathers, sons, brothers and sweethearts were still away fighting for the Confederate cause. "Do you think I would order them out to see your soldiers parade? Sir, I'll be damned if I do!" "Yes, sir, thems the exact words the Mayor said and I heard him say em," emphasized the former slave. [18]

No proclamation was needed to get the colored folk out. An Illinois soldier was impressed by the "capers the darkies cut" as they rushed after the bands, "dancing, hopping and slapping their hands." But the center of attraction at parades was always Sherman himself. The troops saw the General as they never saw him in the field. "Uncle Billy's dolled up like a duke," whispered one drummer-boy of the 10th Michigan to another during the review of the 14th Corps.[19] When the Commanding General passed through the streets of Savannah on one occasion that December, his route was jammed by the inhabitants "as closely as ever the Boulevards of Paris were when Napoleon rode through them," reported the Cincinnati *Gazette.*

The Northern soldiers found much that they liked about Savannah besides oysters. To be sure, there were exceptions. A diarist in the 92nd Illinois rated the city as "third-class," describing the buildings as "old, tumble-down things; the streets, beds of loose sand." The place was "old and dilapidated," wrote a Wisconsin soldier who declared that "the disparity in the width of the streets are in keeping with the extreme conditions of the people—the Oligarch and the 'poor trash.' " An Ohio soldier of few words recorded in his diary after a visit from camp, "See every thing that can be seen and return. Dont think much of the place."[20]

As a whole, however, impressions were favorable. Savannah possessed a quality different from anything that the Midwesterners had ever seen. "Our whole army has fallen in love with this city," said Major Connolly. In the eyes of an Indiana surgeon it possessed "every mark of wealth, intelligence, refinement & aristocracy." A member of the 104th Illinois reported that the soldiers were "charmed with its beautiful appearance, so different from anything seen before."[21]

A correspondent of the Cincinnati *Daily Commercial* was reminded of the "scenery, and grandeur, and romance" of Italy. "A vaery nice Place" was the verdict of Private Essington who reported that "the Buildings look Ancient and appear to be built after some other country stile than America." * To a soldier named

---

* It is a wonder Essington was in the mood to look at architecture. He was still starry-eyed over the accomplishments of Sherman's Army. Describing a review of his brigade at Savannah on December 26, this Indiana private reported that it was "not as Prety as some we have had but the Boys are as Proud over it as eney we ever had some had one

Hoadley the place was "old and rusty" but "it looks as though their was more business done in it than any place we have ever taken." A Methodist preacher who had enlisted in an Illinois regiment described the "senery" around Thunderbolt as "Beautifully grand even beyond Description." [22]

The Northerners were indefatigable sightseers. "This being a seaport and an old city, has many sights new and strange to us," explained a member of the 50th Illinois Regiment. The men "take great interest viewing the surroundings, strolling everywhere." He could not help reflecting how foolish it was that a people living amid such beauty "should desire a change in government, and seek to destroy what has cost so much to build up." [23]

The Pulaski monument in Monterey Square attracted much attention from the strollers. Among those who viewed the work was D. Lieb Ambrose of Illinois. As historian of his regiment, he later conjured up the spectacle of rebel traitors at its base swearing that the Union for which Pulaski gave his life should be "consigned to the wrecks of the dead empires." That fantasy become fact in Ambrose's mind, he could rhetorize, "Oh! wicked men, why stood ye here above the dust of Poland's martyr, seeking to defame his name and tear down what he helped to rear!" The monument was "the nicest thing I have seen yet" (in what was "not a very nice town"), said another soldier who added, "It is a wonder that the rebels have not disfigured it." An Indiana surgeon reported that the inhabitants who were proud of the memorial to this martyr to the cause of American liberty "have been exposing their lives for American slavery." [24]

Everywhere that Chaplain John Hight went in Savannah he seemed to find sermons in stones. On the Pulaski monument the use of the shield of Georgia instead of that of the United States was a manifestation of "the sectional pride" that had brought ruin to the people of the State. The Nathanael Greene monument was

---

Pants Leg alike some did not some had shoes on some did not but all had a crown which is woren onley by those who have Passed through what we have in the Past 3 month."

described by Hight as "an unsightly pile of large, square stones." He attributed its "wretched execution" to the fact that funds with which the monument was erected had been raised by a State-authorized lottery.

This Indiana clergyman could even find a moral in the fountain in Forsyth Place. The "four old satyrs" from which jets of water once flowed were now without occupation, said Hight, "naked, and dirty as a rebel soldier." One of them which had fallen over in the fountain was a symbol of a city attempting to wash herself "in the muddy pool of her own sins." When this good chaplain passed the grave of an Indiana volunteer who had died near Savannah, he left with the sleeping soldier, "solitary and alone, in a strange land," the comforting assurance that "his rest will be as quiet here as anywhere, and the power of the resurrection will be as effectual here as anywhere else; nor will it militate against one's eternal interests to rise in Georgia." [25]

Cemeteries were included in the sight-seeing, particularly Bonaventure. To an Illinois officer it was a "most grandly solemn, & most appropriate, resting place for the dead." However, a correspondent of the Cincinnati *Daily Commercial* thought that the moss-covered oaks, drooping evergreens, mournful shade, murmuring river and "grand, gloomy" surroundings combined to make it the "most weird place" he had ever visited. He was more impressed with Laurel Grove where he saw the tomb of Francis S. Bartow. "A brave man, no doubt," observed the Northern reporter, "but now that he fills a traitor's grave it ought to be so marked, if marked at all." Others, not exactly sight-seers, visited the old Colonial burial ground in town where the inhabitants had, according to rumor, hidden their silver. "Many of the graves and vaults were ransacked," said a resident, "and the bones & skulls scattered about, hoping to find valuables secreted there." [26]

The churches were both admired and frequented by the soldiers. "A beautiful and lovely day for Christmas," one of them wrote on December 25, 1864. "I attend Church in the morning and afternoon at the St. Johns Church (Episcopal) a fine large building and well filled, a good many Ladies in attendance & several Maj

Genls as well as Brig. Genl's." Chaplain George W. Pepper preached "a remarkable sermon," said an Ohio soldier who supposed "he did his best as Gen. Sherman and his staff was present." [27]

Pepper described the Independent Presbyterian Church as easily the finest religious house he had ever seen and Christ Church as "a perfect gem." The rector of the latter church once found himself in trouble as the result of his failure to pray for the President of the United States. The omission caused "considerable commotion among both officers and privates, as well as loyal citizens," reported a local newspaper. Its comment was an outgrowth of a letter from a Federal soldier inquiring why the Reverend Coley should not be required to offer a prayer for the President of the United States and all in civil authority. By way of reply, the editor repeated an anecdote going the rounds. It seems that one of the "rebel Episcopal divines" paid a call upon Sherman to learn whether or not it was permissible for him to pray for the President of the Confederate States. "Pray for Jeff. Davis, why certainly!" said the General. "You ought to pray for him every day, for Jeff. Davis and the d—l need praying for very much." [28]

No such problem existed in the colored churches. "The ministers here will not pray for the President, except the black clergymen," reported a correspondent. "They pray heartily for him and the Government." And, of course, for Sherman, too. "Been prayin' for you all long time, Sir," a freedman told him in Savannah, "prayin' day and night for you, and now, bless God, you is come." [29]

Charles Coffin wrote a lively description of an assembly of several hundred Negroes in the Second African Baptist Church. The meeting was called to explain Sherman's field order authorizing freedmen to occupy abandoned lands. After the singing of hymns, General Rufus Saxon announced that he had come to tell them what the President of the United States had done for them. "God bless Massa Linkum!" they chorused. "You are all free," Saxon informed them. "Glory to God! Hallelujah! Amen!" came a tumultuous response. "God bless General Sherman! Amen! that's so!" they shouted when "Chaplain" Mansfield French (a New

England Abolitionist referred to as their "white Jesus" by some Georgia Negroes) told them, "Your freedom is the gift of God. The President has proclaimed it, and the brave men of General Sherman's army have brought it to you." [30]

What they would do with it remained to be seen. Only time would solve the problem, thought one of Savannah's large slave-holders, of whether freedom would destroy or preserve the African race. "Slavery as it existed may be modified," wrote William B. Hodgson in December, 1864. He believed a state of serfage or ascription to the soil was inevitable, predicting that if the European race could not contract the labor of the African under some form, the latter must die out or the white race be transported to another soil. "The negroes are gone," wrote Richard T. Gibson who ventured the opinion that the conquerors would make them remain with their masters "a certain number of years receiving a certain sum annually for wages." The death of slavery, which he called "our bane," was good riddance. In peace, said this Savannahian, the institution had "prevented the development of the ingenuity and energy of the south" and in war it had proved a source of weakness.

Among the inhabitants Charles Coffin talked to in Savannah was the young lady (already mentioned) who hated Yankees generally. The conversation was on a friendly enough plane though the Southerner spoke with flashing eyes that "added charms to her beauty." They soon got around to the topic of slavery. "I don't care anything about keeping the negroes in slavery," she told the reporter. What worried her and her kind, Coffin concluded, was the fear of social equality. Abolition seemed to represent the breaking down of all such distinctions and to Southerners such a thought was "intolerable." [31]

According to Jane Wallace Howard, "The Yankees and negroes appear to be on the most intimate terms—a perfect equality prevails." Such statements frequently came second and even third hand; for example, the story that Fanny Cohen repeated in her journal on Christmas Day, 1864. "This morning," she wrote, "my uncle Mr Myers and his daughter Mrs Yates Levy came to see us and told us of a party given the evening before by the negroes at Genl Geary's Hd Qrts where the Gen went into the kitchen and desired an introduction to the *ladies* and *gentlemen* there assembled. After the introduction he asked who were slaves and who were free. There was but one slave present a servant girl of my Aunt's who acknowledged the fact. This elegant gentleman enquired into her private history and finding that she was a married woman begged an introduction to her husband Mr *Valentine*. He then presented Mr Valentine, as a Christmas gift, with a *free wife*. The girl was so much amused having always been a favorite servant and treated like one of the family that she told it to her mistress as a good joke."

More immediate than the fear of interracial association was that of the city being garrisoned by Negro troops. The subject was a "perfect bugaboo" to Savannahians, Sherman informed Halleck. Writing from the field, Joseph C. Thompson told his father that he was "nearly crazy" with worry over his mother and sister, especially after Sherman "leaves the place, and it is garrisoned by Foster and his negro troops." He would not think of it, if he could avoid the thought. When William B. Hodgson broached the subject to the General, he replied, "I have not a negro soldier in my army." [32] He respected local feeling on the subject but commented that "people are more influenced by prejudice than by reason."

Politics were distasteful to the Union General. He was fighting a war, not revolutionizing a social order. But cold eyes were watching him. Black Republicanism was ready to have its day. While in Savannah during January, 1865, Secretary of War Stanton spent hours interviewing some Negro clergymen whom he called in to answer the question, "What do you want for your own people?" Stanton personally transcribed their answers. He did Sherman the discourtesy of having him leave the room when he inquired as to the attitude of the colored people concerning the General himself. "His conduct and deportment toward us characterize him as a friend and a gentleman," he was assured. Upon that subject only one was unwilling to express an opinion. He

was also the lone dissenter when others said they preferred that
the colored race live by themselves rather than among the whites.
"There is a prejudice against us in the South that will take years
to get over," the other nineteen believed.[33]

Meanwhile, Sherman had received a friendly admonition from
General Halleck. Everyone was praising him in the North but
there was a certain element possessed of influence with President
Lincoln which was raising a point about him and "Inevitable
Sambo." He was being accused of showing "an almost *criminal*
dislike to the negro," Halleck informed him.[34]

What did they want of him? Had he not allowed several thousand Negroes to tag along behind his Army through Georgia as
virtual wards? He had acted toward them the part of a "Christian"
soldier, a fact to which one of his Negrophile officers, Major
Connolly, could attest. As for the criticism going around about
General Jefferson C. Davis, that officer was strictly a soldier and
disliked having his wagon trains and columns impeded by the
hangers-on, said Sherman. "We all felt a sympathy," he said in
his *Memoirs,* "but a sympathy of a different sort from that of Mr.
Stanton, which was not of pure humanity, but of *politics.*"

His headquarters in Savannah had been thrown wide open to
the freedmen. Hundreds of them had come to see him—"old and
young, men, women and children, black, yellow and cream-
colored, uncouth and well-bred," said Major Hitchcock. "They
gather around me in crowds," Sherman informed Halleck, "and I
can't find out whether I am Moses or Aaron, or which of the
prophets." He generally received his callers in the upstairs room
in the Green house in which he was accustomed to work. "Well,
boys—come to see Mr. Sherman, have you? Well, I'm Mr. Sherman—glad to see you," he would say. After shaking hands he
was wont to offer some advice. They were now free, had "no
master nor mistress to *support*" any more and must be "industrious
and well-behaved, etc." [35]

Sherman was glad when the time came for his Army to get out
of Savannah and back in the field "to get into the pine-woods
again," as he put it, "free from the importunities of rebel women

asking for protection, and of the civilians from the North who were coming to Savannah for cotton and all sorts of profits." [36] And perhaps free, too, from "Inevitable Sambo."

"I am now moving my troops slowly & quietly to the new points from which I can converge rapidly to my intended place of convention," Sherman wrote in January, 1865. The movements preparatory to the campaign in the Carolinas had commenced. Early that month the 17th Corps and two divisions of the 15th were transferred by steamer to Beaufort. A geographically confused soldier informed friends back home that en route from "sivania" they "got so far down on the coast that we was over in south amarica." On January 17 two divisions of the 20th Corps crossed into South Carolina opposite Savannah. Three days later portions of the 14th Corps broke camp and marched up the right bank of the Savannah River. From Sisters Ferry where the troops crossed that stream a Union officer wrote, "Our stay in Savannah had been attended with so much pleasure and good feeling on the part of both soldiers and citizens that we turned our backs on the Forest City with emotions of regret." [37]

No such good feeling existed among the people to whom Sherman's attention was now turned. Letters and diaries of officers and enlisted men, and even chaplains, reveal quite clearly what was in store for South Carolina. A Minnesota private assured his wife that the people of that State would learn to know them "to their Sorrow," declaring that "the Boys have a prejudice against that State and will make their mark wherever they go." General Slocum declared that it would have been a sin for the war to be brought to a close "without bringing upon the original aggressor some of its pains." In a letter from Savannah Orlando Poe informed his wife, "We are on her borders, ready to carry fire & sword into every part of that state." Nor was evidence of William T. Sherman's own state of mind lacking. The march through South Carolina, he said, would be one of the "most horrible things in the history of the world." [38]

23.

"Externally the city is the same"

 ⎰ THE RIFLE honeymoon of Savannah and the North ended when Sherman departed. Conquest and occupation was not merely a bad dream; it was bitter reality. Reflecting philosophically on the new order of things in his journal, William B. Hodgson commented upon the "marked effects of moral depression" among a conquered people. Garrisoning produced a state of things that was "brutifying." Men's minds, touched by fear, hope and distrust, became "excessively distrait." In conversation Hodgson found persons requesting that remarks be repeated a second and even a third time. Men who owned substantial property but had lost every dollar of income therefrom sank "under the incubus of that property," he noted, while those who lived only by salaries or labor were "ingeniously contriving to make these available in the new currency of green-backs."

General Cuvier Grover succeeded Geary in command of the garrison left at Savannah. If it was any part of the duty of this Maine soldier to make the populace content, his regime must be accounted a failure. He possessed a singular capacity to irritate. "The people learned to regret General Geary the more" as his successor "did little to conciliate the people, but much to dishearten them," said a Union officer.[1]

The inhabitants were disheartened enough already. "One thing is certain," wrote a Savannahian, "if the present condition of things is to continue, there are no people on the earth who are more entirely enslaved than we will be, and to live here will be impossible to all who have known the blessings of freedom." In the perspective of defeat it seemed clear to him that "God was against us." "A more unhappy people than were the people of the South at the close of the late War the world had never seen," declared Henry R. Jackson in 1866. Merely to look about the city was depressing. It presented a most deplorable aspect, declared a New Yorker. "The deserted and decaying wharves, the closed warehouses, the total absence of anything like commercial enterprise, or even life" gave "a sombre and forbidden hue to the whole picture." [2]

One business flourished. Hotels were jammed with Northern visitors. Among the dignitaries who visited Savannah during this period were Simon Cameron, Abner Doubleday, William Lloyd Garrison and Henry Ward Beecher. A junketing group from Congress included John Sherman, Lyman Trumbull, B. F. Wade and James W. Grimes. "There is no pretence of business," wrote John Chipman Gray concerning the latter group, describing them and their ladies as "a very cheap looking lot." Later in the spring another politician visited Savannah, Salmon P. Chase. Whitelaw Reid who came with him wrote an interesting account of this Chief Justice of the Supreme Court of the United States catechizing his many Negro callers to ascertain whether they could be depended on to vote correctly if given the ballot.[3]

As if to strike an unhappy opening note for General Grover's administration, a disastrous fire occurred on January 28, 1865—a conflagration that consumed more than a hundred buildings, including the former Confederate arsenal located at West Broad and Broughton Streets. The fire was the work of "an incendiary," claimed the *Republican.* General John Foster blamed it on the rebels. Savannahians attributed it to disgruntled members of the 17th Army Corps.

Whatever the origin, it was a spectacle of "awful grandeur and sublimity," reported the *Republican.* "The flames leaping high in air, thrown up in columns by the thirteen-inch shells" made a "gorgeous" spectacle, according to Charles Coffin. Fragments of shells were thrown all over the city. It was impossible to convince some of the colored inhabitants that the Confederates had not returned. "My God, misstis, marster come shell we all," exclaimed one of them. "Never while I live," wrote William B. Hodgson whose house stood at the verge of the fire, "shall I cease to remember this night of horror." [4]

March saw the arrival of Negro troops. The 33rd, 54th and 102nd Massachusetts colored regiments were sent to assist in garrisoning the city. Well enough behaved, their presence was irritating to the whites. "There were many things that seemed hard for us to bear, such as having our City guarded by negro soldiers," wrote a Savannahian who added, "I must say, however, both white and col[ored] soldiers behaved remarkably well." [5] Conceding that many civilians and "some of our best soldiers" resented Negro troops, the *Republican* argued that the decision to enlist them should not be criticized. The editor complained of instances of colored soldiers being "jostled and sneered at by both soldiers and citizens." When a brickbat battle after a St. Patrick's Day parade occurred between white and Negro boys, the paper claimed that the whites (who objected to the colored youths attending the review of the 9th Connecticut) had started the fighting.

The incidents at Savannah prompted the *Republican* to editorialize, "These black troops are here in this city as United States Soldiers, sworn and enlisted to defend and uphold the Constitution and enforce the Laws of the United States Government, and as such all parties are bound to respect their uniform, if they do not the men who are clothed in them, no matter what their complexion may be." [6]

In March the authorities began to enforce an earlier order that all women whose husbands were in the Confederate service were to be sent beyond the Union line. "Will any of us who passed through the dreadful ordeal," reminisced the wife of an officer, "ever forget the day that the orders came for all Officers' wives and children to be sent across the lines?" A number of women were evacuated by boat up the Savannah River. Protesting against "so cruel and barbarous an order," General P. M. B. Young assured General Grover that friends would welcome them again to their protection. "My!" wrote Mary Drummond, "what a pleasure it was for *us* refugees to see the familiar faces and the dear old uniforms of grey and meet those interested in us; oh, such a meeting!" [7]

Four years later Savannahians were still incensed about the order of deportation. Long after all the charges of wrongdoing against Sherman were forgotten this "crowning act of oppression" would remain a disgrace to the man who years before, as a lieutenant in Savannah, was hospitably received by relatives of the women he now sent from their homes. Sherman was not to blame. While at Savannah he refrained from enforcing a policy that came from higher up. William B. Hodgson wrote during the occupation that the General refused to execute the order—"an evidence" of what he called "his humanity and good feeling." [8]

Removal of the dead rather than the living from their abode seems to have disturbed Bishop Augustin Verot. Immediately east of the Catholic cemetery on the Thunderbolt Road the Confederates had erected an earthwork called Fort Brown. When Sherman's engineers laid out a more constricted line to protect the city against attack while in Northern hands, that fortification became part of the new defenses. The engineers recommended that the most effectual way of protecting communications with the river was to enclose the Fort. (What Confederate force was going to endanger those communications in March, 1865, is a riddle.) At any rate, Fort Brown was closed in and in the process the cemetery was desecrated by removal of some of the dead. Verot bitterly complained. Hearing that General Gillmore (at whose order the work was done) was a Catholic, the Bishop wrote to him, "It imposes on me the obligation to mark you of the censures of the Church against those who usurp her property." [9]

During these weeks Lee's Army was being hacked to pieces in Virginia. "The toils were closing around the lion," said Major Basinger. The winter had been one of great hardship. Living in tents of rotten canvas on rations of one pound of corn meal and one-third pound of inferior bacon a day, "the experiences of Washington's Army at Valley Forge could scarcely have been more severe," declared Basinger. Sherman's march to the sea depressed everyone. Letters from home complaining of dire want and urging the return of husbands, fathers, sons and brothers took their toll from the Volunteer Guards. There were many desertions. "The negro musicians of the Guards to whom every solicitation to desert was offered in vain, were more faithful than they," wrote Basinger.

The Guards' last fight at Sayler's Creek, Virginia, on April 6, 1865, was memorably chronicled by Major Basinger. " 'Charge bayonets, forward, double-quick, march!' Never did such command meet with more willing or more magnificent response. . . . It was a thrilling and inspiring spectacle, that line of leveled steel as it rushed forward to the attack. . . . The shock was irresistible." The fighting became a series of individual combats, continued Basinger, in which "every man of the Guards was engaged in personal conflict with one or more of the enemy." [10] Of the eighty-five men left in the outfit thirty were killed and twenty-two wounded. The survivors were made prisoners when General Ewell surrendered.

Three days later came Appomattox. "Lee has surrendered to Grant!" trumpeted the Savannah *Daily Herald* which called it the "Most Glorious News of the War." The Southern Confederacy "will speedily be but a dark shadow of the past," said the editor. As to whether its shadow was dark men might differ; that it belonged to the past was beyond debate. Two weeks later in North Carolina General Johnston surrendered. It was difficult for Clement Saussy of the Chatham Artillery to believe as he looked about him that the scarecrows he saw, some of them barefooted, were the same men who had gone down to Fort Pulaski in January, 1861, with fine uniforms, polished shoes, trunks of clothing, cases of whiskey and old wines, and cooks and butlers "galore." [11]

On Easter Sunday one of the last battles of the war was fought at Columbus, Georgia. Charles A. L. Lamar, among the first to enlist in the South's cause, was one of the last to fall. The devil-may-care Savannahian epitomized Northern conceptions of his class. He had fought a duel. He had been a party to bringing in one of the last slave ships to enter the country. He was killed at a post of great danger where he stationed himself beyond the call of duty. When the commanding officer protested his presence, telling him that the men had been put there to be sacrificed, Lamar's reply was, "I know it. I heard you were down here and I have come to stay with you." His remains were later reburied at Savannah. "Poor Charley Lamar," reported Mercer, "was interred as he had lived in the midst of storm and tempest." [12]

The storm and tempest were over, too, for Abraham Lincoln. "Saturday," wrote a Savannahian, "we were all startled & electrified by the hopes of peace foreshadowed in Lee's surrender & yesterday by the horrible tidings of the murder of Lincoln." A public meeting was called by the City Council and resolutions of regret and of indignation were adopted. Memorial services for the dead President were held in Johnson Square where the Mayor and aldermen sat on the platform with high-ranking Union officers. The editor of the *Republican* never recalled "so large an assemblage of human beings collected together in our city." But beneath the veneer of official sorrow at Savannah there were dissenting, if silent, opinions about Lincoln. "He was not a martyr," protested William Basinger, "for, much as we may object to and condemn assassination, he committed a monstrous crime in making war upon us, and his tragic death was no more than just punishment for that crime." [13]

One month after Lincoln's death Jefferson Davis came to town. He arrived from Augusta on a tug along with other prisoners, including Alexander Stephens, Clement Clay and General Joseph Wheeler. The party stopped briefly at Savannah before being transferred to a coastal steamer. While there, a captain in the Quartermaster Department undertook an unsuccessful search for milk for the Davis baby. The Union officer later complained to Susan Howard Waring that Savannahians were "not very patriotic" as he could obtain no milk for love or money. "You tried probably, in your name," stated Mrs. Waring. It was true. "Had you used that of Mrs. Davis," she informed him, "there is not in Savannah a Southern woman who would not have felt honored by the application. . . ."[14]

Mrs. Davis was separated from her husband at Hampton Roads. She came back to Savannah where she stayed at the Pulaski House—under military surveillance. Residents of the city were kind to her. According to the wife of Clement C. Clay, "The people of Savannah acted as by one great impulse of generosity."[15] Mrs. Davis was desperately unhappy. When she read in the Savannah *Republican* that her husband had been placed in shackles, she shut herself in her room and gave way to hysterical sobbing.

In May the bedraggled soldiers of Johnston and Lee began to drift back to Savannah. "It was like a dead town," said Olmstead. For want of anything to do the men would gather daily and swap stories of their war experiences. The authorities did not like the looks of the thing and forbade the wearing of the Confederate uniform. After the commanding officer became convinced the men had nothing else to put on the order was rescinded. But the Confederate buttons were to be removed or covered over.[16] "The dear old coats of grey!" wrote Mary A. Drummond. "We covered their buttons with black cloth instead of taking them off."

Whitelaw Reid was embarrassed by a "brutal scene" in a hotel in which a drunken sergeant insisted on cutting the buttons from the coat of a dignified, gray-haired Brigadier just come in from Johnston's Army. Commodore Josiah Tattnall also refused to remove his buttons. When he passed a Negro guard one day without incident, a Savannahian who feared the "gallant gentleman would be insulted," was greatly relieved. The colored soldier stood at attention and respectfully saluted the old naval officer.[17]

In a poem entitled, "Doffing the Gray," Robert Falligant, a former officer in Lee's Army, injected this note of bitterness in the final stanza:

> Down with the vows we've made,
>   Down with each memory—

Down with the thoughts of our noble dead—
   Down, down to the dust where their forms are laid
And down with Liberty.[18]

Among the veterans who returned to Savannah that May was
George Anderson Mercer. Four years and four months had gone
by since he brought down to Fort Pulaski what he had called "the
glorious news of Georgia's secession from a perverted and oppres-
sive government." He now set down in his diary the thoughts of a
Southerner of his walk of life. "It would be difficult to paint in
words the change which has come over Savannah. Externally the
city is the same; but the iron has entered its soul, its whole social
organization has been subverted, and to all intents and purposes
it is a new place. Its rich have become poor, and new aspirants
for wealth and honor rise upon the ruins of its ancient inhabitants.

"I have not yet recovered from the stunning effect of mingled
surprise and grief caused by the sudden prostration of our cause.
The noble structure we had reared was leveled like a house of
cards." The future was sombre and offered only oppression for
"the hearts of our unhappy people." Looking back, there was a single consolation. Impartial history would record, declared Mercer,
that victories were won by the Confederacy as long as there was
a semblance of equality. "The starry cross of the South was never
lowered until a hostile vessel barred every river and inlet on her
coast, until her depots had been destroyed, her means of communication broken up, her finances prostrated, her Brigades reduced to Regiments, her Regiments to Squads, while the wide
world swelled the ranks of her enemies, and the slaves she nour-
ished in her bosom were converted into her foes."

The most poignant of Captain Mercer's sensations was the feeling he experienced of being a man without a country. One night
while his wife was reading *Vanity Fair* aloud to him she came to
the passage that described the enthusiasm evoked among some
English tourists in Germany when an orchestra played "God Save
the King." The tears actually rushed to his eyes, said Mercer in reflecting that there was "now no national song capable of producing similar emotions in me." [19]

Major William Basinger entertained few regrets about disunion. "I did not doubt then, have never doubted since, and have been confirmed in my belief by events since the unhappy result of the war that secession was the only course possible to us." Even if he had clearly foreseen all that had happened, Basinger would still have been in favor of it. His only regret was that he had not been able to "do more for Georgia."

George Washington Stiles of the Savannah Volunteer Guards returned home after the surrender, ill and in rags, accompanied by his faithful colored servant, Frank, who had followed him for more than four years. Thin and weak as the colored man was, he carried his master to his room. "Missus," Frank apologized to the mother of the Confederate officer, "we fought hard but we got beat."

NOTES

[Misspellings and peculiarities of speech in quoted material have been retained throughout this book.]

1. "We will sing the requiem of these United States"

1. Bartow's speech on September 17, 1860, was reported in full in *Southern Banner* (Athens, Ga.), October 11, 1860. See also I. W. Avery, *The History of the State of Georgia from 1850 to 1881* (New York, 1881), 127. Possibly with the passage quoted in mind, a Georgian wrote, "Barring its egotism—execrable under the circumstances—it is a capital speech and must do good." C. C. Jones, Sr., to C. C. Jones, Jr., September 28, 1860, in Charles Colcock Jones, Jr., Collection, University of Georgia Library, Athens.
2. "The Personal Reminiscences of William Starr Basinger, 1827–1910." Hereafter cited as "Personal Reminiscences." The original manuscript is in the University of Georgia Library. A typed copy is in possession of Major Basinger's daughter, Mrs. Edward P. Lawton of Savannah. Quotations appearing in this Chapter are from pp. 121, 140ff., 142 of the typescript.
3. William Howard Russell, "Recollections of the Civil War," *North American Review*, CLXVI, (March, 1898), 369.
4. Olmstead's war-time reminiscences (not to be confused with his Memoirs) are in Adelaide Wilson, *Historic and Picturesque Savannah* (Boston, 1889), 195–204.
5. "Diary and Note Book" of George A. Mercer, entry of "Oct. 31 to Nov. 26," 1860. This manuscript is owned by a grandson, John H. Mercer of Savannah and Hollywood. It is cited hereafter as Diary of G. A. Mercer (No. I) to distinguish it from the portions of his diary in the Southern Historical Collection, University of North Carolina Library, Chapel Hill. For preceding quotations in paragraph, see C. C. Jones, Jr., to parents, November 7, 1860, Charles Colcock Jones, Jr., Collection, University of Georgia Library; Mrs. G. J. Kollock to G. J. Kollock, Jr., November 11, 1860, in Susan M. Kollock, ed.,

"Letters of the Kollock and Allied Families, 1826–1884," *The Georgia Historical Quarterly*, XXXIV, (June, 1950), 155 (hereafter this publication is cited as *G.H.Q.*).

6. Lilla Mills Hawes, ed., "The Memoirs of Charles H. Olmstead," *G.H.Q.*, XLIII, (December, 1959), 389ff.

7. H. C. Wayne to Jefferson Davis, May 10, 1861, Confederate Memorial Literary Society, Confederate Museum, Richmond, Va.

8. H. C. Wayne to A. H. Stephens, November 5, 1861, in Papers of Alexander H. Stephens, The Library of Congress, Washington, D. C.

9. *Letters from Henry R. Jackson to the Hon. Alex. H. Stephens* (Savannah, November 26, 1860), 13.

10. Mrs. Mary Jones to C. C. Jones, Jr., January 3, 1861, in Charles Colcock Jones, Jr., Collection, University of Georgia Library. For preceding quotations in paragraph, see Richard D. Arnold to William C. Lowber, December 7, 1860; Arnold to Dr. James J. Waring, December 28, 1860, in Richard H. Shryock, ed., *Letters of Richard D. Arnold, M.D., 1808–1875* (Durham, N. C., 1929), 99, 100; Henry C. Wayne to Henry Simons, February 9, 1861, in records of Adjutant General's Office, Georgia Department of Archives and History, Atlanta.

11. Father James Hanson to Bishop Patrick N. Lynch, March 9, 1861, Archives, Catholic Diocese of Charleston, S. C. Bishop Verot's statement is quoted in Benjamin J. Blied, *Catholics and the Civil War* (Milwaukee, 1945), 63ff.; George H. Clark, Rector of St. John's Church, is quoted in T. Conn Bryan, *Confederate Georgia* (Athens, Ga., 1953), 231.

12. *Republican*, October 18, 1862. As to such lawlessness, see special presentment of a Chatham County grand jury, January Term, 1861.

13. Alexander R. Lawton to Joseph E. Brown, December 26, 1860, in Lawton folder, Georgia Department of Archives and History.

14. Augusta J. Kollock to G. J. Kollock, Jr., January 22, 1861, "Letters of the Kollock and Allied Families, 1826–1884," *G.H.Q.*, XXXIV, (September, 1950), 229. Hereafter they are cited as Kollock Letters.

15. Isaac W. Avery, *The History of the State of Georgia from 1850 to 1881*, 144ff.; Atlanta *Daily Intelligencer*, December 29, 1860.

16. "Memoranda April to August, 1861," in Edward C. Anderson papers owned by Mrs. Florence Crane Schwalb of Savannah, a great granddaughter of Colonel Anderson. The manuscript includes a resumé by Anderson of his activities up to his departure for England on May 25, 1861, at which time he commenced his war journal. A similar viewpoint concerning South Carolina was expressed by Anderson in later years. See Daniel Ammen, *The Navy in the Civil War. The Atlantic Coast* (London, 1898), 247ff.

17. C. C. Jones, Jr., to his father, October 18, 1860, in Charles Colcock Jones, Jr., Collection, University of Georgia Library.

2. "The Rubicon is passed—a new nation is born!"

1. Olmstead, Memoirs, *G.H.Q.*, XLIII, (December, 1959), 386ff., 388; Olmstead, "Fort Pulaski," *ibid.*, I, (June, 1917), 99; Allen D. Candler, ed., *The Confederate Records of the State of Georgia* (Atlanta, 1909), II, 9–12.
2. *The Wanderer Case: The Speech of Hon. Henry R. Jackson of Savannah, Ga.* (Atlanta, no date), 75.
3. Clement A. Evans, ed., *Confederate Military History* (Atlanta, 1899), VI, 8ff., 15.
4. Olmstead to his wife, January 16, 1861, in Charles H. Olmstead Papers, Southern Historical Collection, University of North Carolina Library.
5. Levi S. D'Lyon to William H. Stiles, January 9, 1861, in Mackay-Stiles Papers, Southern Historical Collection, University of North Carolina Library. For the immediately preceding quotation, see Augusta J. Kollock to G. J. Kollock, Jr., January 22, 1861, in Kollock Letters, *G.H.Q.*, XXXIV, (September, 1950), 229.
6. *Southern Confederacy* (Atlanta, Ga.), March 16, 1861; *Morning News*, March 15, 1861.
7. G. B. Lamar to Howell Cobb, March 25, 1861, in U. B. Phillips, ed., *The Correspondence of Robert Toombs, Alexander H. Stephens, and Howell Cobb*, published in *Annual Report of the American Historical Association for the Year 1911* (Washington, D. C., 1913), II, 552. For seizure of the guns and the ships, see Candler, ed., *The Confederate Records of the State of Georgia*, II, 24–32. For Northern reaction, see Kenneth M. Stamph, *And the War Came, The North and the Secession Crisis, 1860–1861* (Baton Rouge, 1950), 229.
8. Diary of G. A. Mercer (No. I), April 12, 20, 1861.
9. Isabel Habersham to Rev. Samuel D. Denison, May 14, 1861, in Samuel D. Denison Papers, Southern Historical Collection, University of North Carolina Library.
10. "God's Presence with the Confederate States" and "The Silver Trumpets of the Sanctuary," June, 1861, in bound volume in the Georgia Historical Society, Hodgson Hall, Savannah, entitled, "Memoirs & Sermons of Rt. Rev. S. Elliott, D.D., Bishop of Georgia." The charge concerning "star-spangled" idolatry had been earlier made by another minister. Charles C. Jones, Sr., father of the Mayor of Savannah, claimed that the Northern people had gone mad on the subject of the Union.

"The God they are worshipping is worshipped under the image of the 'Star Spangled Banner!'" Jones to his son, May 16, 1861, Charles Colcock Jones, Jr., Collection, University of Georgia Library.

3. "We are a miniature Sparta"

1. A. R. Lawton to H. C. Wayne, February 9, 1861, records of Adjutant General's Office, Georgia Department of Archives and History.
2. William Starr Basinger, "The Savannah Volunteer Guards, 1858–1882," 55. The original manuscript is in the University of Georgia Library. Page references herein are to a typescript in possession of the Guards organization, Savannah.
3. For adoption of color of the uniform, see Basinger, "Personal Reminiscences," 144; Basinger, "The Savannah Volunteer Guards," 53. The two works of Major Basinger are frequently repetitive.
4. Augusta J. Kollock to G. J. Kollock, Jr., January 22, 1861, in Kollock Letters, *G.H.Q.*, XXXIV, (September, 1950), 230.
5. William Howard Russell, *My Diary North and South* (New York, 1863), 62.
6. For the Bartow-Walker exchange, see *The War of the Rebellion: A Compilation of the Official Records of the Union and Confederate Armies* (Washington, D. C., 1880–1901), Series I, LIII, 136, 142–144. This work is hereafter cited as *O.R.* One of the Confederate officers sent to Pulaski was James C. Barrow who had resigned from West Point in January, 1861. In reference to the feeling at the Academy about the secession of Georgia he wrote, "People around here like the way Geo. acted a great deal better than they do the action of So. Ca. They say S. C. seemed as if she had gotten into a fit and run off. . . ." Barrow to a cousin, January 23, 1861, in James C. Barrow letters in possession of Dean Smith, Jr., Savannah.
7. Russell's account of Fort Pulaski was reprinted from the London *Times* in Savannah *Morning News*, June 20, 1861.
8. J. L. Branch to his mother, April 12, 1861, in Margaret Branch Sexton Collection of Family Letters, University of Georgia Library; James C. Barrow to his sister, April 5, 1861, in Colonel David C. Barrow Papers, University of Georgia Library. The Barrow letter is quoted in E. Merton Coulter, *Lost Generation: The Life and Death of James Barrow, CSA* (Tuscaloosa, Ala., 1956), 47; "W.J.N." to his family, April 9, 1861, reprinted from the Columbus *Times* in *Morning News*, April 18, 1861.
9. Olmstead, Memoirs, *G.H.Q.*, XLIV, (March, 1960), 60.
10. A. R. Lawton to H. C. Wayne, January 9, 14, 1861, in Lawton folder, Georgia Department of Archives and History.

11. Report of C.R.P. Rodgers, December 6, 1861, *Official Records of the Union and Confederate Navies in the War of the Rebellion* (Washington, D. C., 1897–1927), Series I, XII, 385. This work is hereafter cited as *O.R.*, Naval.

12. C. C. Jones, Jr., to C. C. Jones, Sr., June 1, 1861, Charles Colcock Jones, Jr., Collection, University of Georgia Library.

13. George Robertson to Simeon, August 25, 1861, in Robertson Papers, Georgia Historical Society. *Cf.* the statement of Charles C. Jones, Jr., to his father on September 14, 1861, that the batteries "are wholly unable to cope either with a fleet or even with a single ship of the line, armed with a battery of heavy guns, such as those now used on board the U. S. sloops and steamers of war."

14. Journal of Edward C. Anderson, November 6, 1864; Basinger, "Personal Reminiscences," 99.

15. Josiah Tattnall to Edward F. Campbell of Augusta, Ga., February 10, 1861, in *Morning News,* February 20, 1861. Tattnall's statement at the banquet and his death-bed remark are from Amos Lawrence Mason, ed., *Memoir and Correspondence of Charles Steedman, Rear Admiral, United States Navy* (Cambridge, Mass., 1912), 300, 301. For another account of Commodore Tattnall's death, see J. F. Kollock to his father, June 17, 1871, in Kollock Letters, *G.H.Q.,* XXXIV, (December, 1950), 324ff.

16. Clipping from the Rochester *Union* in Hanleiter Scrapbooks, Atlanta Historical Society.

17. H. C. Wayne to W. B. Hill, January 15, 1861, Adjutant General's Letter Book, December 22, 1860, to July 18, 1861, in Department of Archives and History.

18. H. C. Wayne to C. Manigault Morris, February 19, 1861; Morris to Wayne, March 4, 1861, in records of Adjutant General's Office, Naval Matters, Department of Archives and History.

19. Specifications of uniform for Georgia Navy, March, 1861, is in records of Adjutant General's Office, Naval Matters, Department of Archives and History.

20. John McIntosh Kell Papers, Duke University Library; Kell, *Recollections of a Naval Life* (Washington, 1900), 140; Munroe d'Antignac, *Georgia's Navy, 1861* (Griffin, Ga., 1945), 10–13.

21. James D. Bulloch, *The Secret Service of the Confederate States in Europe* (London, 1883), I, 143.

22. Bulloch, *The Secret Service of the Confederate States in Europe,* I, 143. For the reputed statement of the Commodore, see report of George W. Davis, a former schoolteacher at Darien, October 14, 1861, in *O.R.,* Naval, VI, 322. For Maffitt's opinion, see Journal in John

Newland Maffitt Papers, Southern Historical Collection, University of North Carolina Library.
23. William H. Russell, "Recollections of the Civil War," *North American Review*, CLXVI, (April, 1898), 501ff.; Russell, *My Diary North and South*, 63ff.

4. "I go to illustrate . . . my native State"

1. Diary of G. A. Mercer (No. I), April 25, May 30, 1861.
2. George Blackshear to his cousin, June 9, 1861, in J. William Blackshear Papers, Duke University Library; Jesse Glenn to Augustus R. Wright quoted in Avery, *The History of the State of Georgia from 1850 to 1881*, 205; George McRae to Martha T. Jones, June 17, 1861, "Letters From Confederate Soldiers," II, Department of Archives and History.
3. Henry C. Wayne to Jefferson Davis, May 3, 1861, in C. C. Jones Papers, Georgia Portfolio, II, 144, Duke University Library. For the immediately preceding quotation, see A. R. Lawton to J. E. Brown, June 17, 1861, Lawton folder, Department of Archives and History.
4. A. McC. Duncan, *Roll of Officers and Members of the Georgia Hussars . . . with Historical Sketch* (Savannah, 1907), 268ff.
5. Avery, *The History of the State of Georgia from 1850 to 1881*, 198. Isaac W. Avery was a member of the Oglethorpes.
6. Levi S. D'Lyon to William H. Stiles, June 24, 1861, in Mackay-Stiles Papers, Southern Historical Collection, University of North Carolina Library.
7. F. S. Bartow to J. E. Brown, May 21, 1861, in *Southern Recorder* (Milledgeville), June 11, 1861.
8. *Morning News*, May 22, 1861.
9. W. S. Rockwell, *The Oglethorpe Light Infantry of Savannah, In Peace and In War* (Savannah, 1894), 3. For letter, see *Morning News*, June 6, 1861.
10. Brown to Bartow, May 29, 1861, in *Southern Recorder*, June 11, 1861; Bartow to Brown, June 14, 1861, in *Morning News*, June 26, 1861.
11. *Proceedings of the Congress on the Announcement of the Death of Col. Francis S. Bartow, of the Army of the Confederate States* (Richmond, 1861), 25ff.
12. B. M. Zettler, *War Stories and School-Day Incidents For Children* (New York, 1912), 46, 58ff., 60ff.; *Morning News*, May 29, 1861.
13. Mrs. John H. S. Branch to James L. Branch, July 17, 1861, in Margaret Branch Sexton Collection of Family Letters, University of Georgia Library.

14. *Morning News,* February 4, 1862. "Who that heard his words," said the editor, "did not feel them sink like lead in his bosom?" For Ferrill, see *ibid.,* August 20, 1861; also G. B. Lamar to J. A. Ferrill, published in New York *Times,* August 12, 1861, and quoted in *Rebellion Record* (New York, 1862), II, 17ff.

15. *Proceedings of the Congress on the Announcement of the Death of Col. Francis S. Bartow . . . , op. cit.,* 12ff., 28.

16. Isabella D. Martin and Myrta Lockett, eds., *A Diary from Dixie as Written by Mary Boykin Chesnut* (New York, 1906), 87ff. On July 26, 1861, a local cabinetmaker and undertaker entered in his ledger book under Bartow's name the item, "1 coffin with trimmings 30.00." Two days later he entered, "To use of hearse horses & extra expenses $50.00." Ledger book of Thomas Henderson from 1857 to 1866, owned by Lindsey P. Henderson, funeral directors, Savannah.

17. C. C. Jones, Jr., to his father, July 24, 1861, Charles Colcock Jones, Jr., Collection, University of Georgia Library.

18. Olmstead to his wife, July 22, 1861, Charles H. Olmstead Papers, Southern Historical Collection, University of North Carolina Library.

19. Journal of Edward C. Anderson, August 4, 1861.

20. William Duncan to Godfrey Barnsley, August 8, 1861, in Barnsley Papers, Emory University Library.

5. Coming of the Vandals

1. Du Pont to Welles, October 29, 1861, in *O.R.,* Naval, XII, 230ff.

2. For quotations in this Chapter from George A. Mercer Diary (No. I), see entries for November 10, 11 and 13, 1861.

3. Albert Bigelow Paine, *A Sailor of Fortune, Personal Memoirs of Captain B. S. Osbon* (New York, 1906), 133ff.

4. Journal of Edward C. Anderson, February 26, 1862.

5. Journal of John Newland Maffitt in John Newland Maffitt Papers, Southern Historical Collection, University of North Carolina.

6. *O.R.,* Naval, XII, 488.

7. Egbert L. Viele, "The Port Royal Expedition, 1861, The First Union Victory of the Civil War," *Magazine of American History,* XIV, (October, 1885), 338. For the preceding quotations in paragraph, see Samuel F. Du Pont to John A. Dahlgren, quoted in *Memoir and Correspondence of Charles Steedman,* 367; Robert Chisholm, "The Battle of Port Royal," in C. R. Graham, ed., *Under Both Flags* (Chicago, 1896), 256.

8. Colonel J. A. Wagener's report is in *O.R.,* Naval, XII, 310. For offi-

cial reports of the expedition to Port Royal and the battle, see *ibid.*, 239–319; *O.R.*, VI, 3–29.

9. *Memoir and Correspondence of Charles Steedman*, 293.

10. Charles Lafferty to his sister, November 15, 1861, in the Lafferty Letters in possession of National Park Service, Fort Pulaski.

11. *War Diary and Letters of Stephen Minot Weld, 1861–1865* (privately printed, 1912), 42ff. For preceding quotation, see *The Diary of Elias A. Bryant of Francestown, N. H.* (privately printed, Concord, N. H., no date), 19.

12. Hawley's letter is quoted in W. A. Croffutt and John M. Morris, *The Military and Civil History of Connecticut During the War of 1861–65* (New York, 1868), 131.

13. C. C. Jones, Jr., to his father, November 9, 1861, Charles Colcock Jones, Jr., Collection, University of Georgia Library; William Duncan to Godfrey Barnsley, November 23, 1861, Emory University Library. For a refutation by Stiles of one of the stories, see *Morning News*, June 3, 4, 1862.

14. Mrs. George W. Anderson to her daughter-in-law, November 11, 1861, in J. Randolph Anderson Papers, Georgia Historical Society.

15. Ammen, *The Old Navy and the New* (Philadelphia, 1891), 349; Maffitt to his daughter, Florie, December 5, 1861, in John Newland Maffitt Papers, Southern Historical Collection, University of North Carolina Library. The affair was later patched up between Maffitt and Tattnall. The former became naval aide to General Lee. "The Commodore is a kind brave and generous man—but impulsive—passionate and ambitious," said Maffitt. *Ibid.*

16. Mrs. George W. Anderson to her daughter-in-law, November 11, 1861.

17. Quoted in James M. Merrill, *The Rebel Shore, The Story of Union Sea Power in the Civil War* (Boston, 1957), 39.

18. Drayton to L. M. Hoyt, January 18, 1862, "Naval Letters from Captain Percival Drayton, 1861–1865," in *Bulletin of the New York Public Library*, X, (November, 1906), 598.

19. George D. Smith to his aunt, November 15, 1861, in Baber-Blackshear Collection, University of Georgia. Smith was then stationed on Green Island. On November 9, 1861, Charles C. Jones, Jr., informed his father that Lee was "represented as severely condemning the policy adopted by our General." Charles Colcock Jones, Jr., Collection, University of Georgia Library.

20. Olmstead, Memoirs, *G.H.Q.*, XLIV, (March, 1960), 63ff. For the quotation concerning Lee at St. Simons, see J. F. Atkinson to his aunt, November 2—, 1861 (date blank), in McDonald-Atkinson-Lawrence

Papers, Georgia Historical Society. Olmstead to his wife, November 21, 1861, in Charles H. Olmstead Papers, Southern Historical Collection, University of North Carolina Library.

21. Diary of John Hart, November 24, 1861, owned by Miss Catherine Moss Pegg, East Orange, N. J. See also *O.R.*, Naval, XII, 324–328.

22. For reconnaissances by Captain Rodgers in Wassaw and Ossabaw, see *O.R.*, Naval, XII, 385ff., 396ff.; Joseph C. Thompson to William Tappan Thompson (the first page of the letter is missing), December ——, 1861, family papers owned by Edward W. Bell, Savannah; Basinger, "The Savannah Volunteer Guards," 89–92.

23. John L. G. Wood to his father, December 20, 1861, in Wood Letters, Department of Archives and History. The typewritten copies also on file in the Department contain numerous errors by the copyist.

24. Charles H. Davis [Jr.], *Life of Charles Henry Davis, Rear Admiral, 1807–1877* (Boston, 1899), 194; Mrs. George W. Anderson to her daughter-in-law, November 29, 1861, in J. Randolph Anderson Papers, Georgia Historical Society.

25. C. C. Jones, Jr., to his parents, March 18, 1862, Charles Colcock Jones, Jr., Collection, University of Georgia Library; Jones, *Historical Sketch of the Chatham Artillery* (New York, 1867), 63.

26. Bulloch, *The Secret Service of the Confederate States in Europe*, I, 143; Percival Drayton to L. M. Hoyt, January 18, 1862, in "Naval Letters," *Bulletin of the New York Public Library*, X, (November, 1906), 597.

27. James Harrison Wilson, *Under the Old Flag* (New York, 1912), I, 74. For other quotations in this Chapter, see Wilson, 80ff., 83ff.

28. Olmstead, Memoirs, *G.H.Q.*, XLIII, (March, 1959), 67.

29. Ammen, *The Old Navy and the New*, 359. Captain Davis' report on the Wilmington Narrows excursion is in *O.R.*, Naval, XII, 523–526. The report of General Wright, commanding the Union land forces involved, is in *ibid.*, 526–528. A Savannah soldier on Green Island wrote on January 28, 1862, "I wish and implor you to leave the city with all the children for some safe place in the country. . . . We are all excitement here." Joseph C. Thompson to his mother, family letters owned by Edward W. Bell. "We expect an attack upon the Batteries at almost any moment," C. C. Jones, Jr., informed his parents on January 27. Charles Colcock Jones, Jr., Collection, University of Georgia Library.

30. Charles K. Cadwell, *The Old Sixth Regiment* (New Haven, 1875), 30–32; Croffutt and Morris, *The Military and Civil History of Connecticut During the War of 1861–65*, 191.

31. *Military Reminiscences of Gen. Wm. R. Boggs, C.S.A.* (Durham, N. C., 1913), 24.

32. Alonzo Williams, "The Investment of Fort Pulaski," in *Personal Narratives of Events of the War of the Rebellion* (Providence, R. I., 1887), 33–38.

33. R. E. Lee to G. W. C. Lee, February 23, 1862, quoted in Douglas Southall Freeman, *R. E. Lee, A Biography* (New York, 1936), I, 627; Journal of Edward C. Anderson, February 11, 12, 1862.

34. Report of Commander John P. Gillis in *O.R.*, Naval, XII, 664.

35. Horace Montgomery, *Howell Cobb's Confederate Career* (Tuscaloosa, Ala., 1959), 50. For Brown's views on defending Savannah, see his letter to R. E. Lee, February 8, 1862, *O.R.*, VI, 377. Augusta *Constitutionalist* quoted in *Morning News,* February 17, 1862.

36. *Life of Charles Henry Davis,* 203ff.

37. Hawley to Gideon Welles, December 30, 1861, in Gideon Welles Papers, 28, 412ff., Library of Congress; Hawley to his wife, March 20, 1862, in Joseph R. Hawley Papers, VIII, The Library of Congress.

38. T. W. Sherman's correspondence is in *O.R.*, VI, 203ff., 209, 211ff., 217, 221, 235, 236.

39. The letters to Du Pont are in *O.R.*, Naval, XII, 485ff.

40. *Ibid.*, 492ff., 501ff.

41. McClellan to Sherman, February 14, 1862, *O.R.*, VI, 225; Sherman to Adjutant General, February 15, 1862, *ibid.*, 226.

6. The Brick Fort and the Rifled Cannon

1. Olmstead to his wife, November 21, 1861, in Charles H. Olmstead Papers, Southern Historical Collection, University of North Carolina Library; Olmstead, Memoirs, *G.H.Q.*, XLIV, (March, 1960), 66ff. It is probable that Lee was at Fort Pulaski on November 18 or 19. He visited Savannah at that period on his way south to inspect the coastal defenses.

2. Olmstead, "Fort Pulaski," *G.H.Q.*, I, (June, 1917), 102; Olmstead, Memoirs, *G.H.Q.*, XLIV, (March, 1960), 64.

3. *The Diary of Elias A. Bryant of Francestown, N. H.,* 28; Gray to his mother, August 21, 1863, in *War Letters, 1862–1865, of John Chipman Gray and John Codman Ropes* (Boston, 1927), 186; Report of Q. A. Gillmore in *O.R.*, VI, 144–165; Gillmore, *Official Report to the United States Engineer Department, of the Siege and Reduction of Fort Pulaski* (New York, 1862); Gillmore, "Siege and Capture of Fort Pulaski," in R. U. Johnson and C. C. Buel, eds., *Battles and Leaders of the Civil War* (New York, 1887), II, 1–12.

4. J. R. Hawley to his wife, December 29, 1861, in Joseph R. Hawley Papers, VIII, The Library of Congress; Gillmore to Greeley, November 12, 1863, in Horace Greeley Papers, The New York Public Library.

5. Wilson, *Under Two Flags,* I, 87. *O.R.,* Naval, XII, 704. See also *ibid.,* 365.

6. Hawley to his wife, March 3, 1862, in Joseph R. Hawley Papers, VIII, The Library of Congress.

7. Hawley to his wife, March 20, 1862, *ibid.* The preceding quotation in the paragraph is from Croffutt and Morris, *The Military and Civil History of Connecticut During the War of 1861–65,* 196.

8. R. E. Lee to C. H. Olmstead, February 17, 1862, in *O.R.,* VI, 389.

9. Stephen Walkey, *History of the Seventh Connecticut Volunteer Infantry . . . 1861–1865* (Southington, Conn., 1905), 44–46.

10. Diary of W. L. Landershine, in possession of National Park Service, Fort Pulaski, Georgia. Journal of Edward C. Anderson. The date of the entry, "Mon. 11/9/1861," is obviously incorrect as Anderson was then on the high seas. The proper date of the entry is clearly Monday, December 9, 1861. It is possible that parts of Anderson's journal were written from contemporary notes at a later period.

11. Olmstead, Memoirs, *G.H.Q.,* XLIV, (March, 1960), 68; Montfort to his family, February 23, 27, March 17, 1861, Theodorick W. Montfort Letters, Georgia Historical Society.

12. Montfort to his wife and children, March 18, 1862, *ibid.*

13. "Private Journal of E. W. Drummond," March 27, 1862. The diary is owned by Eugene D. Drummond of Jackson, Mississippi, a grandson of Major Edward W. Drummond.

14. A. R. Lawton to C. H. Way, April 9, 1862, in Alexander R. Lawton folder, Department of Archives and History; Olmstead, Memoirs, *G.H.Q.,* XLIV, (March, 1960), 68.

15. William Duncan to Godfrey Barnsley, March 11, 1862.

16. Diary of Cornelius R. Hanleiter, April 10, 1862, Atlanta Historical Society. Similar prayerful expressions are found in Edward C. Anderson, Jr., to his wife, April 10, 1862, J. Randolph Anderson Papers, Georgia Historical Society, and in Diary of G. A. Mercer (No. II), April 11, 1862. The Mercer Diary, No. II, is in the Southern Historical Collection, University of North Carolina Library. It covers the periods during the war not included in Diary No. I. See Bibliography.

17. Diary of W. L. Landershine, April 9, 1862; "Private Journal of Edward W. Drummond," March 30, 1862.

18. Wilson, *Under the Old Flag,* 88.

19. Diary of W. L. Landershine, April 10, 1861.

20. Wilson, *Under the Old Flag,* 89.

21. Q. A. Gillmore, "Siege and Capture of Fort Pulaski," in *Battles and Leaders of the Civil War,* II, 7.

22. Report by Captain C. R. P. Rodgers in *O. R.,* Naval, XII, 731.

23. The Confederate flag incident is reported in Landershine's diary,

April 10, 1861, and in F. D. Lee and J. L. Agnew, *Historical Record of the City of Savannah* (Savannah, 1869), 85.

24. Olmstead, "Fort Pulaski," *G.H.Q.*, I, (June, 1917), 103–104.

25. "Private Journal of Edward W. Drummond," April 11, 1862; Croffutt and Morris, *The Military and Civil History of Connecticut During the War of 1861–65,* 196; Hawley to his wife, April 14, 1861, in Joseph R. Hawley Papers, VIII, The Library of Congress.

26. Savannah *Republican,* April 23, 1862.

27. Q. A. Gillmore, "Siege and Capture of Fort Pulaski," in *Battles and Leaders of the Civil War,* II, 12.

28. Jones, *Historical Sketch of the Chatham Artillery,* 68; Jones to his parents, April 11, 1862, Charles Colcock Jones, Jr., Collection, University of Georgia Library. For the preceding quotations in this paragraph, see Harden to Captain Richard M. Cuyler, April [10], 1862, Ordnance Department Records, Confederate, CXXXVIII, 152, Record Group No. 109, The National Archives; William Duncan to Godfrey Barnsley, April 11, 1862, Emory University Library.

29. Olmstead to his wife, April 17, 1862, Georgia Historical Society; Hawley to his wife, April 14, 1862.

30. Jones to his parents, April 14, 1862, Charles Colcock Jones, Jr., Collection, University of Georgia Library.

31. Olmstead, Memoirs, *G.H.Q.*, XLIV, (March, 1960), 73.

32. *Battles and Leaders of the Civil War,* II, 8.

33. *O.R.*, VI, 167. Possibly the signalman was sent from Virginia following Captain E. P. Alexander's offer to establish signal communication between Fort Pulaski and Savannah. See Alexander's letter, January 28, 1862, in *O.R.*, LIII, 215ff. A notable instance of Corporal Law's courage is cited in Olmstead, Memoirs, *G.H.Q.*, XLIV, (March, 1960), 58ff. W. M. Davidson to his wife, April 13, 1862. The letter is in possession of his grandson, William Murray Davidson of Savannah.

34. Diary of G. A. Mercer (No. II), April 14, 1862, Southern Historical Collection, University of North Carolina Library. A typewritten copy of this diary is in the Georgia Historical Society, Savannah.

7. "A stronger place even than Charleston"

1. William Duncan to Godfrey Barnsley, February 14, 1862; James M. Merrill, ed., "Personne Goes to Georgia: Five Civil War Letters," *G.H.Q.*, XLIII, (June, 1959), 203.

2. The letter describing the excitement was reprinted in the New York *Herald,* April 19, 1862.

3. Duncan to Godfrey Barnsley, April 28, 1862. For the preceding quota-

tion, see Alfred L. Hartridge to his mother, April 16, 1862, in Hartridge family letters owned by Walter C. Hartridge, Savannah.

4. For correspondence relating to martial law, see *O.R.,* XIV, 478, 492, 495, 497.

5. Minutes, Mayor and Aldermen of Savannah, April 29, 1862; the Sandersville editor is quoted in Bryan, *Confederate Georgia,* 73.

6. Brown to Secretary of War, February 7, 1863, *O.R.,* LIII, 279; Alfred L. Hartridge to his mother, April 16, 1862, in family letters owned by Walter C. Hartridge.

7. W. H. Hood to parents, February 22, 1862, in "Reminiscences of Confederate Soldiers," II, Department of Archives and History; E. R. Harden to his mother, April 17, 1862, in Edward R. Harden Papers, Duke University Library.

8. "Personne Goes to Georgia," *G.H.Q.,* XLIII, (June, 1959), 205–207.

9. John L. G. Wood to his father, April 4, 1862, in Wood Letters, Department of Archives and History.

10. R. H. Moore to Joseph Espey, March 17, 1862, in Joseph Espey Papers, Southern Historical Collection, University of North Carolina Library; Joseph J. Hardy to Sophia Hardy, March 10, 1862, in "Letters from Confederate Soldiers, 1861–1865," II, Department of Archives and History; John L. G. Wood to a cousin, January 23, 1862.

11. *O.R.,* XIV, 337.

12. *Morning News,* May 9, 1862. A Savannahian wrote that month, "All quiet around our city except now and then the enemy sends up balloons with the expectation, they may discover any other troops to defend us except Georgians." G. F. Palmes to S. W. Nichols, May 28, 1862, in George F. Palmes Papers, Georgia Historical Society.

13. *O.R.,* XIV, 558; LIII, 246.

14. Wilson, *Under the Old Flag,* I, 91ff.; Hunter's orders are in *O.R.,* XIV, 333, 341.

15. John M. Bessmer to John Weissert, May 18, 1862, in Bessmer Letters, Michigan Historical Collections, University of Michigan. The author is indebted to F. A. O. Bahre of Savannah for the translation of this letter which is written in German. Percival Drayton to L. M. Hoyt, June 22, 1862, "Naval Letters from Captain Percival Drayton, 1861–1865," *Bulletin of the New York Public Library,* X, (November, 1906), 604ff.

16. *O.R.,* XIV, 599.

17. Wilson, *Under the Old Flag,* 85ff.

18. For Hunter's message, see *O.R.,* XIV, 335. For skirmish on Whitemarsh Island, April 16, 1862, see *O.R.,* XIV, 4–13; *Morning News,* April 18, 1862; *Republican* quoted in Athens *Southern Banner,*

April 23, 1862. An earlier skirmish which occurred on Whitemarsh on March 30–31, 1862, is reported in *O.R.*, VI, 120–123; LIII, 2ff.

19. John D. Carswell to John W. Carswell, February 28, 1862, in family papers owned by Porter W. Carswell, Bellevue Plantation, Waynesboro, Georgia; the letter of "Personne" in the Charleston *Courier* concerning the defenses of Savannah was reprinted in the *Morning News,* March 2, 1862.

20. For proceedings of the board of general officers, see *O.R.*, XIV, 864–876. Beauregard's reports on defenses are *ibid.*, 645–648, 657–664.

21. William W. Mackall, *A Son's Recollections of His Father* (New York, 1930), 223; Basinger, "The Savannah Volunteer Guards," 107.

22. John L. G. Wood to his father, March 20, 1862, in Wood Letters, Department of Archives and History; R. H. Moore to Joseph Espey, March 17, 1862, in Joseph Espey Papers, Southern Historical Collection, University of North Carolina Library.

23. John L. G. Wood to his father, February 25, 1862.

24. W. Stanley Hoole, *Vizetelly Covers the Confederacy* (Tuscaloosa, Ala., 1957), 68.

25. John W. Carswell to John D. Carswell, August 5, 1862, in family papers owned by Porter W. Carswell.

26. George D. Smith to his aunt, October 1, 1862, Baber-Blackshear Collection, University of Georgia.

27. J. E. Brown to Secretary of War Seddon, February 7, 1863, *O.R.*, LIII, 279.

28. John W. Hagan to his wife, March 19, 1863, in Bell Irvin Wiley, ed., "The Confederate Letters of John W. Hagan," *G.H.Q.*, XXXVIII, (June, 1954), 183; Alfred L. Hartridge to his mother, February 20, 1863. During an earlier visit to Savannah in October, 1862, Beauregard delivered a speech following a serenade in his honor. "He makes a poor out at speaking," reported a witness. C. C. Jones, Jr., to his father, October 21, 1862. Charles Colcock Jones, Jr., Collection, University of Georgia Library.

29. Josephine C. Habersham described a visit in September, 1863, to this "beautiful Battery" and a trip into its hot magazine "where the 120-pound *shells* ranged on the shelves looked like skulls as if it were a Golgotha." Spencer Bidwell King, Jr., ed., *Ebb Tide: As Seen Through the Diary of Josephine Clay Habersham, 1863* (Athens, Ga., 1958), 78.

30. Du Pont to Theodorus Bailey, October 30, 1862, *O.R.*, Naval, XIII, 423.

31. Mitchel's speech was reported verbatim in the *New South* (Port

Royal, S. C.), September 20, 1862. General Mitchel died of yellow fever at Beaufort a few weeks later.

32. Abraham J. Palmer, *The History of the Forty-Eighth Regiment New York State Volunteers* (New York, 1885), 43, 57.

8. The Blockade and Savannah

1. Ammen, *The Old Navy and the New,* 330ff.
2. Bulloch, *Secret Service of the Confederate States in Europe,* I, 122–126; Journal of Edward C. Anderson, November 12–13, 1861.
3. G. F. Palmes to A. L. Shewmake, September 25, 1861, in George F. Palmes Papers, Georgia Historical Society. Mayor Jones wrote on September 18, 1861, "We have intelligence that Capt. Bulloch and Mr. Edward Anderson will soon leave England each in command of fully appointed steam vessels of war." Charles Colcock Jones, Jr., Collection, University of Georgia Library. Mrs. George W. Anderson to her daughter-in-law, November 11, 1861, in J. Randolph Anderson Papers, Georgia Historical Society.
4. Athens *Southern Banner,* November 20, 1861; Diary of G. A. Mercer (No. I), November 13, 1861.
5. William Duncan to Godfrey Barnsley, September 18, 24, 1861, Barnsley Papers, Emory University Library; C. C. Jones, Jr., to his mother, September 18, 1861, Charles Colcock Jones, Jr., Collection, University of Georgia Library; Diary of G. A. Mercer (No. I), September 17, 1861.
6. *O.R.,* Naval, XII, 222ff.
7. Allan Fullerton to Lord Russell, August 22, 1861; John Boston to Secretary of the Treasury Memminger, October 15, 1861, quoted in Marcus W. Price, "Ships That Tested the Blockade of the Georgia and East Florida Ports, 1861–1865," *The American Neptune,* XV, (April, 1955), 104, 105.
8. For an account of the blockade-running activities of Lamar and his son, C. A. L. Lamar, see Thomas Robson Hay, "Gazaway Bugg Lamar, Confederate Banker and Business Man," *G.H.Q.,* XXXVII, (June, 1953), 115–122.
9. *O.R.,* Naval, XII, 324, 380.
10. *Ibid.,* XV, 723.
11. Bulloch, *Secret Service of the Confederate States,* I, 140.
12. Savannah *Republican,* August 23, 1863; *O.R.,* Naval, XIV, 492–494; John McIntosh Kell to N. C. Munroe, March 22, 1861, in Munroe d'Antignac, *Georgia's Navy, 1861,* 12.
13. Wilbur to his wife, August 31, 1862, in Aaron Wilbur Papers, Duke

University Library; *O.R.,* Naval, XIII, 508. For Usina's statement, see Savannah *Morning News,* February 17, 1897. Usina had been a member of the Oglethorpe Light Infantry and was severely wounded at First Manassas. He later entered the Confederate Navy and made a number of successful runs through the blockade at Wilmington.

14. Log book of USS *Cimarron,* September 18, 1863, in The National Archives (Record Group No. 24); *O.R.,* Naval, XIV, 234ff., 644–646, 679.

15. *O.R.,* Naval, XV, 397–399; Reverend Frederick Denison, *Shot and Shell: The Third Rhode Island Heavy Artillery Regiment* (Providence, 1879), 231ff.

16. *O.R.,* Naval, XIII, 236–238; log book of USS *Unadilla,* August 4, 1862, in The National Archives (Record Group No. 24); Diary of C. R. Hanleiter, August 5, 1862.

17. Savannah *Republican,* December 30, 1864; Charles Seton Hardee, *Reminiscences and Recollections of Old Savannah* (Savannah, *ca.* 1928), 28–29, 94–96.

18. Drayton to Alex Hamilton, Jr., February 18, 1863, *Bulletin of the New York Public Library,* X, (November, 1906), 614; *O.R.,* Naval, XIII, 682–687.

19. *O.R.,* Naval, XIV, 220ff.; *ibid.,* XV, 321, 354–356, 364ff.

20. Henry Blun, *Reminiscences of My Blockade Running* (Savannah, 1910). See also Blun's account in Savannah *Morning News,* February 21, 1897.

21. Olmstead, Memoirs, *G.H.Q.,* XLIV, (September, 1960), 307ff.

22. George F. Palmes to his uncle, November 1, 1861, Georgia Historical Society.

23. A. G. Spencer to Sister Mary Loyola, September 6, 1862, in Edward C. Anderson Papers, Duke University Library. For the export and import statistics, see Price, "Ships That Tested the Blockade of the Georgia and East Florida Ports, 1861–1865," 109.

24. Olmstead "Memoirs," *G.H.Q.,* XLIV, (September, 1960), 306; the description of Savannah in April, 1862, originally published in the Columbus *Enquirer,* was reprinted in the *Morning News,* May 16, 1862.

25. Mrs. H. J. Wayne to Mrs. E. J. Harden, March 10, 1861, in Edward J. Harden Papers, Duke University Library.

26. William Duncan to Godfrey Barnsley, June 30, August 5, 1862, Emory University Library.

27. King, *Ebb Tide: As Seen Through the Diary of Josephine Clay Habersham, 1863,* 61, 103; Edmund C. Lee to his wife, January 8, 1863, in "Civil War Letters by Edmund C. Lee, Chaplain in Confederate Army," typescript in Georgia Historical Society. The Indiana clergyman

(S. C. Logan) was quoted in *The New South* (Port Royal), January 17, 1863, and in James M. Nichols, *Perry's Saints, or the Fighting Parson's Regiment* [48th New York] *in the War of the Rebellion* (Boston, 1886), 142.

28. Henry L. Graves to his sister, December 26, 1863, in "Confederate Diaries," VI, Department of Archives and History. The originals of the letters of Henry Graves and Iverson D. Graves are in the Southern Historical Collection, University of North Carolina Library. The letter of General Colston to his daughter, dated October 26, 1863, is in the Raleigh E. Colston Papers in the same collection.

29. Writing in the *Republican* on August 26, 1863, concerning Quartermaster Department policy in supplying shoes for the Confederate soldier, Peter W. Alexander complained, "The same vessels that brought him through the blockade a meagre supply of worthless German shoes, might also have brought him all the necessary machinery for the manufacture of supplies for the troops."

30. Anna Harden to "Grandma," May 14, 1864, in Edward J. Harden Papers, Duke University Library; Mary A. Drummond, "War Memories." These reminiscences were written in 1868. The original is lost. A copy is in possession of Eugene D. Drummond of Jackson, Mississippi, grandson of Mary A. (Mrs. Edward W.) Drummond.

31. Joseph C. Thompson to his father, January 5, 1865.

32. Celathiel Helms to Mary Helms, wife, March 9, 1864, in "Letters from Confederate Soldiers," II, Department of Archives and History.

33. George W. Gift to his wife, August 3, 1864, George W. Gift Papers, Southern Historical Collection, University of North Carolina Library. This letter is paraphrased (with several omissions) under the erroneous date of August 2, 1864, in Harriet Gift Castlen, *Hope Bids Me Onward* (Savannah, 1945), 184.

34. McHenry Howard, *Recollections of a Maryland Confederate Soldier and Staff Officer under Johnston, Jackson and Lee* (Baltimore, 1914), 338.

9. Fort McAllister Versus Lincoln's Navy

1. For the chase of the *Nashville,* see *O.R.,* Naval, XIII, 134. The report of her presence in the Ogeechee River is quoted in Mason, *Memoir and Correspondence of Charles Steedman,* 315ff.

2. *O.R.,* Naval, XIII, 161ff.

3. Admiral Dahlgren's diary, entry for December 15, 1864, in *O.R.,* Naval, XVI, 361.

4. Alfred L. Hartridge to his mother, June 18, 1862, in family letters owned by Walter C. Hartridge, Savannah.
5. *O.R.,* Naval, XIII, 221; Hartridge to his mother, July 31, 1862.
6. Diary of George A. Mercer (No. II), November 21, 1862.
7. Gideon Welles to Du Pont, January 6, 1863, in *O.R.,* Naval, XIII, 503.
8. New York *Herald,* March 13, 1863.
9. Albert Bigelow Paine, *A Sailor of Fortune, Memoirs of Captain B. S. Osbon,* 228–246, *passim.*
10. Felix Gregory De Fontaine ("Personne"), *Marginalia; Or, Gleanings From An Army Note-Book* (Columbia, S. C., 1864), 57; Isaac Hermann, *Memoirs of a Veteran* (Atlanta, 1911), 80–84.
11. Diary of G. A. Mercer (No. II), March 5, 1863.
12. Lieutenant Commander William Gibson's report, *O.R.,* Naval, XIII, 630.
13. Official reports of the destruction of the *Nashville, O.R.,* Naval, XIII, 696–699. The *Montauk's* log is in The National Archives, Record Group No. 24.
14. *O.R.,* Naval, XIII, 700, 708ff., 766.
15. "Naval Letters from Captain Percival Drayton, 1861–1865," in *Bulletin of the New York Public Library,* X, (November, 1906), 590, 600, 603.
16. Du Pont to Assistant Secretary of Navy Fox, March 2, 1863, in *O.R.,* Naval, XIII, 712.
17. *Ibid.,* 717. For reports of attack, March 3, 1863, see *ibid.,* 716–734; *O.R.,* XIV, 218–223.
18. "Naval Letters from Captain Percival Drayton, 1861–1865," *op. cit.,* 616ff. For Drayton's report to Du Pont, see *O.R.,* Naval, XIII, 718.
19. Welles' comment to Du Pont is in a letter dated November 4, 1863, quoted in H. A. Du Pont, *Rear-Admiral Samuel Francis Du Pont, United States Navy* (New York, 1926), 158.
20. Mercer to Mrs. Mary S. Walker, March 11, 1863, in Mercer-Walker Letters, Emory University Library.
21. Letter to "my dear E" from "C," May 28, 1862, in Mackay-Stiles Papers, Southern Historical Collection, University of North Carolina Library.

10. In Camp, Fort and Headquarters

1. Letter of Felix Gregory De Fontaine, March 14, 1862, in James M. Merrill, ed., "Personne Goes to Georgia: Five Civil War Letters," *G.H.Q.,* XLIII, (June, 1959), 208ff.

2. "Reminiscences of Confederate Soldiers," II, Department of Archives and History.

3. Pope Barrow to Mrs. Howell Cobb, June 19, 1861, in Cobb Papers, University of Georgia Library. Quoted with permission of Howell C. Erwin, Jr., of Athens. For the preceding quotations in paragraph, see John L. G. Wood to his father, November 15, 1861, in Wood Letters, Department of Archives and History; Thomas A. Barrow to his sister, May 9, 1861, in Colonel David C. Barrow Papers, University of Georgia Library.

4. Henry L. Graves to his mother, November 18, 1863, in "Confederate Diaries," VI, Department of Archives and History.

5. Henry Hull Carlton to his family, June 8, 1861, in Carlton-Newton-Mell Collection, University of Georgia Library.

6. Howell Cobb, Jr., to his mother, May 10, 1861, in Cobb Papers, University of Georgia Library. For preceding quotations in paragraph, see Joseph J. Hardy to Sophia Hardy, July 2, 1862, in "Letters from Confederate Soldiers," II, Department of Archives and History; William W. Gordon to his wife, June 6, 1861, in Gordon family papers, Georgia Historical Society.

7. William Murray Davidson to his wife, April 13, 1862. For the other quotation in paragraph, see John L. G. Wood to his aunt, February 19, 1862, in Wood Letters, Department of Archives and History.

8. Joseph C. Thompson to his sister, September 25, 1861.

9. Diary of C. R. Hanleiter, December 23, 1861, February 20, 1862, in Atlanta Historical Society.

10. G. W. Nichols, *A Soldier's Story of his Regiment (61st Georgia)* (published, 1898), 16.

11. Diary of G. A. Mercer (No. I), see entries for April 23, August 15, September 30, October 7, December 26, 1861, January 18, 1862.

12. Edward R. Harden to Howell Cobb, July 13, 14, 15, 26, 1861, in Cobb Papers, University of Georgia Library; the court-martial charges against Colonel S. W. Chastain are in "Order book of Gen. H. R. Jackson, 1st Division Georgia Volunteers at Savannah from Decr. 24, 1861 to 16th Aprl. 1862," records of Adjutant General's Office, Department of Archives and History.

13. H. C. Wayne to H. R. Jackson, February 14, 1862, records of Adjutant General's Office; Wayne to Jackson, February 15, 1862, Henry R. Jackson folder, Department of Archives and History.

14. Alfred L. Hartridge to his mother, June 21, 1863.

15. John D. Carswell to his father, March 9, 1862.

16. Ledger book of Thomas Henderson from 1857 to 1866, owned by Lindsey P. Henderson, funeral directors, Savannah.

17. Joseph Espey Papers, Southern Historical Collection, University of North Carolina Library.

18. John L. G. Wood to his father, February 18, 1862; J. H. Graham to his wife, January 16, 1862, in "Confederate Diaries," VIII, Department of Archives and History.

19. A copy of the order, dated July 31, 1861, prohibiting card playing is in the C. R. Hanleiter folder, Atlanta Historical Society; the exchange between William Percy M. Ashley and Thomas J. Perry was published in the *Morning News,* January 27, 1862.

20. John D. Hopkins to his daughter, August 23, 1864, in letters of Lieutenant Hopkins to "Bessie," in possession of Jane D. Hopkins, his granddaughter, Savannah; John W. Bentley to his sister, June 1, 1862, in John W. Bentley Papers, Georgia Historical Society.

21. John L. G. Wood to his father, December 20, 1861; to his aunt, December 9, 1861.

22. Josh C. Bruyn to a friend, October 3, 1861, owned by Ralston B. Lattimore, Savannah. The chaplain's report is quoted in Bryan, *Confederate Georgia,* 236.

23. Henry L. Graves to his sister, December 26, 1863, "Confederate Diaries," VI, Department of Archives and History; William Duncan to Godfrey Barnsley, March 11, 1861, Emory University Library; Journal of Edward C. Anderson, December 24, 1863.

24. Journal of Robert Watson, March 17, 1864; Savannah *Morning News,* June 10, 1934. The diary was published in *Kinfolks, A Genealogical and Biographical Record* (New Orleans, 1935), the drinking episode being omitted.

25. Jones, *Historical Sketch of the Chatham Artillery,* 25; John F. Wheaton, *Reminiscences of the Chatham Artillery During the War 1861–1865* (Savannah, 1887), 3ff.

26. Diary of John Hart, December 25, 1861, owned by Miss Catherine Moss Pegg, East Orange, N. J.; Diary of W. L. Landershine, foreword, dated May 16, 1862. The Landershine diaries are in possession of National Park Service, Fort Pulaski. Writing of the same Christmas Day, a Northern private stationed at Hilton Head said, "We had a merry Christmas down hear. We bought Sassiges of the nigers and hoe cake and build a fir and cooked our sassiges and whent around throu the nigers houses." Letter of Charles Lafferty, December 29, 1861, National Park Service, Fort Pulaski.

27. For General Porter's anecdote, see *Battles and Leaders of the Civil War,* II, 8.

28. Jones, *Historical Sketch of the Chatham Artillery,* 45ff. A hazel-eyed, German-born musician, "old Hetterick" was thirty-five years of age at

the time. "Register Chatham Artillery, 1861–1865," in Georgia Historical Society. For a description of camp life at Isle of Hope, see C. C. Jones, Jr., to his father, October 26, 1861, in Charles Colcock Jones, Jr., Collection, University of Georgia Library. For Charlton, see Clement Saussy, "Humors of Camp in Chatham's Artillery," *Confederate Veteran* (1910), 215.

29. Basinger, "The Savannah Volunteer Guards," 93. In describing the same visit Basinger said that a bottle of genuine Holland gin was brought out. "Gen Lee would not touch it, and the gentlemen with him, though they looked longingly at it, were evidently unwilling to touch it in his presence." Basinger, "Personal Reminiscences," 152ff. For other sources in paragraph, see William Harden, *Recollections of a Long and Satisfactory Life* (Savannah, 1934), 98; I. G. Bradwell, "In Camp Near Savannah, Ga.," *Confederate Veteran* (September, 1923), 338.

30. Walter A. Clark, *Under the Stars and Bars or, Memories of Four Years Service With the Oglethorpes, of Augusta, Georgia* (Augusta, 1900), 86; A. P. Adamson, *Brief History of the Thirtieth Georgia Regiment* (Griffin, Ga., 1912), 25.

31. Edward C. Anderson, Jr., to his wife, April 3, 1862, in J. Randolph Anderson Papers, Georgia Historical Society.

32. I. G. Bradwell, "In Camp Near Savannah, Ga.," *Confederate Veteran* (September, 1923), 339.

33. George Blackshear to his cousin, June 9, 1861, in J. William Blackshear Papers, Duke University Library.

34. Theodorick W. Montfort to members of his family, February 12, March 17, 1862, in Georgia Historical Society. Copies are in "Letters from Confederate Soldiers," II, Department of Archives and History.

35. *Morning News*, November 18, 1861. H.R.W.'s piece appeared in Atlanta *Southern Confederacy*, May 31, 1861.

36. George D. Smith to his aunt, December 8, 1861, June 17, 1862, in Baber-Blackshear Collection, University of Georgia. For preceding quotations in paragraph, see John W. Hagan to his brother, July 27, 1862, in Bell Irvin Wiley, ed., "The Confederate Letters of John W. Hagan," *G.H.Q.*, XXXVIII, (June, 1954), 178; John L. G. Wood to his father, February 4, 1862.

37. Edward C. Anderson, Jr., to his wife, July 26, 1862, in J. Randolph Anderson Papers, Georgia Historical Society.

38. *O.R.*, LIII, 256; John W. Hagan to his brother, July 27, 1862, "The Confederate Letters of John W. Hagan," *G.H.Q.*, XXXVIII, (June, 1954), 179.

39. Jones to his parents, March 18, 1862, Charles Colcock Jones, Jr., Col-

lection, University of Georgia Library. For a post-war tribute to Mercer, see Jones, *Historical Sketch of the Chatham Artillery,* 101.

40. Sarah Alexander Lawton to Henry R. Jackson, September 9, 1861, copy in Georgia Historical Society.

41. Pope Barrow to Mrs. Howell Cobb, June 19, 1861, in Cobb Papers, University of Georgia Library.

42. Jones to his parents, March 18, 1862, Charles Colcock Jones, Jr., Collection, University of Georgia Library. On September 14, 1861, Jones wrote to his father, "I heartily wish that we had some efficient competent leader to take a hand, and vigorously prosecute this whole matter of our sea coast defenses." For Mrs. Anderson's comment, see her letter to her daughter-in-law, November 11, 1861, in J. Randolph Anderson Papers, Georgia Historical Society. General John C. Pemberton complained on May 14, 1862, of Lawton's lack of "pushing energy." *O.R.,* XIV, 502.

43. H. W. Mercer to P. G. T. Beauregard, March 19, 1863; H. C. Wayne to H. W. Mercer, March 16, 1863; *O.R.,* XIV, 836.

44. A. R. Lawton to H. R. Jackson, April 11, 1862, in Jackson folder, Department of Archives and History. For preceding quotations in paragraph, see A. R. Lawton to J. E. Brown, May 7, 1861, in Lawton folder, Georgia Department of Archives and History; H. R. Jackson to R. E. Lee, December 28, 1861, *O.R.,* VI, 362.

45. Clement A. Evans, ed., *Confederate States History,* VI, 327. Concerning Jackson's appointment as a Brigadier in the Confederate Army Mayor Jones had written in June, 1861, "It is a position he has long and most ardently desired, and I doubt not, when the hour of combat comes, he will do the States no little service." C. C. Jones, Jr., to his parents, June 10, 1861, Charles Colcock Jones, Jr., Collection, University of Georgia Library. For other quotations, see C. C. Jones, Jr., to his parents, February 10, 1862; Alfred L. Hartridge to his mother, April 16, 1862.

11. Webb Attacks the Monitors

1. J. Thomas Scharf, *History of the Confederate Navy from its Organization to the Surrender of Its Last Vessel* (Atlanta, 1887), 653.

2. The description of the *Macon* by Lieutenant Colonel Edward Bloodgood is in *O.R.,* XLIV, 346.

3. Mrs. E. F. Neufville to G. J. Kollock, September 2, 1862, in Kollock Letters, *G.H.Q.,* XXXIV, (September, 1950), 242. For the preceding descriptions of the *Georgia,* see Charles Nordoff, "Two Weeks at Port Royal," *Harper's New Monthly Magazine,* XXVII, (June, 1863), 116; *O.R.,* Naval, XIII, 776–777.

4. Report dated February 3, 1864, in *O.R., Naval*, XV, 709.

5. H. F. Willink, Jr., to Thomas Brent, July 23, 1862, in Savannah Squadron Papers, Emory University Library.

6. H. B. Littlepage to Lieutenant Catesby ap R. Jones, February 16, 1863, in *O.R., Naval*, XIII, 819ff.; Edward C. Anderson's account of the conversion of the *Fingal* into an ironclad is in the family papers owned by Mrs. Florence Crane Schwalb of Savannah.

7. Jones, *The Life and Services of Commodore Josiah Tattnall* (Savannah, 1878), 227.

8. Diary of G. A. Mercer (No. II), April 23, 1863.

9. *O.R.,* Naval, XIII, 417, 767.

10. Jones, *The Life and Services of Commodore Josiah Tattnall*, 224; G. J. Kollock to his wife, April 5, 1863, in Kollock Letters, *G.H.Q.*, XXXIV, (September, 1950), 256.

11. Duncan to Godfrey Barnsley, June 26, 1862. For the preceding quotations, see Bulloch, *The Secret Service of the Confederate States in Europe*, I, 143ff., 146.

12. Mrs. E. F. Neufville to G. J. Kollock, February 9, 1863, Kollock Letters, *G.H.Q.*, XXXIV, (September, 1950), 249.

13. S. R. Mallory to R. L. Page, April 6, 1863, Savannah Squadron Papers, Emory University Library.

14. Webb's statements concerning his plans are in *O.R., Naval*, XIV, 698ff., 710ff.

15. For statement as to Webb's speech, see John W. Carey quoted in *Morning News*, June 27, 1863; for statement as to flag, see E. D. Townsend, *Anecdotes of the Civil War in the United States* (New York, 1884), 208ff.; *History of the Rebel Steam Ram "Atlanta," Now on exhibition at foot of Washington Street . . . with an interesting account of the engagement which resulted in her capture* (Philadelphia, 1863). The pamphlet contains an account of the engagement written by Robert S. Davis, correspondent of the Philadelphia *Inquirer*. Davis' dispatch was printed in *Morning News*, July 3, 1863.

16. Captain Rodgers' comment is from his testimony in *The Atlanta* (District Court, Mass., 1864), 2 *Federal Cases*, 116–121.

17. Letter of T. F. Egan, June 19, 1864, in *Morning News*, June 29, 1864.

18. *History of the Rebel Steam Ram "Atlanta," op. cit.*

19. 3 *Wallace* 425 (1866). The log of the *Nahant*, perhaps written with an eye to prize money, read: "At 4:20 a.m. saw a steamer about 3 miles distant up the river which proved to be a rebel Ram standing toward us. Called to quarters. At 4:30 weighed anchor and stood for the Ram. At 4:45 she commenced the action by firing the first gun at us and continued to direct her fire at the Nahant." The log is in The National Archives (Record Group No. 24).

20. *O.R.*, Naval, XIV, 288; J. Thomas Scharf, *History of the Confederate States Navy*, 645. A writer in the *Republican* on June 19, 1863, analyzed Kennard's theory of mutiny and accurately surmised what had occurred.

21. The story in the Richmond *Examiner* about Webb fainting is refuted in Scharf, *op. cit.*, 645.

22. Report of Webb, October 19, 1864, in *O.R.*, Naval, XIV, 291. For the statement about Webb by a member of the crew, see *Morning News*, June 27, 1863. An account by another member of the crew ("W.B.M.") appeared in the *Republican* on the same date.

23. This was apparently an incident that occurred in March, 1863, when five deserters from the transport *Savannah* overpowered a master's mate and carried him to Fort Pulaski. *O.R.*, Naval, XIII, 767. While disloyalty played no part in the loss of the *Atlanta*, thirty members of her crew later took the oath of allegiance to the "Lincoln Government," claiming that their families resided in the North, according to an item in the *Morning News*, July 9, 1863.

24. Extract of a private letter from a Union officer reprinted in *Morning News*, July 3, 1863.

12. Ladies at War

1. Diary of G. A. Mercer (No. I), August 17, 1861.

2. Olmstead's reminiscences in *Historic and Picturesque Savannah*, 200; Jones, *Historical Sketch of the Chatham Artillery*, 28.

3. *The New South* (Port Royal, S. C.), January 17, 1863. For another example of sensitiveness on the subject of alleged spying see letter to Mayor Jones from his father, October 5, 1861, concerning Dr. James J. Waring who had recently returned to Savannah after several years' residence at Washington, D. C. The manuscript is in the Charles Colcock Jones, Jr., Collection, University of Georgia Library.

4. King, *Ebb Tide: As Seen Through the Diary of Josephine Clay Habersham, 1863*, 24ff., 38, 64.

5. Charles Carleton Coffin, *Four Years of Fighting* (Boston, 1866), 427.

6. Quoted by Mrs. A. A. Campbell in *Confederate Veteran* (November, 1920), 420.

7. Mary A. Drummond, "War Memories."

8. Russell, *My Diary North and South*, 61.

9. The roster of the Savannah Ordnance Depot was published in Savannah *Evening Press*, April 15, 1932.

10. The letter of "P.M.L." to Governor Brown, December 18, 1862, is quoted by Bryan in *Confederate Georgia*, 70. A copy is in the folder

of the Henry R. Jackson papers, designated "Unsigned Letters," Georgia Department of Archives and History.

11. On May 28, 1862, Charles C. Jones, Jr., wrote, "We will soon be returning the compliment of the Enemy, by reconnoitering with our own balloon. A member of our company made it, and will make the ascensions." The member of the Chathams concerned was Charles Cevor, a Savannah aeronaut. He made several ascensions in Virginia. See *Republican*, July 4, 7, 17, 1862.

12. Hermann, *Memoirs of a Veteran*, 80. For gifts of gray uniforms to Madame Cazier see *Morning News*, January 20, February 3, 1862; *Republican*, April 17, 1862.

13. Frances Thomas Howard, *In and Out of the Lines, An Accurate Account of Incidents during the Occupation of Georgia by Federal Troops in 1864–65* (New York, 1905), 176. The names of persons used in this book are fictitious; the people are real. The diaries and the reminiscences (the latter were written in 1870) are authentic. A note attached to the copy of *In and Out of the Lines* in the Georgia State Library, Atlanta, identifies the actual persons for whom pseudonyms are used in the book.

14. For the reputed inspiration of Marie Le Coste's "Somebody's Darling" (January, 1864), see clipping from Savannah newspaper (July 28, 1938) in Thomas Gamble Scrapbooks, I, 165, Savannah Public Library; clipping from *The Musical Courier* in John Hill Hewitt Scrapbooks, Emory University Library.

15. George Arthur Gordon, "Eleanor Kinzie Gordon, A Sketch," in *G.H.Q.*, I, (September, 1917), 186ff., 189.

16. Mrs. Cornelia A. Screven's reminiscences in *"Our Women in the War," The Lives they Lived; the Deaths they Died* (Charleston, 1885), 136.

13. The Taking of the Water Witch

1. Alfred T. Mahan, *From Sail to Steam* (New York, 1907), 174, 188.

2. Ammen, *The Old Navy and the New*, 368ff.; *O.R.*, Naval, XV, 471.

3. *O.R.*, Naval, XV, 734–736; Reports dated February 11, 17, 1864, Savannah Squadron Papers, Emory University Library; Iverson D. Graves to his sister, May 3, 1864, in "Confederate Diaries," VI, Department of Archives and History.

4. E. M. Anderson to E. C. Anderson, November 18, 1862, in Anderson family papers owned by Mrs. Florence C. Schwalb, Savannah.

5. *O.R.*, Naval, XIV, 717.

6. Palmer, *The History of the Forty-eighth Regiment, New York State Volunteers,* 34ff.
7. *O.R.,* Naval, XV, 481.
8. The description of Pelot is quoted in a newspaper article written by John T. Boifeuillet entitled, "New Light on a Hero of the Confederate Navy." A clipping is in the Thomas Gamble Scrapbooks, I, 94, Savannah Public Library. For Hanleiter's comment about his diary, see *The Joseph Thompson Artillery—Recollections of Captain C. R. Hanleiter* (published, with other articles, by Kimsey's Book Shop, Atlanta, 1956), 73ff.
9. Arthur C. Freeman's reminiscences appeared in a letter, dated July 26, 1873, published in the Norfolk *Virginian.* The article was reprinted that year in a Savannah newspaper. An undated clipping is in the Georgia Historical Society.
10. John R. Blocker, "Capture of Blockader Water Witch," as related by Amos Sherritt, in *Confederate Veteran* (December, 1909), 604.
11. The official reports of the capture of the *Water Witch* are in *O.R.,* Naval, XV, 469–506. See also *Republican,* June 7, 1864.
12. The poem signed "M.E.B." was printed in the article by J. T. Boifeuillet. See note 8, *supra.*
13. George Noble Jones, ed., *Journal of Anna Wylly Habersham, 1864* (Savannah, 1926), 6. See also F. B. Culver, "The War Romance of John Thomas Scharf," *Maryland Historical Magazine,* XII, (September, 1926), 295–302.
14. For Warley's reports on fighting and for his request for transfer, see letters to Flag Officer Hunter, September 30, August 29, 1864, respectively, Savannah Squadron Papers, Emory University Library; George W. Gift to his wife, July 13, 1864, in Harriet Gift Castlen, *Hope Bids Me Onward,* 181.

14. "A general deep-felt weariness of war"

1. Diary of G. A. Mercer (No. II), May 24, August 31, 1863; Elisha Wylly to "Habbie," July 13, 1863, in family papers owned by L. Ralston Wylly, Sr., Savannah.
2. Diary of C. R. Hanleiter, June 4, 1862.
3. William Duncan to Godfrey Barnsley, March 8, 1862, in Barnsley Papers, Emory University Library.
4. E. C. Lee to his wife, November 6, 1863, in "Civil War Letters by Edmund C. Lee, Chaplain in Confederate Army," typescript in Georgia Historical Society.
5. Henry L. Graves to his mother, November 3, 1863, in "Confederate

Diaries," VI, Department of Archives and History. Graves referred to Davis' remarks as a "pretty little speech." In the course of it the President said that his father had fought at the Siege of Savannah in 1779.

6. King, *Ebb Tide: As Seen Through the Diary of Josephine Clay Habersham, 1863,* 103ff.

7. R. T. Gibson to Mrs. E. B. Richardsone, May 15, 1865, owned by Pearson Hardee, Haverford, Pa.; Thomas Robson Hay, "Gazaway Bugg Lamar, Confederate Banker and Business Man," *G.H.Q.,* XXXVII, (June, 1953), 126ff.

8. *O.R.,* Naval, XV, 487.

9. Susie King Taylor, *Reminiscences of My Life in Camp With the 33D United States Colored Troops Late 1st S. C. Volunteers* (Boston, 1902), 65; *New South* (Port Royal, S. C.), August 15, 1863.

10. *O.R.,* Naval, XV, 108.

11. *Ibid.,* 248; Journal of Edward C. Anderson, January 12, 1864.

12. Celathiel Helms to his wife, August 31, 1863, January 19, March 5, 1864, in "Letters from Confederate Soldiers," II, Department of Archives and History.

13. Diary of G. A. Mercer (No. I), January 15, 1864.

14. Reports on the abortive mutiny and the engagement on Whitemarsh Island are in *O.R.,* XXXV, part 1, 529–531 and 361–364, respectively.

15. *The Diary of Elias A. Bryant of Francestown, N. H.,* 135ff.

16. Mrs. William H. Stiles to her husband, January 22, 1864, in Mackay-Stiles Papers, Southern Historical Collection, University of North Carolina Library. Mrs. Stiles believed, however, that God's deliverance of the country might not come until after her time. Mrs. George Anderson's letter, dated August 2, 1863, is in J. Randolph Anderson Papers, Georgia Historical Society.

17. Augustin Verot to Bishop Lynch, March 28, 1863, in Willard E. Wight, ed., "Letters of the Bishop of Savannah, 1861–1865," *G.H.Q.,* XLII, (March, 1958), 105. He had written a few months before, "Sometimes I wish I was in France to represent things there in their true light & cause perhaps an intervention from the Emperor." *Ibid.,* 99. G. B. Lamar to H. J. Hartstein and C. A. L. Lamar, July 31, 1863, in New York *Times,* January 16, 1864.

18. Carrie Bell Sinclair to an unknown admirer, October 30, 1864, in Carrie Bell Sinclair Papers, Georgia Historical Society; William Duncan to Godfrey Barnsley, October 25, 1862, in Emory University Library; Olmstead to his wife, July 31, 1864, in Charles H. Olmstead Papers, Southern Historical Collection, University of North Carolina Library.

19. I. T. Hardy to Sally Smith, July 30; same to Mrs. S. C. Hardy, Sep-

tember 2, 1864, in "Letters of Confederate Soldiers, 1861–1865," II, Department of Archives and History; Henry L. Graves to his mother, September 5, 1864, *ibid.*, VI.

20. George W. Gift to his wife, July 24, 1864, in George W. Gift Papers, Southern Historical Collection, University of North Carolina Library.

21. *O.R.*, Naval, XV, 487.

15. "I die in the best cause a man could fall in"

1. W. B. C. Coker to brother, September 15, 1864, *The Georgia Review*, XIV, (Winter, 1960), 359. The letter of the unidentified Savannahian, dated July 23, 1864, appeared without signature in a Savannah newspaper at that period. It was reprinted in the Savannah *Morning News*, July 31, 1938. Olmstead's observations on Johnston are found in his Memoirs and in a letter to his wife, July 31, 1864, in Charles H. Olmstead Papers, Southern Historical Collection, University of North Carolina Library.

2. An account of Lieutenant Saussy's exploit appeared in the Richmond *Examiner* in August, 1863, under the signature "Sabre."

3. *Roll of Officers and Members of the Georgia Hussars . . . with Historical Sketch*, 496–499.

4. Wheaton, *Reminiscences of the Chatham Artillery During the War 1861–1865*, 14–17; *Republican*, February 23, March 2, 1864.

5. Robert Stiles, *Four Years Under Marse Robert* (New York, 1910), 275–278. Falligant's promotion is referred to in *Morning News*, October 16, 1862.

6. G. Moxley Sorrel, *Recollections of a Confederate Staff Officer* (New York, 1905), 241–245. Putnam Smith's letter, written in 1892, was quoted in Savannah *Morning News*, August 12, 1901.

7. Journal of Edward C. Anderson, July 5, 17, 24, August 1, 1864.

8. King, *Ebb Tide: As Seen Through the Diary of Josephine Clay Habersham, 1863*, 113, 115ff. Fifty-three years later David B. Morgan, formerly of the 5th Georgia Cavalry which was sent from the coast to join Joe Wheeler in 1864, could still well recall "the jeers we met with." Morgan's reminiscences are in a letter to Otis Ashmore, July 28, 1917, Georgia Historical Society.

9. Edward S. Willis to his mother, June 14, 1862, in *Southern Historical Society Papers*, XVII (Richmond, 1889), 172–177.

10. Stiles, *Four Years Under Marse Robert*, 120–124. For citations of Willis after Chancellorsville, see *O.R.*, XXV, part 1, 941, 946, 967, 968.

11. Sorrel, *Recollections of a Confederate Staff Officer*, 260.

12. A. S. Pendleton, to F. T. Willis, May 31, 1864, quoted in W. G. Bean,

Stonewall's Man, Sandie Pendleton (Chapel Hill, 1959), 200ff. A copy of this letter is in the Department of Archives and History.

16. In Which Sherman Heads East

1. George W. Hanger to family, December 14, 1864, in *G.H.Q.*, XLII, (December, 1958), 440ff.; Moses Harter to family, December 23, 1864, Letters of Moses Harter, Co. A, 25th Indiana, typescripts in The William Henry Smith Memorial Library of The Indiana Historical Society, Indianapolis.
2. For the source of quotations in this paragraph, see Charles Ewing to Thomas Ewing, December 15, 1864, in George C. Osbon, ed., "Sherman's March through Georgia: Letters from Charles Ewing to his Father Thomas Ewing," *G.H.Q.*, XLII, (September, 1958), 326; Alpheus S. Williams to S. E. Pittman, April 21, 1865, in Milo M. Quaife, ed., *From the Cannon's Mouth, the Civil War letters of General Alpheus S. Williams* (Detroit, 1959), 385; O. M. Poe to his wife, December 16, 1864, in Orlando M. Poe Papers, The Library of Congress.
3. Henry W. Slocum to Joseph Howland, January 6, 1865, in Miscellaneous Manuscripts, The New York Historical Society. Quoted by courtesy of the Society.
4. Divine (143rd New York) to J. H. Everett, December 19, 1864, copy in Georgia Historical Society; C. S. Brown to family, December 16, 1864, in the Charles S. Brown Papers, Duke University Library. Brown had helped himself to some "Rebel music" and also to some jewelry from the plundered and burned house of "Reb. Gen. Irwin"; "Jo" (15th Iowa) to Linda McNeill, December 24, 1864, owned by M. N. Deffenbaugh, Waynesboro, Va.
5. Wayne's report, February 6, 1865, in *O.R.*, LIII, 36.
6. The telegram, dated November 21, 1864, is in *O.R.*, XLIV, 877.
7. Frederick Emil Schmitt, "Prisoner of War: Experiences in Southern Prisons," in *Wisconsin Magazine of History*, XLII, (Winter, 1958–1959), 90–91.
8. C. C. Jones, Jr., to his mother, September 9, 1864, in Charles Colcock Jones, Jr., Collection, University of Georgia Library; Journal of Edward C. Anderson, September 4, 1864; McLaws to Major Stringfellow, September 8, 1864, in *O.R.*, VII, (Series 2), 788. See also McLaws' report, August 18, 1864, in *O.R.*, XXXV, part 2, 610–612.
9. "The Immortal Six Hundred," *Confederate Veteran* (April, 1897), 148; Ralston B. Lattimore, *Fort Pulaski National Monument, Georgia* (Washington, D. C., 1954), 38–40. For comments on the hardships of imprisonment at Hilton Head written by George P. Harrison, Sr. (he

was captured near Savannah in December, 1864), see his letter to Congressman Hartridge, January 9, 1865, in *O.R.*, VIII, (Series 2), 50ff.

10. George D. Smith to his aunt, March 26, 1863, in Baber-Blackshear Collection, University of Georgia. For preceding quotations in paragraph, see Henry L. Graves to a cousin, October 10, 1864, "Confederate Diaries," VI, Department of Archives and History; Diary of G. A. Mercer (No. II), January 20, 1863.

11. Edmund C. Lee to his wife, undated letter written in the winter of 1864, and letter to his daughter, May 5, 1864, in "Civil War Letters by Edmund C. Lee, Chaplain in Confederate Army."

12. A. O. Abbott, *Prison Life in the South, at Richmond, Macon, Savannah* . . . (New York, 1866), 99ff.; *Morning News,* September 13, 1864. The Union officer was W. L. Greenwood.

13. F. Buntyn to Elizabeth Buntyn, December 4, 1864, in Elizabeth Buntyn Papers, Duke University Library; C. C. Jones, Jr., to his mother, November 23, 1864, Charles Colcock Jones, Jr., Collection, University of Georgia Library.

14. James S. Robinson to L. G. Hunt, December 24, 1864, in Gen. J. S. Robinson Collection, The Ohio Historical Society, Columbus; T. H. Pendergast, "Journal of Sherman's Grand March through Georgia," December 6, 1864, in William W. Pendergast and Family Papers, Minnesota Historical Society, St. Paul.

15. Reminiscences of Mrs. Mary Copp Wilbur in Aaron Wilbur Papers, Emory University Library.

16. Edward C. Anderson, Jr., to his mother, December 3, 1864, in J. Randolph Anderson Papers, Georgia Historical Society.

17. William Harden, "Recollections of a Private in the Signal Corps," in *Addresses Delivered Before the Confederate Veterans Association, of Savannah, Ga.* (Savannah, 1898), 24.

18. The thrust was part of Sherman's strategy. On November 11, 1864, he had telegraphed Halleck that he would like to have General Foster break the railroad line at Pocotaligo about December 1. *O.R.,* XXXIX, 740.

19. For diversion of Georgia militia and the Battle of Honey Hill, see Gustavus W. Smith, "The Georgia Militia During Sherman's March to the Sea," in *Battles and Leaders,* IV, 667–669; report of General Smith, December, 1864, in Gustavus Woodson Smith Papers, Duke University Library; Richard Taylor, *Destruction and Reconstruction, Personal Experiences of the Late War* (New York, 1955), 261–263, edited by Richard B. Harwell; William A. Courtenay, "Heroes of Honey Hill," *Southern Historical Society Papers,* XXVI, (Richmond, 1898), 232–241.

20. Luis F. Emilio, *History of the Fifty-Fourth Regiment of Massachusetts Volunteer Infantry, 1863–1865* (Boston, 1894), 248.

21. Joseph C. Thompson to his father, December 2, 1864; General John K. Jackson's account of the "Augusta Battalion" at Honey Hill is in the C. C. Jones Papers, Duke University Library.

17. Sherman at the Gate

1. Journal of Edward C. Anderson, June 29, August 26, 1864.

2. *Army Life of an Illinois Soldier . . . Letters and Diary of the Late Charles W. Wills,* compiled by Mary E. Kellogg (Washington, D. C., 1906), 334; Francis R. Baker, 78th Ohio Infantry, transcript of his memoirs, 1861–1865, in Illinois State Historical Library.

3. John C. Van Duzer Papers, journal, December 7, 1864, in Duke University Library.

4. Charles C. Jones, Jr., *The Siege of Savannah in December, 1864* (Albany, N. Y., 1874), 115; *O.R.,* XLIV, 974. Writing to C. C. Jones, Jr., in 1866, Hardee stated that he had lost all of his papers relating to the siege of Savannah. "I chance, however, to remember that on the day we left Savannah My Field Report showed 7,300 men for duty, which included every effective man in Savannah, in the trenches, and at the Forts." W. J. Hardee to C. C. Jones, Jr., May 14, 1866, in William Joseph Hardee Papers, Duke University Library. The defensive line is described in detail in *The Siege of Savannah,* 78–91, and in Jones, "The Siege and Evacuation of Savannah, Georgia," *Southern Historical Society Papers,* XVII, (Richmond, 1889), 68–73.

5. U. R. Brooks, ed., *Stories of the Confederacy* (Columbia, S. C., 1912), 313–327. General Hugh Mercer was later arrested on the charge of murder of the two deserters. His son wrote on December 15, 1865, "When I saw my honored gray-headed Father, whose own Grand Father fell on the field of Princeton in defence of American liberty, marched yesterday before a Military tribunal, between two soldiers, my heart swelled with inexpressible emotions, and the bitterness of the vanquished filled my very soul." Mercer was acquitted. See G. A. Mercer Diary (No. I), January 28, 1866.

6. "Daily Record" of Peter Ege, Captain 34th Illinois Volunteers, December 8, 1864, in Peter Ege Papers, State Historical Society, Wisconsin, Madison.

7. S. F. Fleharty, *Our Regiment, A History of the 102d Illinois Infantry Volunteers* (Chicago, 1865), 123. The Smith anecdote is from Edwin E. Bryant, *History of the Third Regiment Wisconsin Veteran Volunteer Infantry, 1861–1865* (Madison, 1891), 389.

8. In the history of the *Ninety-second Illinois Volunteers* (Freeport, Ill.,

1875), 208–211, the authors state, "Many of the wealthy people living in Savannah had gone to the plantations on Taylor's Creek, to escape Sherman's troops, taking their elegant city furniture with them. The Ninety-Second boys made saddle cloths of their beautiful Brussels and Turkey carpets." For an account of depredations in Liberty County, see Haskell Monroe, "Men Without Law: Federal Raiding in Liberty County," *G.H.Q.*, XLIV, (June, 1960), 154–171; Haskell Monroe, ed., Mary Sharpe Jones and Mary Jones Mallard, *Yankees A'Coming: One Month's Experience during the Invasion of Liberty County Georgia, 1864–1865* (Tuscaloosa, Ala., 1959). Diary of G. B. Mc-Millan, 16th Wisconsin Volunteers, December 11, 1864, in George B. McMillan Papers, State Historical Society, Wisconsin; Harvey Reid to his parents, December 11, 1864, in Papers of Harvey Reid, 22nd Wisconsin Volunteers, State Historical Society, Wisconsin.

9. Henry H. Wright, *A History of the Sixth Iowa Infantry* (Iowa City, 1923), 380.

10. M. A. DeWolfe Howe, ed., *Marching with Sherman, Passages From The Letters and Campaign Diaries of Henry Hitchcock* (New Haven, 1927), 174ff. Hereafter cited *Hitchcock*.

11. General Hardee to Flag Officer Hunter, December 10, 1864, in Savannah Squadron Papers, Emory University Library.

12. George S. Bradley, *The Star Corps; Or, Notes of an Army Chaplain, During Sherman's Famous "March to the Sea"* (Milwaukee, 1865), 210–211.

13. Hunter's report of the engagement is in *O.R.*, Naval, XVI, 486. Union versions are in *O.R.*, XLIV, 235, 250, 357. Scharf's account is in *History of the Confederate States Navy*, 652.

14. Diary of Levi A. Ross, Captain, Co. K, 86th Illinois Infantry, December 11, 1864, in Illinois State Historical Library, Springfield. The chaplain was George S. Bradley.

15. William Worth Belknap, ed., *History of the Fifteenth Regiment, Iowa Veteran Volunteer Infantry* (Keokuk, Iowa, 1887), 423ff.

16. George W. Hanger to his family, December 14, 1864, in *G.H.Q.*, XLII, (December, 1958), 440ff.

17. Frederick Price to his wife, December 18, 1864, in Savannah *Morning News*, December 18, 1960. For other quotations in paragraph, see diary of John L. Hostetter, Regimental Surgeon, quoted in Edwin W. Payne, *History of the Thirty-fourth Regiment of Illinois Infantry, September 7, 1861–July 12, 1865* (Clinton, Iowa, 1902), 170; Bruce Hoadley to "Cousin Em," December 15, 1864, Robert Bruce Hoadley Papers, Duke University Library.

18. Bryant, *History of the Third Regiment Wisconsin Veteran Volun-*

teer Infantry, 1861–1865, 296; Alfred G. Hunter, *History of the Eighty-second Indiana Volunteer Infantry, its Organization, Campaigns and Battles* (Indianapolis, 1893), 142ff.

19. John Henry Otto, "Diary of an ex-Prussian soldier, Captain Otto, Co. D, 21st Wisconsin Volunteer Infantry," in State Historical Society, Wisconsin. The immediately preceding reference is from Rufus Mead, Jr., to his family, December 28, 1864, in James A. Padgett, ed., "With Sherman Through Georgia and the Carolinas: Letters of a Federal Soldier" in *G.H.Q.,* XXXIII, (March, 1949), 61.

18. Fort McAllister Again

1. W. E. Strong, "Capture of Fort McAllister," December 30, 1864, in William T. Sherman Papers, The Library of Congress. Strong was Inspector General and Chief of Staff, Army of the Tennessee.
2. For Captain Duncan's exploit, see George W. Pepper, *Personal Recollections of Sherman's Campaign in Georgia and the Carolinas* (Zanesville, Ohio, 1866), 257–259; *O.R.,* Naval, XVI, 127ff., 361; *O.R.,* XLIV, 658, 671, 699. For an alleged instance of drunkenness, see *ibid.,* 622.
3. Charles Cowley, *Leaves from a Lawyer's Life Afloat and Ashore* (Lowell, Mass., 1879), 141ff.
4. Diary of E. P. Burton, Surgeon, 7th Regiment, Illinois, December 11, 1864. A typescript is in the Illinois State Historical Library.
5. *O.R.,* XLIV, 751–754.
6. John C. Van Duzer Papers, journal, December 13, 1864, in Duke University Library.
7. J. E. P. Doyle's account appeared in the *Herald,* December 22, 1864.
8. Major Anderson's account was published in Jones, *Historical Sketch of the Chatham Artillery,* 140–144.
9. Diary of Major James A. Connolly in *Transactions of the Illinois State Historical Society for the Year 1928,* 426.
10. George W. Nichols, "How Fort M'Allister was taken," *Harpers New Monthly Magazine,* XXXVII, (August, 1868), 370; William B. Hazen, *A Narrative of Military Service* (Boston, 1885).
11. Joseph A. Saunier, *A History of the Forty-Seventh Regiment Ohio Veteran Volunteer Infantry* (Hillsboro, Ohio, 1903), 363.
12. For Hazen's report, see *O.R.,* XLIV, 109–111.
13. Account by Captain J. H. Brown quoted in Saunier, *op. cit.,* 372.
14. Clinch's hand-to-hand duel with Captain Stephen F. Grimes is described (with much embellishment) by George W. Pepper in his *Personal Recollections, op. cit.,* 255. See also *O.R.,* XLIV, 122, and Major Anderson's account in Jones, *Sketch of the Chatham Artillery,* 143.

15. Sherman to his wife, December 16, 1864, in M. A. DeWolfe Howe, ed., *Home Letters of General Sherman* (New York, 1909), 319. For Sherman's joyous comment, see *Hitchcock,* 179ff.; Sherman, *Memoirs,* II, 198; J. E. P. Doyle's account, New York *Herald,* December 22, 1864. Captain L. M. Dayton's message is in *O.R.,* XLIV, 704.

16. John C. Gray, Jr., to John C. Ropes, December 14, 1864, *War Letters, 1862–1865, of John Chipman Gray and John Codman Ropes,* 427.

17. *Hitchcock,* 194ff. For the preceding quotations in this paragraph, see John C. Arbuckle, *Civil War Experiences of a Foot-Soldier Who Marched With Sherman* (Columbus, Ohio, 1930), 116; Diary of Captain Eli J. Sherlock, of the 100th Indiana, December 13, 1864, typescript in Records of the Adjutant General's Office (Record Group No. 94), The National Archives.

19. The Plank Road

1. *Hitchcock,* 188; Gray to John C. Ropes, December 14, 1864, in *War Letters, 1862–1865, of John Chipman Gray and John Codman Ropes,* 427.

2. *O.R.,* XLIV, 718.

3. Diary of William Lomax, Surgeon, 12th Indiana Regiment, December 12, 1864, typescript in The William Henry Smith Memorial Library of The Indiana Historical Society, Indianapolis.

4. John C. Van Duzer Papers, journal, December 17, 1864, in Duke University Library; Oscar Osburn Winther, ed., *With Sherman to the Sea, the Civil War Letters, Diaries & Reminiscences of Theodore F. Upson* (Baton Rouge, 1943), 139ff.

5. George W. Nichols, "How Fort M'Allister was taken," *Harpers New Monthly Magazine,* XXXVII, (August, 1868), 368–369.

6. Charles Brown to his family, December 16, 1864, in Charles Brown Papers, Duke University Library.

7. H. C. Wayne to W. T. Sherman, October 23, 1875, in *Memoirs of Gen. W. T. Sherman* (New York, 1891), II, 568. Wayne's recollection may have been faulty. See Beauregard's letter to President Davis, December 13, 1864, in *O.R.,* XLIII, 381ff.

8. The Hardee-Beauregard telegrams are in the William Joseph Hardee Papers, Duke University Library. See also *O.R.,* XLIV, 942ff.

9. M. H. Turrentine to his sister, December 22, 1864, in Michael H. Turrentine Papers, Duke University Library. See also John G. Clark to P. G. T. Beauregard, April 16, 1875, in Alfred Roman, *The Military Operations of General Beauregard* (New York, 1884), II, 622ff.

10. For the summons to surrender and Hardee's answer, see *O.R.*, XLIV, 737–738.

11. Sherman to Grant, December 18, 1864, *O.R.*, XLIV, 741ff.; General Sherman mistakenly referred to the "Exchange" instead of the court-house.

12. Ezra A. Carman, *General Hardee's Escape from Savannah* (Washington, D. C., 1893), 16ff.; Slocum to Sherman, December 15, 1864, *O.R.*, XLIV, 719ff.

13. *O.R.*, XLIV, 720ff., 792.

14. For reports as to vulnerability of Confederate line, see *O.R.*, XLIV, 57, 73, 166, 209, 330.

15. G. W. Smith to Hardee, December 31, 1864, in *O.R.*, LIII, 38; Jones, *The Siege of Savannah in December, 1864*, 115.

16. W. T. Sherman to John Sherman, December 31, 1864, in Rachel Sherman Thorndike, ed., *The Sherman Letters, Correspondence Between General and Senator Sherman from 1837 to 1891* (New York, 1894), 241ff. For Sherman's letter to his wife, see *Home Letters of General Sherman*, 319.

17. *With Sherman to the Sea, the Civil War Letters, Diaries & Reminiscences of Theodore F. Upson*, 141. The immediately preceding quotation is from a letter of Charles Albertson, 15th Iowa, to his brother, December 17, 1864, in Miscellaneous Manuscripts, The Georgia Historical Society.

20. Exit Hardee

1. Reminiscences of Mary Wragg Bond. The original is owned by J. Sullivan Bond of Savannah; Mary A. Drummond, "War Memories"; Reminiscences of Mary Copp Wilbur in Aaron Wilbur Papers, Emory University Library.

2. Ezra A. Carman, *General Hardee's Escape from Savannah*, 25. Carman's account was based on what General Joseph Wheeler told him after the war.

3. Edward C. Anderson to his wife, January 2, 1865, in family papers owned by Mrs. Florence C. Schwalb, Savannah. For preceding quotation, see "Diary of an ex-Prussian soldier, Captain Otto, Co. D, 21st Wisconsin Volunteer Infantry . . ." in State Historical Society of Wisconsin.

4. R. D. Chapman, *A Georgia Soldier in the Civil War, 1861–1865* (Houston, Texas, 1923), 101.

5. A. S. McCollum's recollections are in "Reminiscences of Confederate Soldiers," III, Department of Archives and History.

6. Berry Benson Papers, Reminiscences, X, 336ff., in Southern Historical Collection, University of North Carolina Library.

7. Walter Clark, ed., *Histories of the Several Regiments and Battalions from North Carolina in the Great War, 1861–1865* (Goldsboro, N. C., 1901), IV, 322; Diary of C. R. Hanleiter, December 20, 1864, Atlanta Historical Society. Mrs. Hanleiter and her brood fared very well under the Goths due to the fact, her husband later explained, that the Union officer who boarded with her was "no drawling down-easter, but a bluff, manly Ohioan." See *The Joe Thompson Artillery—Recollections of Captain C. R. Hanleiter* (published with other sketches by Kimsey's Book Shop, Atlanta, 1956), 74. Other Savannah ladies had similar experiences with their Northern boarders. The mother of Augustus G. Guerard, a Confederate soldier, wrote to him on January 20, 1865, concerning Captain Coleman, a Federal officer: "His gentlemanly generous conduct entitles him to our respect & esteem. Most faithfully has he fulfilled his office of protector to your mother & sisters." Guerard Family Papers, Georgia Historical Society. See also Eliza Alice West, "Long Ago," 51, typescript in Georgia Historical Society.

8. Henry L. Graves to his mother, December 28, 1864, in "Confederate Diaries," VI, Department of Archives and History; F. Buntyn to Elizabeth Buntyn, December 24, 1864, January 1, 1865, in Elizabeth Buntyn Papers, Duke University Library.

9. "Statement by Elizabeth Georgia Basinger of the experiences of her mother Jane Susan Starr Basinger and herself during the occupation of Savannah by Sherman's army on December 20, 1864," in Basinger, "Personal Reminiscences," Appendix IV.

10. John C. Van Duzer Papers, journal, December 22, 1864, in Duke University Library.

11. Reverend George A. Blount's reminiscences (dated May 25, 1902) appeared in Savannah *Morning News,* December 25, 1932. The manuscript was in possession of Mrs. S. B. DuBose of Ludowici in 1932.

12. The instructions to Hunter to fight his vessels out and the inability to remove the torpedoes are in *O.R., Naval,* XVI, 481, 483ff.

13. For operations of the *Savannah* on December 21, 1864, see *O.R., Naval,* XVI, 484; for firing on her from the city, see *O.R.,* XLIV, 357. The shelling of Fort Jackson is mentioned in *ibid.,* 280. See Baltimore *American and Commercial Advertiser,* January 6, 1865, for an account of damage to houses in Savannah.

14. Robert Watson's Journal, December 20–21, 1864, in William Curry Harllee, ed., *Kinfolks, A Genealogical and Biographical Record,* 1898; Savannah *Morning News,* June 10, 1934.

15. John C. Gray, Jr., to his mother, December 25, 1864; Gray to John C.

Ropes, January 7, 1865, in *War Letters, 1862–1865, of John Chipman Gray and John Codman Ropes,* 431, 434.

16. Iverson D. Graves to his mother, January 20, 1864, in "Confederate Diaries," VI, Department of Archives and History.

17. M. H. Turrentine to his sister, December 22, 1864, in Michael H. Turrentine Papers, Duke University Library; W. J. Hardee to C. C. Jones, Jr., May 14, 1866, William Joseph Hardee Papers, Duke University Library.

18. Sherman's letter to Halleck and Stanton's to Grant are in *O.R.,* XLIV, 800, 809.

19. Jones, *Siege of Savannah,* 178.

20. Alexander Robert Chisholm, "Some Corrections of Sherman's Memoirs," *Southern Historical Society Papers,* VII (Richmond, 1879), 296; Chisholm, "The Failure to Capture Hardee," *Battles and Leaders of the Civil War,* IV, 679. For statement of Union officer, see John C. Van Duzer Papers, journal, December 22, 1864, in Duke University Library.

21. Carman, *General Hardee's Escape from Savannah,* 30; Slocum to Joseph Howland, January 6, 1865, in Miscellaneous Manuscripts, The New York Historical Society. Quoted by courtesy of the Society.

21. Enter Sherman

1. Carman, *General Hardee's Escape from Savannah,* 27.

2. *O.R.,* XLIV, 279, 309, 315.

3. Letters of Wesley W. De Haven, a Union soldier, in "Confederate Letters, Diaries and Reminiscences, 1860–1865," X, Department of Archives and History; John Henry Otto, "Diary of an ex-Prussian soldier, Captain Otto, Co. D, 21st Wisconsin Volunteer Infantry," in State Historical Society, Wisconsin; *With Sherman to the Sea, the Civil War Letters, Diaries & Reminiscences of Theodore F. Upson,* 141ff.

4. For Barnum's reconnaissance, see George W. Nichols, *The Story of the Great March, From the Diary of a Staff Officer* (New York, 1865), 96ff.; New York *Evening Post,* January 2, 1865.

5. John W. Geary to John H. Estill, Secretary, July 13, 1866, in Archives of Solomons Lodge, No. 1, AFM, Savannah. The preceding account of the surrender of the city follows Lee and Agnew, *Historical Record of the City of Savannah,* 95–98. The allusion to Tattnall is from the journal of William B. Hodgson entitled, "Journal of the events connected with Gen'l. Sherman's Capture of Savannah, December 21, 1864," in Charles Colcock Jones, Jr., Collection, University of Georgia Library. Hereafter cited Hodgson, Journal.

6. T. H. Pendergast, "Journal of Sherman's Grand March through Georgia," December 6, 1864, in William S. Pendergast and Family Papers, Minnesota Historical Society, St. Paul. The preceding quotations are from Robert G. Athearn, ed., "An Indiana Doctor Marches with Sherman: The Diary of James Comfort Patten," *Indiana Magazine of History,* XLIX, (December, 1953), 422; Rufus Mead to "Folks at Home," December 28, 1864, in *G.H.Q.,* XXXIII, (March, 1949), 62.

7. "Statement by Elizabeth Georgia Basinger" in Basinger, Personal Reminiscences," Appendix IV.

8. *O.R.,* XLIV, 319.

9. Diary of James G. Essington, Co. D, 75th Indiana, December 22, 1864, typescript in The William Henry Smith Memorial Library of The Indiana Historical Society.

10. Hodgson, Journal, December 20, 1864, in Charles Colcock Jones, Jr., Collection, University of Georgia Library. The Savannah resident is quoted in Cincinnati *Daily Commercial,* January 11, 1865.

11. Reminiscences of Reverend George A. Blount (1902), in Savannah *Morning News,* December 25, 1932; M. H. Turrentine to his sister, December 22, 1864, in Michael H. Turrentine Papers, Duke University Library.

12. *O.R.,* XLIV, 280; Minutes of Solomon's Lodge, No. 1, AFM, Savannah, March 15, 1866.

13. William Grunert, *History of the One Hundred and Twenty-ninth Regiment Illinois Volunteer Infantry* (Winchester, Ill., 1866), 158–159. In his *Memoirs* (II, 216ff.) Sherman stated that the subject discussed was the movement of one of Foster's divisions on Bluffton, S. C., in order to cut the plank road. The version he gave on December 23, 1864, seems more reliable. In a letter that day Sherman stated, "I arranged with General Foster and the admiral for immediately bringing round a sufficient force from the Ogeechee to unite with General Foster's troops, then lying at the head of Broad River for this purpose." *O.R.,* XLIV, 792. An account of the trip from Port Royal is in Admiral Dahlgren's diary, December 19–21, 1864, *O.R., Naval,* XVI, 362ff.

14. Sherman to James Harrison Wilson, January 21, 1861, excerpt published in Mary A. Benjamin, ed., *The Collector* (June, 1954), LXVII, 54.

15. *Hitchcock,* 201. Called on by Richmond for an explanation of why he did not burn the cotton, Hardee explained that to do so would have destroyed the city. See *O.R.,* XLVII, part 2, 1105; *O.R.,* LIII, 412.

16. Hodgson, Journal, December 28, 1864, in Charles Colcock Jones, Jr., Collection, University of Georgia Library. Sherman's reply to Molyneux's representative is quoted in his letter to E. M. Stanton, January 2, 1865, *Memoirs,* II, 265ff.

17. The damage to the Molyneux house and contents is described in an affidavit by William Taskersmith, April 14, 1866, British Consulate Papers, Georgia Historical Society. For the complaint of Molyneux's housekeeper, see Howard, *In and Out of the Lines*, 188–191. Wimer Bedford, "Real Life in the Civil War," 62ff. A transcript of Captain Bedford's reminiscences (and his diary) is in The Library of Congress. The originals are in the Bedford Family Collection, Valley Forge Museum of American History. The statement as to non-use of liquor in Howard's headquarters is in Nichols, *The Story of the Great March*, 143.

18. Spencer B. King, Jr., ed., "Fanny Cohen's Journal of Sherman's Occupation of Savannah," *G.H.Q.*, XLI, (December, 1957), 414.

19. Gilbert R. Stormont, ed., *History of the Fifty-eighth Regiment of Indiana Volunteer Infantry . . . From the Manuscript Prepared by the Late Chaplain John J. Hight* (Princeton, Ind., 1895), 452.

20. Edward C. Anderson to his wife, January 2, 1865, in family papers owned by Mrs. Florence C. Schwalb, Savannah. For Sherman's letters to Halleck and Grant, see *O.R.*, XLIV, 841–842.

21. The original of the letter from "Jake," February 2, 1865, is owned by Beverly M. DuBose, Jr., of Atlanta. For preceding quotations in paragraph, see Sherman to Thomas Ewing as quoted in Anna McAllister, *Ellen Ewing, Wife of General Sherman* (New York, 1936), 293; Recollections of William A. Pigman in Savannah *Evening Press*, December 26, 1932; Samuel Garrett, of the 147th Pennsylvania, to Jefferson Hartman, January 15, 1865, in Jefferson Hartman Papers, Duke University Library; Diary of George Lemon Childress, Co. D., 66th Illinois, December 23, 26, 29, 1864, January 6, 9, 1865, Illinois State Historical Society.

22. J. W. Geary to J. H. Estill, Secretary, July 13, 1866, in archives of Solomon's Lodge, No. 1, AFM, Savannah; Nichols, *The Story of the Great March*, 98.

23. Albert Stearns, *Reminiscences of the Late War* (Brooklyn, 1881), 33–35; Lee and Agnew, *Historical Record of the City of Savannah*, 133n; John M. Glidden to W. H. Gardiner, January 29, 1865, edited by Frank Otto Gatell, in *G.H.Q.*, XLIII, (December, 1959), 429, 430. For some equally unenthusiastic observations on Glidden himself, see Howard, *In and Out of the Lines*, 216ff.

24. Correspondent of the New York *World*, writing from Savannah on December 23, 1864, quoted in Chicago *Tribune*, January 7, 1865. The latter newspaper stated that the notice was "understood to be from the Mayor."

25. The seizure of the property of the *Republican* is described in a suit in Chatham Superior Court, a copy of which is in the C. R. Hanleiter

folder, Atlanta Historical Society. On the subject of the Union press at Savannah during this period, see John E. Talmadge, "Savannah's Yankee Newspapers," *The Georgia Review,* XII, (Spring, 1958), 66–73.

26. Sherman to General Webster, December 23, 1864, *O.R.,* XLIV, 793. For the immediately preceding quotation, see James S. Robinson to L. G. Hunt, December 24, 1864, in Gen. J. S. Robinson Collection, The Ohio Historical Society.

27. Diary of G. B. McMillan, December 22, 1864, in George B. McMillan Papers, State Historical Society, Wisconsin. For preceding quotations in paragraph, see George W. Pepper, *Personal Recollections,* 285; George S. Bradley, *The Star Corps; Or, Notes of an Army Chaplain,* 244; Willie J. Baugh, Co. I, 76th Ohio, to his parents, December 25, 1864. The Baugh letters are owned by William T. Mahoney, Wilmington, Delaware. Transcripts are in possession of Bell I. Wiley, Atlanta.

28. "Alderman Henry Frederick Willink" in *The Times* (Savannah), May 31, 1879. A clipping is in possession of Miss Daisy B. Willink, Savannah. For Glidden's letter, see note 23, *supra.*

29. Isaac H. Boyle to "Bro. Reynolds," January 6, 1865, copy of letter in possession of Allen E. Roberts, Highland Springs, Va.; Julian Wisner Hinkley, *A Narrative of Service with the Third Wisconsin Infantry* (published by Wisconsin Historical Library, 1912), 165; Diary of Captain Eli J. Sherlock, 100th Indiana, January 8, 1865, in Adjutant General's Office (Record Group No. 94), The National Archives; John Henry Otto, "Diary of an ex-Prussian soldier, Captain Otto, Co. D, 21st Wisconsin Volunteer Infantry," in State Historical Society, Wisconsin.

30. Howard, *In and Out of the Lines,* 211ff.; undated note from Mrs. Emma P. Hopkins to Lieutenant Colonel York, photostat in possession of Katherine L. Hopkins, Lexington, Kentucky.

31. R. D. Arnold to Harrison O. Briggs, March 17, 1865, *The Arnold Letters,* 115. In April, 1865, Arnold wrote, "The city in a large majority, is anxious for a termination of the war. . . . She must stand or fall in the United States of America." Arnold to Aaron Wilbur, April 4, 1865, typescript in Aaron Wilbur Papers, Duke University Library.

32. Howell Cobb to Jefferson Davis, January 6, 1865, quoted in Montgomery, *Howell Cobb's Confederate Career,* 127.

33. Robert M. Stiles to W. H. Stiles, January 9, 1861, in Mackay-Stiles Papers, Southern Historical Collection, University of North Carolina Library; Earl Schenck Miers, ed., *When the World Ended: The Diary of Emma Le Conte* (New York, 1957), 11.

34. George D. Smith to his aunt, January 31, 1865, Baber-Blackshear Collection, University of Georgia Library. Lieutenant Smith's death is

described in F. W. DuPrée to a cousin, May 28, 1865. Sources of other quotations in this paragraph are: Joseph C. Thompson to his father, January 6, 1865, and William S. Basinger to his mother, February 23, 1865, in "Personal Reminiscences," Appendix XI.

35. Hodgson, Journal, December 28, 1864, in Charles Colcock Jones, Jr., Collection, University of Georgia Library. Some Northern soldiers found bundles of Confederate currency outside a printing office in Savannah. One of them wrote, "The boys are offering $1,000 to citizens for a loaf of bread, and some of the officers have offered from $4,000 to $5,000 for some one to curry their horses, but they can find no one who will accept their offers." Olynthus C. Clark, ed., *Downing Civil War Diary by Sergeant G. Downing* (Des Moines, Iowa, 1916), 240.

36. For Northern aid, see *O.R.*, XLVII, part 2, 166–169; pamphlet entitled, *Savannah and Boston, Account of the Supplies Sent to Savannah* (Boston, 1865); New York *Tribune*, January 7, 10, 11, 13, 1865; John P. Dyer, "Northern Relief for Savannah during Sherman's Occupation," *The Journal of Southern History*, XIX, (November, 1953), 457–472.

37. L. E. Chittenden, *Personal Reminiscences, 1840–1890* (New York, 1893), 248, 255–258.

38. The article in the New York *Times* was reprinted in *Frank Leslie's Illustrated Newspaper,* February 25, 1865.

22. In Occupied Savannah

1. Mrs. W. H. Stiles to her husband, March 2, 1865, Mackay-Stiles Papers, Southern Historical Collection, University of North Carolina Library. Mrs. Stiles conceded that the "larger portion of our people are anxious for submission."

2. O. M. Poe to his wife, December 21, 1864, in Orlando M. Poe Papers, The Library of Congress.

3. "Five Brothers Saussy in the C.S. Army," *Confederate Veteran* (December, 1911), 558.

4. Coffin, *Four Years of Fighting,* 430ff.

5. "Fanny Cohen's Journal of Sherman's Occupation of Savannah," *G.H.Q.,* XLI, (December, 1957), 411–415. As the occupation proceeded, Miss Cohen's attitude possibly mellowed. Her journal stops abruptly on January 3, 1865, the day General Hazen arrived to stay with the Cohens. He proved "very considerate" and said "nothing offensive," Fanny reported. In his *Memoirs* Hazen speaks of his stay with this "interesting and estimable family."

6. Charles Cowley, *Leaves from a Lawyer's Life Afloat and Ashore,* 147ff.

7. Mahan, *From Sail to Steam*, 192.

8. Ammen, *The Old Navy and the New*, 416ff.

9. *Hitchcock*, 207ff. In *Recollections of a Confederate Staff Officer* Moxley Sorrel wrote, "Sherman as a young lieutenant had shared my father's hospitality and had not forgotten it." 282ff.

10. A. S. Williams to his daughters, January 6, 1865, in *From the Cannon's Mouth, The Civil War letters of General Alpheus S. Williams*, 355.

11. George Arthur Gordon, "Eleanor Kinzie Gordon, A Sketch," *G.H.Q.*, I, (September, 1917), 186ff., 189.

12. Hodgson, Journal, December 27, 1864, Charles Colcock Jones, Jr., Collection, University of Georgia Library; recollections of George B. Pritchard as told to Savannah *Press*, December 20, 1928. A clipping is in the Thomas Gamble Scrapbooks, V, 42, Savannah Public Library.

13. The copy of Connolly's letter, December 18, 1864, which he sent to General Baird, is in Box 1, War, 1861–65, Letters, No. 6, The New York Historical Society (quoted by courtesy of the Society); diary and letters of James A. Connolly in *Transactions of the Illinois State Historical Society for the Year 1928*, 374, 435. In connection with the conduct of Davis see also "An Indiana Doctor Marches with Sherman: The Diary of James Comfort Patten," *Indiana Magazine of History*, XLIX, (December, 1953), 419.

14. Diary of Charles W. Wills, 103rd Illinois Infantry, January 9, 1865, in Illinois State Historical Society.

15. George Secor Geer to his wife, June 9, 1865, in Miscellaneous Manuscripts, Georgia Historical Society.

16. "Statement of Elizabeth Georgia Basinger" in Basinger, "Personal Reminiscences," Appendix IV. The immediately preceding quotation is from Edward J. Thomas, *Memoirs of a Southerner, 1840–1923* (Savannah, 1923), 53.

17. Letters of James A. Connolly in *Transactions of the Illinois State Historical Society for the Year 1928*, 371; Edwin E. Bryant, *History of the Third Regiment Wisconsin Veteran Volunteer Infantry*, 300ff.

18. "Uncle" George Carter's recollections are in "Reminiscences of Confederate Soldiers," II, Georgia Department of Archives and History.

19. *With Sherman to the Sea, A Drummer's Story of the Civil War as related by Corydon Edward Foote to Olive Deane Hormel* (New York, 1960), 229ff. The preceding quotation is from William Grunert, *History of the One Hundred and Twenty-ninth Regiment Illinois Volunteer Infantry*, 159ff.

20. Diary of Captain William C. Marlatt, 70th Ohio Infantry, January 4, 1865. The original is owned by James J. McDonald of Madison, Wis-

consin. A copy is in the Atlanta Historical Society. The preceding quotations in the paragraph are from *Ninety-second Illinois Volunteers,* 211; Diary of Benjamin F. Heuston, 23rd Wisconsin Infantry, December 22, 1864, in State Historical Society, Wisconsin.

21. William Wirt Calkins, *The History of the One Hundred and Fourth Regiment of Illinois Volunteer Infantry, War of the Great Rebellion, 1862–1865* (Chicago, 1895), 274. For preceding quotations in paragraph, see letters of James A. Connolly in *Transactions of the Illinois State Historical Society for the Year 1928,* 375; Diary of William Lomax, Surgeon, 12th Indiana, December 23, 1864, in The Indiana Historical Society.

22. *The Diary of James T. Ayers, Civil War Recruiter* (Springfield, Ill., 1947), 73. For other quotations in paragraph, see Diary of James G. Essington, Co. D, 75th Indiana, December 23, 1864, in The Indiana Historical Society; Bruce Hoadley to "Cousin Em," December 31, 1864, in Robert Bruce Hoadley Papers, Duke University Library.

23. Charles F. Hubert, *History of the Fiftieth Regiment, Illinois Volunteer Infantry, in the War of the Union* (Kansas City, Mo., 1894), 337ff.

24. D. Lieb Ambrose, *History of the Seventh Regiment, Illinois Volunteer Infantry* (Springfield, Ill., 1868), 290ff.; "An Indiana Doctor Marches with Sherman: The Diary of James Comfort Patten," *Indiana Magazine of History,* XLIX, (December, 1953), 421; Frederick Downs to his mother, January 15, 1865, in Downs Papers, Brown University Library, Providence, Rhode Island.

25. *History of the Fifty-eighth Regiment of Indiana Volunteer Infantry . . . From the Manuscript Prepared by the Late Chaplain John J. Hight,* 440, 447, 455, 456.

26. Diary of Charles W. Wills, January 11, 1865, in Illinois State Historical Society; Reminiscences of Mary Wragg Bond.

27. Diary of G. B. McMillan, 16th Wisconsin Volunteers, December 25, 1864, George B. McMillan Papers, State Historical Society, Wisconsin; Nixon B. Stewart, *Dan. McCook's Regiment, 52nd O.V.I., A History of the Regiment* (Alliance, Ohio, 1900), 150.

28. *Republican,* January 8, 1865. According to the Cincinnati *Daily Commercial* of February 11, 1865, Dr. I. S. K. Axson of the Presbyterian Church offered a prayer "for all Presidents that their minds might be illuminated to see the right and follow it." See also *Hitchcock,* 199ff.

29. *Hitchcock,* 202.

30. Coffin, *Four Years of Fighting,* 419–421; see also *Republican,* February 3, 1865.

31. *Cf.* the views of Miss Lizzie Frew of Savannah. In 1865 she was apparently living in the North. "A thousand pities it is," she wrote a

young friend in Savannah, "that the mass of the population for the sake of slavery allowed themselves to be hurled by a few leaders into this fatal conflict from which nothing is to be gained. . . ." Lizzie Frew to Lizzie Lachlison, March 23, 1865, letter owned by Mrs. Harriet Train Blake of Savannah.

32. Hodgson, Journal, December 27, 1865, Charles Colcock Jones, Jr., Collection, University of Georgia Library; Joseph C. Thompson to William Tappan Thompson, January 6, 1865, in family papers owned by Edward W. Bell.

33. For Stanton's interview with the Negro preachers, see *O.R.,* XLVII, part 2, 37–41; Nichols, *The Story of the Great March,* 101–103; Sherman, *Memoirs,* II, 245–247.

34. For the Sherman-Halleck correspondence as to Negroes, see Halleck to Sherman, December 30, 1864, *O.R.,* XLIV, 836; Sherman to Halleck, December 31, 1864, *ibid.,* XLIV, 842; Sherman, *Memoirs,* II, 247–250.

35. *Hitchcock,* 202ff.

36. Sherman, *Memoirs,* II, 252. A Union officer wrote in January, 1865, "There are a great many citizens here from the North, all striving to make money. . . ." Gus Van Dyke to his brother, January 21, 1865, in Civil War Letters of Gus Van Dyke, Lieutenant 14th Indiana, The William Henry Smith Memorial Library of The Indiana Historical Society. As to this phase of the occupation, see George Winston Smith, "Cotton from Savannah in 1865," *The Journal of Southern History,* XXI (November, 1955), 496–498.

37. Sherman to Halleck, January 8, 1865, in William T. Sherman Papers, William L. Clements Library, Ann Arbor, Michigan; Moses Harter to "friends," January 7, 1865, in Letters of Moses Harter, Co. A, 25th Indiana, typescript in The Indiana Historical Society; the letter from Levi A. Ross, dated February 1, 1865, was copied out in Ross's diary. The original diary is in the Illinois State Historical Library.

38. *War Letters, 1862–1865, of John Chipman Gray and John Codman Ropes,* 428; Sherman, *Memoirs,* II, 227ff. For preceding quotations in paragraph, see Henry W. Slocum to Joseph Howland, January 6, 1865, in Miscellaneous Manuscripts, The New York Historical Society, quoted by courtesy of the Society; Poe to his wife, December 26, 1864, in Orlando M. Poe Papers, The Library of Congress; M. R. Dresbach to his wife, January 29, 1865, in Michael R. Dresbach Papers, Minnesota Historical Society.

23. "Externally the city is the same"

1. David P. Conyngham, *Sherman's March Through the South, with Sketches and Incidents of the Campaign* (New York, 1865), 294.

2. Dr. E. Lathrop's letter in the New York *Examiner and Chronicle* was reprinted in the *Republican,* March 25, 1865. For preceding quotations in paragraph, see Henry R. Jackson, *Eulogy on the Late Right Rev. Stephen Elliott, Bishop of Georgia* (Savannah, 1867), 17; R. T. Gibson to Mrs. E. B. Richardsone, May 15, 1865.

3. Whitelaw Reid, *After the War: A Southern Tour* (Cincinnati, 1866), 142–145; John C. Gray, Jr., to his mother, March 21, 1865, *War Letters, 1862–1865, of John Chipman Gray and John Codman Ropes,* 463.

4. For other accounts of the fire, see Coffin, *Four Years of Fighting,* 418ff.; L. E. Chittenden, *Personal Reminiscences, 1840–1890,* 262–264; New York *Tribune,* February 6, 1865. Howard, *In and Out of the Lines,* 204.

5. Reminiscences of Mrs. Mary Wragg Bond.

6. Savannah *Republican,* March 19, 1865.

7. Mary A. Drummond, "War Memories"; P. M. B. Young to Cuvier Grover, March 25, 1865, *O.R.,* XLVII, part 3, 23.

8. Hodgson, Journal, January 12 [16?], 1865, Charles Colcock Jones, Jr., Collection, University of Georgia Library. On April 6, Hodgson wrote, "The order of expulsion has been deemed severe by Gen'l Grover. He requested Secy Stanton to revoke it." For the strictures against Sherman, see Lee and Agnew, *Historical Record of the City of Savannah,* 102.

9. For the cemetery controversy, see *O.R.,* XLVII, part 3, 202ff., 204, 205, 566.

10. Basinger, "Personal Reminiscences," 240, 254–258; Basinger, "Savannah Volunteer Guards," 208ff., 232ff.

11. Clement Saussy, "Humors of Camp in Chatham's Artillery," *Confederate Veteran* (1910), 215ff.

12. Diary of G. A. Mercer (No. I), June 3, 1866. The reference to Lamar's death is from Pope Barrow's Memorial Day Address, 1896, in *Addresses Delivered before the Confederate Veterans Association of Savannah, Ga.* (Savannah, 1896).

13. Mary E. Copp Wilbur to her husband, April 19, 1865, in Aaron Wilbur Papers, Duke University Library; Basinger, "Personal Reminiscences," 146.

14. Howard, *In and Out of the Lines,* 223ff.

15. Ada Sterling, ed., *A Belle of the Fifties, Memoirs of Mrs. Clay, of Alabama* (New York, 1905), 274.

16. Olmstead's reminiscences, *Historic and Picturesque Savannah,* 203ff.

17. Howard, *In and Out of the Lines,* 222.

18. Robert Falligant's "Doffing the Gray" is in William Gilmore Simms, ed., *War Poetry of the South* (New York, 1866), 461ff. Falligant also wrote "The Man of the Twelfth of May."

19. Diary of George A. Mercer (No. I), June 11, 1865.

BIBLIOGRAPHY

I. UNPUBLISHED LETTERS AND DIARIES

Confederate

Journal and papers of Edward C. Anderson, owned by his great granddaughter, Mrs. Florence Crane Schwalb of Savannah. The papers include a reminiscence by Anderson of his activities during the early weeks of the war.

Letters of Edward C. Anderson, Jr., (nephew of Edward C. Anderson) and Mrs. George W. Anderson, in J. Randolph Anderson Papers, Georgia Historical Society, Hodgson Hall, Savannah.

Godfrey Barnsley Papers, letters of William Duncan, 1861–1862, Emory University Library, Atlanta.

Colonel David C. Barrow Papers, University of Georgia Library, Athens. The collection includes some letters of James C. Barrow.

Letters of James C. Barrow, owned by Dean Smith, Jr., Savannah.

John W. Bentley Letters, Georgia Historical Society, Savannah.

J. William Blackshear Papers, Duke University Library, Durham.

Letters of John L. Branch and Mrs. John H. S. Branch, in Margaret Branch Sexton Collection of Family Letters, University of Georgia Library, Athens.

Letters of F. Buntyn, in Elizabeth Buntyn Papers, Duke University Library, Durham.

Letters of John Devine Carswell and John Wright Carswell, family papers owned by Porter W. Carswell, Bellevue Plantation, Waynesboro, Georgia.

Cobb Papers, on deposit in University of Georgia Library, Athens. This collection includes letters written from Savannah by Howell Cobb, Jr., Pope Barrow and Edward R. Harden.

Raleigh E. Colston Papers, Southern Historical Collection, University of North Carolina Library, Chapel Hill.

"Private Journal of E. W. Drummond." The original is owned by Major Drummond's grandson, Eugene D. Drummond, of Jackson, Mississippi.

Joseph Espey Papers, Southern Historical Collection, University of North Carolina Library, Chapel Hill.

George W. Gift Letters, in Southern Historical Collection, University of North Carolina Library, Chapel Hill. The Savannah letters of Lieutenant Gift in this collection vary from those quoted or paraphrased in Harriet Gift Castlen, *Hope Bids Me Onward* (Savannah, 1945).

William Washington Gordon letters, in Gordon family papers, Georgia Historical Society, Savannah.

J. H. Graham letters, in "Confederate Diaries," VIII, Georgia Department of Archives and History, Atlanta.

Henry L. Graves (and Iverson D. Graves) letters, in "Confederate Diaries," VI, Georgia Department of Archives and History, Atlanta. The originals are in the Southern Historical Collection, University of North Carolina Library, Chapel Hill.

Diary of Cornelius R. Hanleiter, 1861–1864, Atlanta Historical Society, Atlanta.

William Joseph Hardee Papers, Duke University Library, Durham.

Edward J. Harden Papers, Duke University Library, Durham.

Joseph J. Hardy and I. T. Hardy letters, in "Letters from Confederate Soldiers," II, Georgia Department of Archives and History, Atlanta.

Diary of John Hart, owned by Miss Catherine Moss Pegg, East Orange, New Jersey. A copy is in possession of Hugh H. Grady, Savannah.

Alfred L. Hartridge letters, owned by Walter C. Hartridge, Savannah.

Celathiel Helms letters, in "Letters from Confederate Soldiers," III, Georgia Department of Archives and History, Atlanta.

William B. Hodgson, "Journal of the events connected with Gen'l. Sherman's Capture of Savannah," Charles Colcock Jones, Jr., Collection, University of Georgia Library, Athens.

W. H. Hood letters, in "Reminiscences of Confederate Soldiers," II, Georgia Department of Archives and History, Atlanta.

Henry R. Jackson, Order Book, December 24, 1861–April 16, 1863, and Henry R. Jackson folder in Georgia Department of Archives and History, Atlanta.

Charles Colcock Jones, Jr., Collection, University of Georgia Library, Athens.

C. C. Jones Papers, Duke University Library, Durham.

John McIntosh Kell Papers, Duke University Library, Durham.

Diary of W. L. Landershine, in possession of the National Park Service, Fort Pulaski, Georgia.

Alexander R. Lawton letters, Georgia Department of Archives and History, Atlanta.

"Civil War Letters by Edmund C. Lee, Chaplain in Confederate Army." A typescript is in the Georgia Historical Society, Savannah. At the time the letters were copied by the Florida Historical Records Survey in 1937 the originals were owned by E. L. Vanderipe of Manatee, Florida.

Mackay-Stiles Papers, in Southern Historical Collection, University of North Carolina Library, Chapel Hill. Another collection of Mackay-Stiles papers is in Emory University Library, Atlanta.

John Newland Maffitt Papers, Southern Historical Collection, University of North Carolina Library, Chapel Hill.

"Diary and Note Book" of George A. Mercer, covering the period from June 15, 1860, to February 28, 1862; September 18, 1863, through April 17, 1864, and resuming June 11, 1865, is owned by Mercer's grandson, John H. Mercer of Savannah and Hollywood. Another of Mercer's war diaries commences March 3, 1862, runs through September 17, 1863, resumes April 30, 1864, and terminates May 20, 1865. The original of the latter is in the Southern Historical Collection, University of North Carolina Library, Chapel Hill.

Mercer-Walker Letters, Emory University Library, Atlanta.

Theodorick W. Montfort Letters. The originals are in the Georgia Historical Society, Savannah. Copies are in "Letters from Confederate Soldiers," II, Georgia Department of Archives and History, Atlanta.

Charles H. Olmstead Papers, Southern Historical Collection, University of North Carolina Library, Chapel Hill.

Confederate Ordnance Department Letters (Savannah), in Confederate Ordnance Papers, The National Archives, Washington, D. C.

George F. Palmes Papers, in Georgia Historical Society, Savannah.

Savannah Squadron Papers, Emory University Library, Atlanta.

Carrie Bell Sinclair Papers, Georgia Historical Society, Savannah.

Letters of George D. Smith, 1860–1865, in Baber-Blackshear Collection, University of Georgia Library, Athens.

Gustavus Woodson Smith Papers, Duke University Library, Durham.

Joseph C. Thompson letters, owned by Edward W. Bell, Savannah.

Michael H. Turrentine Papers, Duke University Library, Durham.

Henry C. Wayne letters and Adjutant General Wayne's Letter Books, 1862–1864, in Georgia Department of Archives and History, Atlanta.

Aaron Wilbur Papers, in Duke University Library, Durham, and in Emory University Library, Atlanta.

John L. G. Wood letters, mss. in Georgia Department of Archives and History, Atlanta.

Union

Letters of Willie J. Baugh, 76th Ohio Regiment. The originals are owned by William T. Mahoney of Wilmington, Delaware. Copies are in possession of Bell I. Wiley, Atlanta.

Diary and reminiscences of Captain Wimer Bedford. Transcripts are in The Library of Congress, Washington, D. C. The originals are in the Bedford Family Collection, Valley Forge Museum of American History, Valley Forge, Pennsylvania.

John M. Bessmer Letters, Michigan Historical Collections, University of Michigan, Ann Arbor. The letters are written in German.

Charles S. Brown Papers, Duke University Library, Durham.

Diary of Elijah P. Burton, Surgeon, 7th Illinois Regiment. A typescript is in the Illinois State Historical Library, Springfield.

Diary of George Lemon Childress, Co. I, 66th Illinois, in Illinois State Historical Library, Springfield.

Michael R. Dresbach Papers, 1864–'65, in Minnesota Historical Society, St. Paul.

Diary of Peter Ege, Captain, 34th Illinois Volunteers, in Peter Ege Papers, State Historical Society, Wisconsin, Madison.

Diary of James G. Essington, Co. D, 75th Indiana, typescript in The Indiana Historical Society, Indianapolis.

Diary of Colonel Douglas Hapeman, 104th Illinois Infantry, in Illinois State Historical Library, Springfield.

Letters of Moses Harter, Co. A, 25th Indiana, typescripts in The Indiana Historical Society, Indianapolis.

Jefferson Hartman Papers, Duke University Library, Durham.

Joseph R. Hawley Papers, The Library of Congress, Washington, D. C.

Diary and letters of Benjamin F. Heuston, 23rd Wisconsin Infantry, State Historical Society, Wisconsin, Madison.

Robert Bruce Hoadley Papers, Duke University Library, Durham.

Charles Lafferty letters, in possession of National Park Service, Fort Pulaski, Georgia.

Diary of William Lomax, Surgeon, 12th Indiana Regiment, typescript in The Indiana Historical Society, Indianapolis.

Diary of George B. McMillan, 16th Wisconsin Volunteers, State Historical Society, Wisconsin, Madison.

Diary of William C. Marlatt, Captain, 70th Ohio Veteran Volunteer Infantry. The original is owned by James J. McDonald, of Madison, Wisconsin. A copy is in the Atlanta Historical Society, Atlanta.

"Diary of an ex-Prussian soldier, Captain [John Henry] Otto, Co. D, 21st Wisconsin Volunteer Infantry . . . ," in State Historical Society, Wisconsin, Madison.

"Journal of Sherman's Grand March through Georgia," in William W. Pendergast and Family Papers, Minnesota Historical Society, St. Paul.

Correspondence of Captain O. M. Poe, USA, with his wife during the Civil War, Orlando M. Poe Papers, Library of Congress, Washington, D. C.

Papers of Harvey Reid, 22nd Wisconsin Volunteers, State Historical Society, Wisconsin, Madison.

J. S. Robinson Collection, The Ohio Historical Society, Columbus.

Diary of Levi A. Ross, Captain, 86th Illinois Infantry, Illinois State Historical Library, Springfield.

Diary of Captain Eli J. Sherlock, 100th Indiana, in Records of the Adjutant General's Office (Record Group No. 94), The National Archives, Washington, D. C. This typescript is not identical in certain places to the manuscript in the Eli J. Sherlock Papers, The Indiana Historical Society, Indianapolis.

William T. Sherman Papers, Library of Congress, Washington, D. C.

"Capture of Fort McAllister" by Lieutenant Colonel William E. Strong, December 30, 1864, in William T. Sherman Papers, The Library of Congress, Washington, D. C.

John C. Van Duzer Papers, Duke University Library, Durham.

Letters of Gus Van Dyke, Lieutenant, 14th Indiana, in Eli J. Sherlock Papers, Henry Smith Memorial Library of The Indiana Historical Society, Indianapolis.

John Weissert letters, in Michigan Historical Collections, The University of Michigan, Ann Arbor. These letters, in German, have been translated in a few cases.

Diary of Charles W. Wills, 103rd Illinois Infantry, in Illinois State Historical Library, Springfield.

II. UNPUBLISHED REMINISCENCES

Francis R. Baker, 78th Ohio Infantry, transcript of Civil War Memoirs in the Illinois State Historical Library, Springfield.

William S. Basinger, "The Personal Reminiscences of William Starr Basinger, 1827–1910." The original is in the University of Georgia Library, Athens. A typewritten copy is in possession of his daughter, Mrs. Edward P. Lawton, Savannah.

"Statement by Elizabeth Georgia Basinger of the experiences of her mother Jane Susan Starr Basinger, and herself during the occupation of Savannah by Sherman's army on December 20, 1864." This memoir is in "The Personal Reminiscences of William Starr Basinger," Appendix IV.

Berry Benson Papers, Reminiscences, in Southern Historical Collection, University of North Carolina Library, Chapel Hill.

Reminiscences of Mrs. Mary Wragg Bond, owned by J. Sullivan Bond, Savannah.

Mary A. (Mrs. Edward W.) Drummond, "War Memories." These reminiscences were written in 1866. A copy made in 1910 is in possession of her grandson, Eugene D. Drummond of Jackson, Mississippi.

General John K. Jackson's account of the operations of his command at Honey Hill in C. C. Jones Papers, Duke University Library, Durham.

Reminiscences of David B. Morgan of Wheeler's Cavalry, dated July 28, 1917, in Georgia Historical Society, Savannah.

Reminiscences of Mrs. Mary E. Copp Wilbur, Aaron Wilbur Papers, Emory University Library, Atlanta.

Roger W. Woodbury, Captain, 3rd New Hampshire Volunteers, "Personal Recollections of the War for the Union," written about 1877. For a description, see publication of Emily Driscoll, manuscripts dealer, New York City, *Autographs, Manuscripts* (December, 1960), 23ff. Chapters are included on Port Royal and Hilton Head. (The author did not have access to Woodbury's reminiscences.)

III. PUBLISHED LETTERS AND DIARIES

Confederate

Letters of Richard D. Arnold, M.D., 1808–1876 (Durham, N. C., 1929), edited by Richard H. Shryock.

"Diary of George Bell," edited by J. Whitfield Bell, *The Georgia Historical Quarterly,* XXII, (June, 1938).

"Fanny Cohen's Journal of Sherman's Occupation of Savannah," edited by Spencer B. King, Jr., *The Georgia Historical Quarterly,* XLI, (December, 1957).

Felix Gregory De Fontaine, see "Personne Goes to Georgia: Five Civil War Letters," edited by James M. Merrill, *The Georgia Historical Quarterly,* XLIII, (June, 1959).

Harriet Gift Castlen, *Hope Bids Me Onward* (Savannah, 1945). This volume contains some of the Civil War correspondence of Lieutenant George W. Gift of the Confederate Navy.

Journal of Anna Wylly Habersham, 1864 (Savannah, 1926), edited by George Noble Jones.

Ebb Tide: As Seen Through the Diary of Josephine Clay Habersham, 1863 (Athens, Ga., 1958), edited by Spencer Bidwell King, Jr.

"The Confederate Letters of John W. Hagan," edited by Bell Irvin Wiley, *The Georgia Historical Quarterly,* XXXVIII, (June and September, 1954).

Frances Thomas Howard, *In and Out of the Lines, An Accurate Account of Incidents during the Occupation of Georgia by Federal Troops in 1864–65* (New York, 1905). The names used in this book are fictitious, the persons are real.

Letters from Henry R. Jackson to the Hon. Alex. H. Stephens (Savannah, November 26, 1860).

Mary Sharpe Jones and Mary Jones Mallard, *Yankees A'Coming: One Month's Experiences during the Invasion of Liberty County, Georgia, 1864–1865* (Tuscaloosa, Ala., 1959), edited by Haskell Monroe.

Letters of Bishop Augustin Verot, see "Letters of the Bishop of Savannah, 1861–1865," edited by Willard E. Wight, *The Georgia Historical Quarterly,* XLII, (March, 1958).

Journal of Robert Watson in *Kinfolks, A Genealogical and Biographical Record* (New Orleans, 1935), edited by William Curry Harllee. Portions of Watson's diary were published in Savannah *Morning News,* June 6, 1934.

Letters of Edward S. Willis, *Southern Historical Society Papers* (Richmond, 1889), XVII.

Union

The Diary of James T. Ayers, Civil War Recruiter (Springfield, Ill., 1947).

The Diary of Elias A. Bryant of Francestown, N. H. (privately printed, Concord, N. H., no date).

Major James A. Connolly's diary and letters to his wife published in *Transactions of the Illinois State Historical Society for the Year 1928* (Springfield, Ill., 1928); *Three Years in the Army of the Cumberland, The Letters and Diary of Major James A. Connolly* (Bloomington, Ill., 1959), edited by Paul M. Angle.

Downing Civil War Diary by Sergeant Alexander G. Downing (Des Moines, Iowa, 1916), edited by Olynthus B. Clark.

"Naval Letters from Captain Percival Drayton, 1861–1865," in *Bulletin of the New York Public Library,* X, (November, 1906).

"Sherman's March through Georgia: Letters from Charles Ewing to his Father Thomas Ewing," edited by George C. Osborn, *The Georgia Historical Quarterly*, XLII, (September, 1958).

Letter of John M. Glidden, edited by Frank Otto Gatell, *The Georgia Historical Quarterly*, XLIII, (December, 1959).

War Letters, 1862–1865, of John Chipman Gray and John Codman Ropes (Boston, 1927).

Letter of George W. Hanger, *The Georgia Historical Quarterly*, XLII, (December, 1958).

Marching With Sherman, Passages From The Letters and Campaign Diaries of Henry Hitchcock (New Haven, 1927), edited by M. A. DeWolfe Howe.

Letters of Rufus Mead, Jr., "With Sherman Through Georgia and the Carolinas: Letters of a Federal Soldier," edited by James A. Padgett, *The Georgia Historical Quarterly*, XXXIII, (March, 1949).

"An Indiana Doctor Marches with Sherman: The Diary of James Comfort Patten," *Indiana Magazine of History*, XLIX, (December, 1953), edited by Robert G. Athearn.

Home Letters of General Sherman (New York, 1909), edited by M. A. DeWolfe Howe.

With Sherman to the Sea, the Civil War Letters, Diaries & Reminiscences of Theodore F. Upson (Baton Rouge, 1943), edited by Oscar Osburn Winther.

War Diary and Letters of Stephen Minot Weld, 1861–1865 (privately printed, 1912).

From the Cannon's Mouth, the Civil War letters of General Alpheus S. Williams (Detroit, 1959), edited by Milo M. Quaife.

Army Life of an Illinois Soldier . . . Letters and Diary of the Late Charles W. Wills, compiled by Mary E. Kellogg (Washington, D. C., 1906).

IV. PUBLISHED MEMOIRS AND REMINISCENCES

Confederate

Reverend George A. Blount, reminiscences of Hardee's evacuation, dated May 25, 1902, Savannah *Morning News,* December 25, 1932.

Henry Blun, *Reminiscences of My Blockade Running* (Savannah, 1910); also his recollections in Savannah *Morning News,* February 21, 1897.

Military Reminiscences of Gen. Wm. R. Boggs, C.S.A. (Durham, N. C., 1913).

James D. Bulloch, *Secret Service of the Confederate States in Europe* (London, 1883), I.

R. D. Chapman, *A Georgia Soldier in the Civil War, 1861–1865* (Houston, 1923).

Alexander Robert Chisholm, "Some Corrections of Sherman's Memoirs," *Southern Historical Society Papers,* VII (Richmond, 1879); A. R. Chisholm, "The Failure to Capture Hardee," *Battles and Leaders of the Civil War* (New York, 1887), II, edited by R. U. Johnson and C. C. Buel.

Robert Chisholm, "The Battle of Port Royal," *Under Both Flags* (Chicago, 1896).

Charles Seton Hardee, *Reminiscences and Recollections of Old Savannah* (Savannah, *ca.* 1928).

William Harden, "Recollections of a Private in the Signal Corps," in *Addresses Delivered Before the Confederate Veterans Association of Savannah, Ga.* (Savannah, 1898); Harden, *Recollections of a Long and Satisfactory Life* (Savannah, 1934).

Isaac Hermann, *Memoirs of a Veteran* (Atlanta, 1911).

McHenry Howard, *Recollections of a Maryland Confederate Soldier and Staff Officer under Johnston, Jackson and Lee* (Baltimore, 1914).

John McIntosh Kell, *Recollections of a Naval Life* (Washington, D. C., 1900).

Lilla Mills Hawes, ed., "The Memoirs of Charles H. Olmstead," *The Georgia Historical Quarterly,* XLII, XLIII, XLIV, XLV, (December, 1958, through March, 1961).

Charles H. Olmstead, reminiscences of war-time Savannah in Adelaide Wilson, *Historic and Picturesque Savannah* (Boston, 1889); Olmstead, *Reminiscences of Service with the First Volunteer Regiment of Georgia, Charleston Harbor, in 1863* (Savannah, 1879).

G. Moxley Sorrel, *Recollections of a Confederate Staff Officer* (New York, 1905).

Robert Stiles, *Four Years Under Marse Robert* (New York, 1910).

Richard Taylor, *Destruction and Reconstruction, Personal Experiences of the Late War* (New York, 1955), edited by Richard B. Harwell.

Edward J. Thomas, *Memoirs of a Southerner, 1840–1923* (Savannah, 1923).

B. M. Zettler, *War Stories and School-Day Incidents for the Children* (New York, 1912). Zettler was a member of the Oglethorpe Light Infantry.

Union

A. O. Abbott, *Prison Life in the South: At Richmond, Macon, Savannah* . . . (New York, 1866).

Daniel Ammen, *The Old Navy and the New* (Philadelphia, 1891).

John C. Arbuckle, *Civil War Experiences of a Foot-Soldier Who Marched with Sherman* (Columbus, Ohio, 1930).

George S. Bradley, *The Star Corps: Or, Notes of an Army Chaplain, During Sherman's Famous "March to the Sea"* (Milwaukee, 1865).

Ezra A. Carman, *General Hardee's Escape from Savannah* (Washington, D. C., 1893).

L. E. Chittenden, *Personal Reminiscences, 1840–1890* (New York, 1893).

Charles Carleton Coffin, *Four Years of Fighting* (Boston, 1866).

David P. Conyngham, *Sherman's March Through the South With Sketches and Incidents of the Campaign* (New York, 1865).

Elbridge J. Copp, *Reminiscences of the War of the Rebellion, 1861–1865* (Nashua, N. H., 1911).

Charles Cowley, *Leaves from a Lawyer's Life Afloat and Ashore* (Lowell, Mass., 1879).

[Corydon Edward Foote], *With Sherman to the Sea, A Drummer's Story of the Civil War as related by Corydon Edward Foote to Olive Deane Hormel,* with a foreword by Elizabeth Yates (New York, 1960).

William B. Hazen, *A Narrative of Military Service* (Boston, 1885).

Julian Wisner Hinkley, *A Narrative of Service with the Third Wisconsin Infantry* (Wisconsin Historical Library, 1917).

Autobiography of Oliver Otis Howard, Major General, United States Army (New York, 1908), II.

Daniel G. Kelley, *What I Saw and Suffered in Rebel Prisons* (Buffalo, N. Y., 1868).

Alfred T. Mahan, *From Sail to Steam* (New York, 1907).

George W. Nichols, *The Story of the Great March, From the Diary of a Staff Officer* (New York, 1865).

Albert Bigelow Paine, *A Sailor of Fortune, Personal Memoirs of Captain B. S. Osbon* (New York, 1906).

George W. Pepper, *Personal Recollections of Sherman's Campaign in Georgia and the Carolinas* (Zanesville, Ohio, 1866).

Whitelaw Reid, *After the War: A Southern Tour* (Cincinnati, 1866).

Frederick Emil Schmitt, "Prisoner of War: Experiences in Southern Prisons," *Wisconsin Magazine of History,* XLII, (Winter, 1958–1959).

Memoirs of Gen. W. T. Sherman Written by Himself (New York, 1891), II. The 1891 edition contains an appendix which was not in the earlier edition of 1875.

Susie King Taylor, *Reminiscences of My Life in Camp With the 33D United States Colored Troops Late 1st S.C. Volunteers* (Boston, 1902).

Alonzo Williams, "The Investment of Fort Pulaski," in *Personal Narratives of Events of the War of the Rebellion* (Providence, R. I., 1887).

James Harrison Wilson, *Under the Old Flag* (New York, 1912), I.

V. REGIMENTAL AND COMPANY HISTORIES

Confederate

A. P. Adamson, *Brief History of the Thirtieth Georgia Regiment* (Griffin, Ga., 1912).

William Starr Basinger, "The Savannah Volunteer Guards, 1858–1882." The original manuscript is at the University of Georgia, Athens. A typewritten copy is in the archives of the Guards at Savannah.

Walter Clark, ed., *Histories of the Several Regiments and Battalions from North Carolina in the Great War, 1861–65* (Goldsboro, N. C., 1901), IV.

Walter A. Clark, *Under the Stars and Bars or, Memories of Four Years Service With the Oglethorpes, of Augusta, Georgia* (Augusta, 1900).

A. McC. Duncan, *Roll of Officers and Members of the Georgia Hussars . . . with Historical Sketch* (Savannah, 1907).

The Joe Thompson Artillery—Recollections of Captain C. R. Hanleiter (published, with other articles, by Kimsey's Book Shop, Atlanta, 1956).

Charles C. Jones, Jr., *Historical Sketch of the Chatham Artillery* (Albany, N. Y., 1867).

G. W. Nichols, *A Soldier's Story of his Regiment* (*61st Georgia*) (1898).

Official Programme and Guide Book, Reunion Georgia Division U.C.V., Savannah, Georgia, November 22, 23, 24, 1899, contains a list of troops contributed by Savannah and its vicinity.

W. S. Rockwell, *The Oglethorpe Light Infantry of Savannah, In Peace and In War* (Savannah, 1894).

The issues of Savannah *Morning News* for May 3 and May 5, 1886, contain histories of various independent companies of the city.

Historical Sketch of the Savannah Volunteer Guards Battalion (Savannah, 1886).

John F. Wheaton, *Reminiscences of the Chatham Artillery During the War 1861–1865* (Savannah, 1887).

Union

D. Lieb Ambrose, *History of the Seventh Regiment, Illinois Volunteer Infantry* (Springfield, Ill., 1868).

William Worth Belknap, ed., *History of the Fifteenth Regiment, Iowa Volunteer Infantry* (Keokuk, Iowa, 1887).

Edwin E. Bryant, *History of the Third Regiment Wisconsin Infantry, 1861–1865* (Madison, Wisc., 1891).

Charles K. Cadwell, *The Old Sixth Regiment* (New Haven, Conn., 1875).

William Wirt Calkins, *The History of the One Hundred and Fourth Regiment of Illinois Volunteer Infantry, War of the Great Rebellion, 1862–1865* (Chicago, 1895).

Reverend Frederick Denison, *Shot and Shell: The Third Rhode Island Heavy Artillery Regiment* (Providence, 1879).

Daniel Eldridge, *The Third New Hampshire, And All About It, 1861–1865* (Boston, 1893).

Luis F. Emilio, *History of the Fifty-Fourth Regiment of Massachusetts Volunteer Infantry, 1863–'65* (Boston, 1891).

The Story of the Fifty-fifth Illinois Volunteer Infantry in the Civil War, 1861–1865 (Clinton, Mass., 1887), prepared by a committee on publication.

S. F. Fleharty, *Our Regiment, A History of the 102d Illinois Infantry Volunteers* (Chicago, 1865).

William Grunert, *History of the One Hundred and Twenty-ninth Regiment Illinois Volunteer Infantry* (Winchester, Ill., 1866).

Charles F. Hubert, *History of the Fiftieth Regiment, Illinois Volunteer Infantry, in the War of the Union* (Kansas City, Mo., 1894).

Alfred J. Hunter, *History of the Eighty-second Indiana Volunteer Infantry, its Organization, Campaigns and Battles* (Indianapolis, 1893).

James M. Nichols, *Perry's Saints, or the Fighting Parson's Regiment* [48th New York] *in the War of the Rebellion* (Boston, 1886).

Ninety-second Illinois Volunteers (Freeport, Ill., 1875), prepared by a committee on publication.

Abraham J. Palmer, *The History of the Forty-eighth Regiment, New York State Volunteers* (New York, 1885).

Edwin W. Payne, *History of the Thirty-fourth Regiment of Illinois Infantry, September 7, 1861–July 12, 1865* (Clinton, Iowa, 1902).

Joseph A. Saunier, *A History of the Forty-Seventh Regiment Ohio Volunteer Infantry* (Hillsboro, Ohio, 1903).

Eli J. Sherlock, *Memorabilia of the Marches and Battles in Which the One Hundredth Regiment of Indiana Infantry Volunteers Took an Active Part* (Kansas City, Mo., 1896).

Nixon B. Stewart, *Dan. McCook's Regiment, 52nd O.V.I., A History of the Regiment, Its Campaigns and Battles From 1862 to 1865* (Alliance, Ohio, 1900).

Gilbert R. Stormont, ed., *History of the Fifty-eighth Regiment of Indiana Volunteer Infantry . . . From the Manuscript Prepared by the Late Chaplain John J. Hight* (Princeton, Ind., 1895).

Stephen Walkey, *History of the Seventh Connecticut Volunteer Infantry . . . 1861–1865* (Southington, Conn., 1905).

Henry H. Wright, *A History of the Sixth Iowa Infantry* (Iowa City, Ia., 1923).

VI. GENERAL WORKS, BIOGRAPHIES AND PUBLISHED RECORDS

History of the Rebel Steam Ram "Atlanta," Now on exhibition at foot of Washington Street . . . with an interesting account of the engagement which resulted in her capture (Philadelphia, 1863).

I. W. Avery, *The History of the State of Georgia from 1850 to 1881* (New York, 1881).

Proceedings of the Congress on the Announcement of the Death of Col. Francis S. Bartow, of the Army of the Confederate States (Richmond, 1861).

U. R. Brooks, ed., *Stories of the Confederacy* (Columbia, S. C., 1912).

T. Conn Bryan, *Confederate Georgia* (Athens, Ga., 1953).

Allen D. Candler, ed., *The Confederate Records of the State of Georgia* (Atlanta, 1909–1911), I–III.

Confederate Veteran. The files of this periodical were used in conjunction with the unpublished index prepared by Ray D. Smith of Chicago, Illinois.

Addresses Delivered Before the Confederate Veterans Association, of Savannah, Ga. (Savannah, 1896, 1898).

E. Merton Coulter, *Lost Generation: The Life and Death of James Barrow, CSA* (Tuscaloosa, Ala., 1956).

W. A. Croffutt and John M. Morris, *The Military and Civil History of Connecticut During the War of 1861–65* (New York, 1868).

Madeline V. Dahlgren, *Memoir of John A. Dahlgren, Rear-Admiral United States Navy* (Boston, 1882).

Munroe d'Antignac, *Georgia's Navy, 1861* (Griffin, Ga., 1945).

Charles H. Davis [Jr.], *Life of Charles Henry Davis, Rear Admiral, 1807–1877* (Boston, 1899).

H. A. Du Pont, *Rear-Admiral Samuel Francis Du Pont, United States Navy* (New York, 1926).

"Memoirs & Sermons of Rt. Rev. S. Elliott, D. D., Bishop of Georgia," bound volume of sermons in Georgia Historical Society, Savannah.

Clement A. Evans, ed., *Confederate Military History* (Atlanta, 1899). Volume VI, entitled *Georgia,* was written by Joseph T. Derry.

Q. A. Gillmore, *Official Report to the United States Engineer Department, of the Siege and Reduction of Fort Pulaski* (New York, 1862); Gillmore, "Siege and Capture of Fort Pulaski," in *Battles and Leaders,* II.

George Arthur Gordon, "Eleanor Kinzie Gordon, A Sketch," *The Georgia Historical Quarterly,* I, (September, 1917).

Letters and Family Documents Relating to Charles Green of Savannah, Georgia, and Greenwich, Virginia (Privately printed, 1941).

W. Stanley Hoole, *Vizetelly Covers the Confederacy* (Tuscaloosa, Ala., 1957).

Charles C. Jones, Jr., *The Siege of Savannah in December, 1864* (Albany, N. Y., 1874); Jones, "The Siege and Evacuation of Savannah, Georgia," in *Southern Historical Society Papers,* XVII (Richmond, 1889).

Charles C. Jones, Jr., *The Life and Services of Commodore Josiah Tattnall* (Savannah, 1878).

Ralston B. Lattimore, *Fort Pulaski National Monument, Georgia* (Washington, D. C., 1954).

F. D. Lee and J. L. Agnew, *Historical Record of the City of Savannah* (Savannah, 1869).

William W. Mackall, *A Son's Recollections of His Father* (New York, 1930).

Amos Lawrence Mason, *Memoir and Correspondence of Charles Steedman, Rear Admiral, United States Navy* (Cambridge, Mass., 1912).

Frank Moore, ed., *Rebellion Record, A Diary of American Events* (New York, 1861–1873), I, II, VI.

The War of the Rebellion: A Compilation of the Official Records of the Union and Confederate Armies (Washington, D. C., 1880–1901), Series I, vols. VI, VII, XIV, XXIX, XXXV (part 1), XLIV, XLVII (parts 2 and 3), LIII; and Series II, vols. VII, VIII.

Official Records of the Union and Confederate Navies in the War of the Rebellion (Washington, D. C., 1897–1927), Series I, vols. VI, XII–XVI inclusive.

Alfred Roman, *The Military Operations of General Beauregard* (New York, 1884), II.

William Howard Russell, *My Diary North and South* (New York, 1863); "Recollections of the Civil War," in *North American Review,* CLXVI, (March, 1898).

J. Thomas Scharf, *History of the Confederate Navy from its Organization to the Surrender of Its Last Vessel* (Atlanta, 1887).

James W. Silver, *Confederate Morale and Church Propaganda* (Tuscaloosa, Ala., 1957).

VII. ARTICLES

R. Jervis Cooke, "Sand and Grit, The Story of Fort McAllister; A Confederate Earthwork on the Great Ogeechee River, Genesis Point, Georgia" (*ca.* 1938). A typed copy is in the Georgia Historical Commission, Atlanta.

John P. Dyer, "Northern Relief for Savannah during Sherman's Occupation," *The Journal of Southern History,* XIX, (November, 1953).

Earl W. Fornell, "The Civil War Comes to Savannah," *The Georgia Historical Quarterly,* XLIII, (September, 1959).

William Harden, "The Capture of the U. S. Steamer 'Water Witch' in Ossabaw Sound, Ga., June 2–3, 1864," *The Georgia Historical Quarterly,* III, (March, 1919).

Thomas Robson Hay, "Gazaway Bugg Lamar, Confederate Banker and Business Man," *The Georgia Historical Quarterly,* XXXVII, (June, 1953).

W. E. Jackson, "The Siege and Capture of Fort Pulaski, Cockspur Island, Georgia" (National Park Service, Washington, D. C., 1951). A typed copy is in the Savannah Public Library.

Malcolm Maclean, "The Last Cruise of the C. S. S. Atlanta," *The Georgia Historical Quarterly*, XL, (June, 1956).

Haskell Monroe, "Men Without Law: Federal Raiding in Liberty County, Georgia," *The Georgia Historical Quarterly*, XLIV, (June, 1960).

Charles H. Olmstead, "Fort Pulaski," *The Georgia Historical Quarterly*, I, (June, 1917).

Marcus W. Price, "Ships That Tested the Blockade of the Georgia and East Florida Ports, 1861–1865," *The American Neptune*, XV, (April, 1955).

George Winston Smith, "Cotton from Savannah," *The Journal of Southern History*, XXI, (November, 1955).

John E. Talmadge, "Savannah's Yankee Newspapers," *The Georgia Review*, XII, (Spring, 1958).

Rogers W. Young, "Two Years at Fort Bartow, 1862–1864," *The Georgia Historical Quarterly*, XXIII, (September, 1939).

VIII. NEWSPAPERS AND MISCELLANEOUS SOURCES

Ledger Book, Thomas Henderson, undertaker and cabinetmaker, Savannah, 1857–1866, in possession of Lindsey P. Henderson, Funeral Directors, Savannah.

Log books of U. S. Naval vessels in The National Archives (Record Group No. 24), Washington, D. C.

Minute Book, Mayor and Aldermen of Savannah, 1862, City Hall; Annual Reports of Mayor of Savannah, 1861–1864, 1866.

Minute Book, Solomon's Lodge, No. 1, AFM, 1866, Savannah.

Newspaper clippings in Georgia Historical Society, Savannah, and in the Savannah Public Library.

Photographic collections: The National Archives, The Library of Congress, Navy Department at Washington, New York Public Library, Boston Public Library and the Frederick Hill Meserve Collection owned by Mrs. Dorothy Meserve Kunhardt of Morristown, New Jersey.

Savannah *Daily Morning News,* October 1, 1861—December 20, 1864. A useful digest of this newspaper, prepared by the Works Progress Administration, is in the Savannah Public Library.

Savannah *Republican,* October 1, 1860—December 21, 1864; its successor of that name, December 30, 1864—December 31, 1865.

Scrapbooks of the late R. P. Daily of Savannah, in possession of his widow.

Thomas Gamble Scrapbooks and the Gamble collection of pictures from *Harpers Weekly,* the Frank Leslie publications and the *Illustrated London News.* The Gamble collections are in the Savannah Public Library.

C. R. Hanleiter Scrapbooks, Atlanta Historical Society, Atlanta.

INDEX

toon bridge erected, 192; demand
and refusal of surrender of, 192–
193; Union trans-Savannah River
operation, 194–195; opinions on
weakness of Confederate line,
195–197; final days of Confederate occupation, 198; night of
Hardee's evacuation, 199–202;
shelling by CSS Savannah and
destruction of ironclad, 203–204;
views on escape of Hardee's Army
from, 204–205; surrender of Savannah by city officials, 207–208;
entry of Union troops, 208–209;
elation of Federals, 208–209; disorders at, 209–210; Sherman's
arrival at, 210–211; his message
to Lincoln, 211; captured cotton,
211–212; housing of officers and
soldiers, 212–213; good order in,
213–214; General Geary commands city, 214; physical condition of city, 215; Union press at,
215–216; pro-Union feeling in,
217–219; absence of bitterness of
inhabitants, 217–219; meeting of
citizens, 218–219; withdrawal
from the war, 219; Southern reaction to, 219–220; Northern relief for people of, 220–222; Confederate sympathies at, 223–225;
consorting with Union soldiers,
225–228; troop reviews by Sherman, 229–230; Northern opinions of Savannah, 230–232;
Negro churches in, 233; garrisoning by Negro soldiers, 235; Sherman and the Negro, 235–237;
Edwin M. Stanton at, 235–236;
departure of Sherman's Army,
237; lack of commercial activity
at, 238–239; Northern visitors
to, 239; conflagration, 239–240;
deportation of officers' wives from,
240–241; memorial services for
Lincoln at, 243; arrival of Jefferson Davis and A.H. Stephens,
243–244; Varina Davis at, 244;
effect of war on, 245.
Savannah Cadets, 18.
Savannah, CSS (former Everglade),
23, 24, 25, 35, 38, 44, 84.

Savannah, CSS (ironclad), 112, 121,
122, 126, 139, 141, 194, 202–
204, 217, 270.
Savannah Daily Herald, 216, 222,
242.
Savannah Daily Morning News,
quoted, 4, 5, 12, 13, 14, 18, 21,
27, 28, 29, 32, 33, 41, 48, 57,
62, 69–70, 77, 78, 83, 90, 91,
101, 102, 128, 129–130, 131,
132, 133, 134, 146, 148, 149,
150, 164, 166, 167, 168, 175,
203, 215, 216.
Savannah Republican, quoted, 7, 8,
9, 21, 28, 44, 45, 61, 62, 68, 70,
82–83, 86, 89, 95, 98, 101, 102,
104, 125, 129, 130, 133, 134,
139, 143, 145, 146, 147, 152,
153, 166, 167, 215.
Savannah Republican (Union), 216,
224, 228, 229, 239, 240, 243,
244.
Savannah River, 4, 20, 24, 41, 43,
44, 48, 49, 74, 75, 77, 78, 81,
85, 86, 109, 112, 124, 139–141,
147, 171, 172, 173, 175, 176,
177, 179, 192, 194, 195, 198,
202, 206, 215, 240.
Savannah Volunteer Guards, 11, 17,
26, 105, 109, 114, 117, 242, 246.
Saxon, Rufus, 233.
Sayler's Creek, 242.
Scharf, John Thomas, 121, 128–129,
144, 178.
Schmitt, Frederick E., 164.
Schreiner, Hermann L., 87.
Scott, Winfield, 118.
Screven, Cornelia A., 136–137.
Screven, John, 21.
Screven's Ferry, 193, 198, 199, 202,
204.
Selma, Ala., 73.
Seneca, USS, 38, 40, 80, 96.
Sharpsburg, Battle of, 71, 112, 158.
Shaw's Dam, 173.
Sherlock, Eli J., 218.
Sherman, John, 239.
Sherman, Thomas W., 34, 43, 47, 48,
49, 50, 53.
Sherman, William T., 34, 132, 154,
156, 162, 167, 173, 176, 178,
179, 181, 182, 183, 184, 186,